Maine Mountain Guide

8th Edition

Maine Mountain Guide

8th Edition

The hiking trails of Maine
featuring Baxter State Park

APPALACHIAN MOUNTAIN CLUB
BOSTON, MASSACHUSETTS

Cover Photograph: Paul David Mozell
Book Design: Carol Bast Tyler

Distributed by the Globe Pequot Press, Old Saybrook, CT.

Library of Congress Cataloging-in-Publication Data

Maine mountain guide: the hiking trails of Maine, featuring Baxter
State Park.—8th ed.
p. cm.
Includes index.
ISBN 1-878239-74-0 (alk. paper)
1. Hiking—Maine Guidebooks. 2. Maine Guidebooks.
I. Appalachian Mountain Club.
GV199.42.M2M35   1999
917.4104'43—dc21   99-21954
                                                         CIP

The paper used in this publication meets the minimum requirements of the American National Standard for Information Sciences—Permanence of Paper for Printed Library Materials, ANSI Z39.48-1984. ∞

**Due to changes in conditions, use of the information
in this book is at the sole risk of the user.**

Printed in the United States of America.

Printed on recycled paper using soy-based inks.

10 9 8 7 6 5 4 3 2 1   99 00 01 02 03 04

Contents

Key to Maps

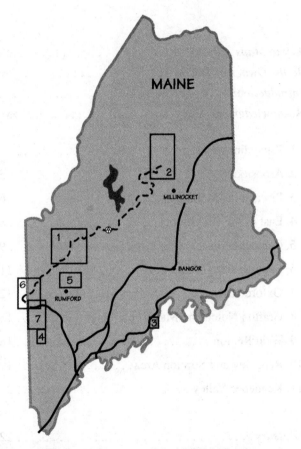

To the Owner of This Book

With the object of keeping pace with the constant changes in mountain trails, the Appalachian Mountain Club publishes a revised edition of this guide at intervals of about five years.

Hiking and climbing in the Maine mountains should provide a combination of outdoor pleasure and healthful exercise. Plan your trip schedule with safety in mind. Determine the overall distance, the altitude to be reached, and the steepness of the footway. If you are returning to the starting point the same day, allow ample time, as your morning quota of energy will have lost some of its get-up-and-go. Read the caution notes where they appear in this book. They are put there for your guidance and protection.

We request your help in preparing future editions. When you go over a trail, please check the description in the book. If you find errors or can suggest improvements, send a note to the committee. Even if the description is satisfactory, "Description of such-and-such trail is okay" will be appreciated. Do not be deterred by a lack of experience. The viewpoint of one unfamiliar with the trail is especially valuable. Address: Maine Mountain Guidebook Committee, Appalachian Mountain Club, 5 Joy St., Boston, MA 02108.

Introduction

This, the eighth edition of the Appalachian Mountain Club's guide to the mountains and trails of Maine, describes nearly two hundred summits in all sections of Maine—from Mt. Agamenticus in the southwestern corner of the state to Deboullie Mtn. in northern Aroostook County, and from Mt. Aziscohos close to the New Hampshire line in northwestern Maine to Pocomoonshine Mtn. near the St. Croix River, which forms the New Brunswick border. Some examples are the compact and scenic Camden Hills, the low but frequently climbed hills in southwestern Maine, and the isolated and interesting mountains close to the Quebec and New Brunswick boundaries.

This guide is intended for use as a pathfinder; it therefore does not include extended historical references or descriptions of views. In general, it describes trail ascents. Any difficulties going down a trail that you would not have encountered going up are mentioned at the end of the description. Where a trail follows a range, this guide describes it for the direction usually traveled. Signs mark many paths, but hikers cannot rely on them, because they often fall down or disappear. Also, trails are constantly changing. Logging may destroy them; heavy storms, such as the ice storm of 1998, may obscure them; and new trails are occasionally added. This guide strives to remain current by adding or deleting trails or mountains depending on present conditions.

MAINE FOREST SERVICE FIRETOWERS

For years, the Maine Forest Service maintained firetowers on many mountains. The trails built to these summit towers made excellent hiking paths. During the last two decades, these towers have been abandoned as the MFS has switched to aircraft for forest fire patrol. Several of the towers have been removed or converted to other uses, such as microwave or cable television relay. Others have been tipped over and left in an unsightly mess.

Some of the firewardens' cabins have been sold to private owners; others are in disrepair or have been vandalized or torn down. Do not expect to use them for camping or emergency shelter.

In many cases, continued use by hikers or adoption by volunteers has kept trails to firetowers open; in other, more remote regions, the trails are becoming overgrown. No group has offered to maintain them. Before you head for the more isolated areas with summit towers, then, check trail conditions with the local MFS office.

DISTANCES AND TIMES

The distances and times that appear in the tables at the end of trail descriptions are cumulative from the starting point at the head of each table. Estimated distances are preceded by *est.*

Times are based on a speed of 2 mph, plus an additional half-hour for every 1000 ft. gained in elevation. Times are included only to provide a consistent measure for comparison among trails and routes. When no time is given, the route described may be considered a leisurely walk or stroll. With experience, you will learn how to correct these standard times for your own normal pace. Bear in mind, however, that if your average pace is faster than the standard time, it will not necessarily be so on trails with steep grades, in wet weather, if you are carrying a heavy pack, or if you are hiking with a group. And in winter, you should roughly double the time it would normally take for you to complete a hike.

The final entry in the distance-time summaries at the end of trail descriptions gives the metric equivalent of the total distance. The metric equivalent for the elevation of each summit is also listed.

GUIDELINES FOR WILDERNESS HIKERS AND CAMPERS

Below are some fundamentals of living in the outdoors without destroying it. Following these simple rules will help preserve the backcountry for all to enjoy.

Camp in Designated Areas

The backcountry can no longer withstand indiscriminate camping and hiking. Please cooperate.

Bring Your Own Tent or Shelter

Shelter buildings are often full, so each group should carry all needed equipment for shelter, including whatever poles, stakes, ground insulation, and cord are required. Do not cut boughs or branches for bedding.

Use a Portable Stove

In some camping areas, a "human browse line" is quite evident, because people have gathered firewood over the years: Limbs are gone from trees, the ground is devoid of deadwood, and vegetation has been trampled by people scouring the area. A carefully operated stove puts the least pressure on the forest.

Help Preserve Nature's Ground Cover

If a shelter is full, or if you camp away from shelters, find a clear, level site on which to pitch your tent, away from trails and streams. Site clearing and ditching around tents are too damaging to soil and vegetation.

Hammock Camping

Some campers use hammocks rather than tents. Hanging between trees eliminates even that crushing of ground cover caused by tents.

(Hammocks, however, have certain limitations during bug season!) We can all practice low-impact camping by making conscious efforts to preserve the natural forest.

Water for Drinking and Washing

Wash your dishes and yourself well away from streams, ponds, and springs. A handy practice is carrying a small screen or cloth to filter the dishwater, so that you do not leave food remnants strewn about the woods.

Most hikers drink from streams without ill effect, and indeed, the pleasure of quaffing a cup of water fresh from a (presumably) pure mountain spring is one of the traditional attractions of the mountains. Unfortunately, in many mountain regions the cysts of the intestinal parasite *Giardia lamblia* are present in some of the water. A conservative practice is to boil water for 20 min. or to use an iodine-based disinfectant. Chlorine-based products, such as Halazone, are ineffective in water that contains organic impurities, and they deteriorate quickly in your pack. Remember to allow extra contact time (and use twice as many tablets) if the water is cold.

Think About Human Waste

Keep it at least 200 ft. away from water sources. If there are no toilets nearby, dig a trench 6–8 in. deep for a latrine and cover it completely when you break camp. The bacteria in the organic layer of the soil will then decompose the waste naturally. (Do not dig the trench too deep, or you will be below the organic layer.)

Carry In–Carry Out

Trash receptacles are not available in trail areas (except at some trailheads), and visitors are asked to bring trash bags and carry out everything—food, paper, glass, cans—they carry in. Cooperation with the "carry in–carry out" program so far has been outstanding, and the concept has grown to "carry out more than you carried in." We hope you will join in the effort.

Use Special Care Above Timberline

Extreme weather and a short growing season make these areas especially fragile. Footsteps alone can destroy the toughest natural cover, so please try to stay on the trail or walk on rocks. And, of course, do not camp above timberline.

Limit the Size of Your Group

The larger the group, the greater the impact on the environment and on others. Please limit the size of your group to a dozen or fewer.

CAUTION

Hikers should always carry a map and compass, knife or small ax, waterproof matches, water, adequate food, a windbreaker, rain gear, a spare sweater or shirt, gloves or mittens, a hat, and extra socks. In addition, at least one member of the group should carry a lightweight survival kit that includes first aid supplies (Band Aids, gauze pads, and adhesive tape; moleskin or a similar blister preventive; an antiseptic; and an analgesic), high-energy emergency food, a flashlight with extra batteries, a large plastic trash bag, some foil, a needle and thread, safety pins, cord, paper and a pencil, and perhaps a space blanket.

Before entering the woods, tell someone where you are going and when you plan to return, and get to know the area. Study a good map and know how to use your compass. Pick out reference points along the trail after you start your hike and check your compass from time to time. Dress for the terrain and weather. Do not depend on cotton clothing for warmth; once it is dampened by perspiration or precipitation, it will pull warmth from your body. Wool and some synthetics such as polypropylene provide better insulation even when wet. Dress in layers: Remember, you can always take off what you have on, but you cannot put on what you do not have with you.

Unless otherwise labeled, compass directions given in this text are based on true north instead of magnetic north. This is important information, because in Maine the compass needle points up to 20 degrees west of true north.

Note: With reference to streams, the terms *right bank* and *left bank* mean right and left when you face downstream. Other abbreviations used frequently in the text are listed on page xxii.

HYPOTHERMIA

Hypothermia, the most serious danger to hikers, is the inability to stay warm because of injury, exhaustion, lack of sufficient food, or inadequate or wet clothing. Most cases occur in temperatures above freezing; the most dangerous conditions involve rain with wind. The symptoms are stumbling, poor coordination, garbled speech, amnesia, disorientation, and agitated behavior. Progressive lethargy, uncontrollable shivering, and coma will follow if no treatment is given. The result is death, unless the victim (who usually does not understand the situation) is treated, and it is not unusual for the victim to resist treatment and even combat the rescuers.

If you suspect a person is hypothermic, find the victim shelter from the wind and rain, and remove any wet clothing. Place the victim in a sleeping bag without clothes or with dry garments. Be sure to cover the head and neck, and provide insulation from the ground. If the victim is fully conscious, supply quick-energy food and warm (not hot), nonalcoholic drinks. Keep the victim inactive until signs of improvement appear. Allow adequate rest before moving on; do not hesitate to send for help if there is any doubt that the victim should proceed.

Uncontrollable shivering is evidence of advanced hypothermia. This shivering will eventually cease on its own, but this is an indication that the hypothermia is becoming even more severe. In severe cases, only professional treatment offers hope for survival. Reduce exposure to wind and rain, prevent further heat loss, and send for help. Do not try to rewarm in the field.

The prevention of hypothermia is infinitely easier than its treatment and should be a prime concern of hikers during any season.

Sources of detailed information on causes, prevention, and current treatment are available through the AMC's Boston or Pinkham Notch headquarters.

GETTING LOST

If you get lost in the Maine woods, it is not necessarily a serious matter. First *stop*, sit down, and think. If you are familiar with the territory, you may be able to find your way back to the trail or to a high spot to survey the area. If you are unsure which direction to take, *stay where you are!* If you have informed someone of your trip plan, then you will probably be found quickly. Do not panic. If you have the proper equipment, you can improvise a shelter (near water if possible) and wait for help. Build a fire for warmth and to draw attention. (Be careful to keep the fire under control, of course.) The main thing to remember is to stay put and stay calm.

SEARCH AND RESCUE

The Department of Inland Fisheries and Wildlife is empowered to conduct search-and-rescue operations in Maine. All Maine telephone books carry the 800 number of the nearest Warden District.

The text of the relevant sections of Maine law is given below; for more information, write to the Safety Division, Department of Inland Fisheries and Wildlife, 41 State House Station, 284 State St., Augusta ME 04333.

Title 12, Sec. 7035, No. 4; Powers

Search and rescue. Whenever the commissioner receives notification that any person has gone into the woodlands or onto the inland waters of the State on a hunting, fishing or other trip and has become lost, stranded or drowned, the commissioner shall exercise the authority to take reasonable steps to ensure the safe and timely recovery of that person; except in cases involving downed or lost aircraft covered by Title 6, section 303.

A. The commissioner may summon any person in the State to assist in those search and rescue attempts. Each person summoned shall be paid at a rate set by the commissioner with the approval of the Governor and shall be provided with subsistence while engaged in these activities.

B. The expenses of the department in search and rescue efforts shall be paid from the General Fund. The Joint Standing Committee of the Legislature having jurisdiction over Inland Fisheries and Wildlife shall report out a bill during each regular session requesting General Fund monies for the full cost of the search and rescue.

C. The commissioner may enter into written agreements with other agencies or corporations, including commercial recreational areas, allowing partial search and rescue responsibility within specified areas.

D. The commissioner may terminate a search and rescue operation by members of his department when, in his opinion, all reasonable efforts have been exhausted.

Any person who has knowledge that another person is lost, stranded or drowned in the woodlands or inland waters of the State shall notify the Warden Service Division of the Department of Inland Fisheries and Wildlife.

Sec. 7036, No. 4; Prohibited Acts

Failure to notify. Except as otherwise provided through written agreement, a person is guilty of failure to report a lost, stranded or drowned person if he has knowledge that a person is lost, stranded or drowned in the woodlands or inland waters of the State and fails to give notice of the incident by quickest means to the Warden Service Division of the Department of Inland Fisheries and Wildlife.

FIRES AND FIRE CLOSURE

The following is a summary of regulations that govern building fires in various areas:

1. In Acadia National Park and in state parks, regulations permit fires at designated places only. In Acadia National Park, consult a park ranger before building any fire.

2. In the White Mountain National Forest, permits are no longer required, but hikers who build fires are still legally responsible for any damage they may cause.

3. In other areas:
   a. In *organized* territory (i.e., within the boundaries of a township with its own local civil government), fires may be kindled on private land only with written permission from the landowner. The landowner's permission must be presented to the town firewarden, who may then issue a permit.

   b. In *unorganized* territory (i.e., where the local government function is performed by state or county authorities), a permit for outdoor cooking and warming fires may be obtained free of charge from any MFS ranger.

   c. Fires may be built without a permit at the following places:
      (1) MFS-authorized campsites and lunch grounds
      (2) State Highway Commission roadside picnic areas
      (3) Appalachian Trail shelter sites
      (4) Baxter Park and Recreation campgrounds and campsites   (but see park regulations and discuss with rangers)
      (5) Maine Bureau of Parks and Recreation campsites and picnic areas
      (6) Maine Bureau of Public Lands–authorized campsites

   d. Specific and detailed information on fire permits may be
      obtained from any MFS ranger or the Forest Service's
      Augusta office (in-state telephone number: 800-750-9777).

During periods when the danger of fires is high, the governor,
through proclamation, may prohibit all outdoor fires or may close the
woods altogether. Check with the MFS before embarking on a trip for
any restrictions that may be in effect. It will have the most up-to-date
and accurate information regarding fires and required permits.

We cannot stress enough the importance of care when you use fire
in the woods. Hikers as a group have compiled a fine record, but a forest fire traced to the carelessness of a hiker could result in the closing
of much land and many trails.

CAMP TRIP LEADERS' PERMITS

Those who lead summer-camp trips in Maine should be aware of a law
that regulates issuing permits for camp trip leaders. The text of the
legislation is given below; for more information, write to the Safety
Division, Department of Inland Fisheries and Wildlife, 41 State House
Station, 284 State St., Augusta ME 04333.

Title 12, Sec. 7322; Permits for Camp Trip Leaders

Boys' and girls' camps licensed by the Department of Human Ser-
vices, or located in another state and licensed in a similar manner, if
the laws of the other state so require, conducting trip camping shall:
provide at least one staff member over 18 years of age for each 6
campers and ensure that the staff member in charge of the trip holds a
valid trip leader permit. Any person wishing a permit shall submit an
application on forms provided by the commissioner and shall pay the
application fee. To qualify initially for a permit, an applicant must
show successful completion of an approved trip leader safety course
or complete an application provided by the commissioner outlining in
detail the applicant's experience and training as a trip leader; and meet

any other requirements adopted by rule of the commissioner. Waiver of the course requirement by the commissioner on the basis of the applicant's experience and payment of the application fee shall qualify the applicant for a trip leader permit.

With the advice of the board, the commissioner shall review and adopt a trip leader safety course curriculum which shall include, but not be limited to: training in first aid; training in water safety, including life saving techniques as appropriate; and trip leader qualifications and required experience for the special waiver procedure in subsection 4. The commissioner shall publish the curriculum adopted or approved by the board and a current list of courses, with the approved curriculum, by name and address.

Wardens of the department and the rangers of the Forestry Service and rangers of the Bureau of Parks and Lands may terminate any trip which is considered unsafe or in violation of this section.

The initial qualifying fee for a trip leader permit is $18. The permit may be renewed upon payment of $13 if requirements of the department are met.

POLICIES OF LANDOWNERS IN NORTHERN MAINE

Maine's economy depends very much upon its woodlands. These lands are owned by a large number of small-lot owners and by a small number of companies that own large areas. These private holdings include many of Maine's mountains; generally, owners allow recreational use of their land.

The opening of the Allagash Wilderness Waterway and improved highways and roads leading to northern and northwestern Maine have increased the flow of hikers, hunters, anglers, canoeists, and others to the forest country. At the same time, continuing technological advances in logging have led to greater use of trucks to haul lumber and pulpwood. The timberland owners constantly extend their system of private roads, many of which are open to the public. These roads offer access to many areas that used to be difficult to reach. In 1971, North Maine Woods, an association of landowners, was established to control recreational use of the area west of ME 11 and north of a line that starts several miles north of Baxter State Park and runs around Telos and Caucomgomoc lakes and then west to the Canadian border. The line extends north along the border to Estcourt, south to St. Francis, southwest to Fish River, south into T 8 R 6, and west toward Baxter State Park. The Katahdin Ironworks/Jo-Mary (Gulf Hagas) area is also under the association's management. The MFS has transferred control and management of most of its forest campsites in this area to North Maine Woods, which operates traffic-control centers on the major private roads into the area. Users must register at the control centers and pay fees, which vary somewhat from year to year and are at times higher for out-of-state residents. There are also fees for use of campsites within the controlled area.

The landowners have established some basic rules for their roads. Speed limits are posted. Trucks always have the right-of-way on these private roads. Do not leave unattended cars that block passage on any road; large logging trucks may need to pass, or access could suddenly be needed to fight a forest fire. Pull well off the road when stopping, even for a few minutes.

Each land-owning company has particular rules, and prior permission is often needed to use a company's roads. For instance, some companies do not allow trailers or RVs on their roads, and others limit vehicle length and width. Anyone coming from a distance to enter an area should check ahead of time with the companies concerned.

For a map showing the locations of control centers and for the latest regulations and information, send a written request and $2 to North Maine Woods, P.O. Box 421, Ashland ME 04732 (207-435-6213). The Sportsman's Alliance of Maine, RR1 Box 1174, Augusta, ME 04330, (207-623-5503), email sam@ime.net, offers information on public and private lands issues including access.

MAINE'S MOUNTAINS IN WINTER

For those who are properly prepared, winter hiking and climbing in Maine offer challenge and satisfaction. The general comments in the *AMC White Mountain Guide*'s section on winter climbing apply equally well to winter climbing in Maine. An added factor in Maine winter climbing is that unplowed access roads frequently lengthen a trip. Many trips that take only a day in summer may take two or more in winter and require camping.

Snowshoes are a must. (The bear-paw type is best for climbing.) Climbers should also carry crampons if they are likely to travel on ice or "boilerplate" snow. Other required gear includes an ice ax or ski pole if you are climbing on open slopes. For brisk snowshoeing, a light shell over a wool shirt is usually sufficient, even in very cold weather. At rest or above timberline, you will usually need an insulated parka and wind pants, and perhaps a face mask and goggles also. Be sure to carry spare pairs of wool socks and warm mittens along with an extra hat. Ordinary leather boots are inadequate. Waterproof insulated boots are recommended, and they should not be too tight.

Deep snow can make route finding difficult. In steep areas or when snow is not compacted, hiking time is much longer than in summer. Be prepared to make an early start and to return after dark using artificial light. Trips should be planned carefully.

The trail descriptions given in various sections of this guide usually apply in winter, with the qualifications that unplowed roads may add distance and trail markers may be hidden. Winter hikers should avoid high peaks and steep rocky slopes unless they have a lot of experience.

Any hikers climbing the higher and longer routes in winter should be fully aware of the danger of low temperatures and high winds. This danger is infinitely greater in winter than in summer. The windchill chart in this guide gives some indication of how cold hiking can be. Plan your trips with such weather in mind.

SKIING

A number of Maine's downhill ski areas are mentioned briefly in the text. To locate them easily, refer to the index under *Skiing*.

In summer, ski trails offer routes that, because of their width and their usually zigzag course on the steeper slopes, are likely to have better views than do regular summer trails. On the other hand, ski trails are less shady, the footing may be poor and rough, and some of them cross swampy places.

BUSHWHACKING IN THE MAINE MOUNTAINS

This guide deals mainly with mountains in Maine that have trails, but it does include a few peaks where you must bushwhack for short distances. It leaves out countless other bushwhacking sites, ranging from rather low hills to mountains approaching 4000 ft. The AMC Maine Mountain Guide Committee feels that such areas should remain without trails so that interested hikers can gain experience in bushwhacking. Some of these mountains are close to existing roads and trails, but many others are accessible only by water or long approach walks. Various topographic maps will show many of these named and unnamed trailless peaks.

Only people who are fully experienced in route finding, using a compass, and map reading should try to bushwhack the higher and more distant mountains. Bushwhackers can encounter a variety of problems and should take extra care to carry sufficient food, clothing, shelter, compasses, first aid equipment, and similar supplies. Bushwhacking is much more time consuming than ordinary hiking, and you should be prepared to spend the night out if necessary.

Since most trailless mountains are located on private property, you should obtain permission from an authorized person prior to starting out. You should also be extra careful to leave word with a responsible party of your routes and destinations.

Bushwhackers should not mark their routes. The usual markers, such as rags and tapes, deteriorate rapidly. Missing markers may mislead those who subsequently attempt to follow them. Markers also destroy the concept of a mountain without trails. If you plan to take the same route out that you take in and you want to mark it to save time on the return, please remove your markers as you leave.

MAPS

Extra copies of the maps at the back of this guide can be purchased separately from the Appalachian Mountain Club, 5 Joy St., Boston MA 02108. Elevations of mountaintops and other points can be found on the maps. Remember, though, that a map cannot indicate the condition of a trail. This is a function of the text. Never assume the existence of a usable route merely because there is a dotted line on the map. Consult both the text and the map.

Other Maps, Guides, and Literature

Among many maps and books covering the mountainous areas of Maine, the following may be particularly valuable.

See the *AMC Guide to Acadia and Mt. Desert* for coverage of those areas.

USGS topographic quadrangles have been published for all of Maine. The 7.5-min. series has replaced the old 15-min. series. In this book, the text indicates the quadrangle available for a given mountain. An index map showing all USGS maps is available at many sporting-goods stores and bookstores throughout the state. The index map and individual maps are also available from USGS Map Sales, Federal Center, Box 25286, Denver CO 80225 (800-USA-MAPS).

DeLorme Map Store, 2 DeLorme Dr., P.O. Box 298, Yarmouth ME 04096 (207-846-7100 and 800-642-0970) publishes *The Maine Map and Guide,* an accurate and regularly updated map of Maine. The *Maine Atlas and Gazetteer,* from the same publisher, provides detailed sectional maps indicating roads, trails, and significant topographic features.

The 13th (1996) edition of the *Appalachian Trail Guide to Maine* contains further information about the Appalachian Trail and maps (seven) for this trail's entire length in Maine. Copies are available at many retail outlets and from the Maine Appalachian Trail Club, P.O. Box 283, Augusta ME 04330-0283.

For further detail on Baxter State Park, see *Katahdin,* by Stephen Clark, published by North Country Press, Unity ME 04988.

Information about state parks, public lands, and fire permits can be obtained from the Maine Forest Service (207-287-2275); Bureau of Public Lands (207-287-3061); and Bureau of Parks and Recreation (207-287-3821).

The AMC's journal, *Appalachia,* periodically publishes material on the mountains of Maine, and the *AMC Maine Mountain Guide* contains references to some of these articles.

COOPERATION

The AMC earnestly requests that those who use the trails, shelters, and campsites on public lands know the rules and follow them, especially those pertaining to fires. The same consideration should be shown to private landowners.

The New England Trail Conference advises that trails should not be blazed or cut on private property without the consent of the owners and definite provision for maintenance. Trails should not be cut or marked on public lands without the approval of the park or forest officials.

The main purpose of this book is to furnish accurate details, both in the text and on the maps; we will gratefully accept corrections from any source. If you find inaccuracies, signs missing, obscure places on the trails, or a map that needs correcting, please send a report to Maine Mountain Guidebook Committee, Appalachian Mountain Club, 5 Joy St., Boston MA 02108.

ABBREVIATIONS

The following abbreviations are used in the trail descriptions:

min.	minute(s)
hr.	hour(s)
mph	miles per hour
in.	inch(es)
ft.	foot, feet
yd.	yard(s)
mi.	mile(s)
m.	meter(s)
km.	kilometer(s)
est.	estimate
AMC	Appalachian Mountain Club
AT	Appalachian Trail
BSP	Baxter State Park
CTA	Chatham Trail Association
FR	Forest Route
MATC	Maine Appalachian Trail Club
ME	Maine
MFS	Maine Forest Service
NH	New Hampshire
NPS	National Park Service
US	United States
USFS	United States Forest Service
USGS	United States Geological Survey
WMNF	White Mountain National Forest

ABBREVIATIONS

The following abbreviations are used in the trail descriptions:

min.	minute(s)
hr.	hour(s)
mph	miles per hour
ft.	foot/feet
ยา	?
yd.	yard(s)
mi.	mile(s)
m.	meter(s)
km.	kilometer(s)
?	?
AMC	Appalachian Mountain Club
AT	Appalachian Trail
BSP	Baxter State Park
CTA	Chatham Trails Association
FR	Forest Road
MATC	Maine Appalachian Trail Club
NF	National Forest
NFS	National Forest Service
NH	New Hampshire
NPS	National Park Service
US	United States
USFS	United States Forest Service
USGS	United States Geologic Survey
WMNF	White Mountain National Forest

Acknowledgments

This updated book is built on the work of volunteers who have participated in the past seven editions. We recognize their contributions, as well as those of the many chapter members and others who generously hiked miles of trails, wrote down data, and came up with more accurate and understandable trail descriptions and guidebook format for this eighth edition. We thank you all.

Particular thanks are due Nancy Houlihan, Lester Kenway, Paul Lones, and Joyce Mailman for taking over whole sections of the work. Among the others who contributed helpful information and energy were: Shirley Helfrich, Ginger Lang, Janet Myers, Wayne Newton, and Roy Schweiker.

Thanks to Cindy Bastey for organizing the Maine Bureau of Parks and Lands's response to our text, to others in the bureau who furnished information, and to Al Cressey, president of the Chatham Trails Association.

Special thanks to Mark Russell and the Joy Street staff for assistance, support, and patience throughout this endeavor, and to Larry Garland, who worked out new digital maps to accompany the book.

The Guidebook Committee, Elliott Bates, chair

WIND CHILL CHART

Estimated Wind Speed in MPH	Actual Thermometer Reading (°F)											
	50	40	30	20	10	0	-10	-20	-30	-40	-50	-60
				Equivalent Temperature (°F)								
calm	50	40	30	20	10	0	-10	-20	-30	-40	-50	-60
5	48	37	27	16	6	-5	-15	-26	-36	-47	-57	-68
10	40	28	16	4	-9	-21	-33	-46	-58	-70	-83	-95
15	36	22	9	-5	-18	-36	-45	-58	-72	-85	-99	-112
20	32	18	4	-10	-25	-39	-53	-67	-82	-96	-110	-124
25	30	16	0	-15	-29	-44	-59	-74	-88	-104	-118	-133
30	28	13	-2	-18	-33	-48	-63	-79	-94	-109	-125	-140
35	27	11	-4	-20	-35	-49	-67	-82	-98	-113	-127	-145
40	26	10	-6	-21	-37	-53	-69	-85	-100	-116	-132	-148

(wind speeds greater than 40 mph have little additional effect)

LITTLE DANGER (for properly clothed person)	INCREASING DANGER	GREAT DANGER
	Danger from freezing of exposed flesh	

Section 1

Katahdin Area

Katahdin, at 5267 ft. the highest mountain in Maine, is about 80 mi. north of Bangor, between the East and West branches of the Penobscot River. It is as wild and alluring as any mountain in the East. The name, in Indian dialect, means "greatest mountain." Katahdin lies within Baxter State Park (BSP), created by a gift of former governor Percival P. Baxter in 1931. By the time of his death in 1969, Governor Baxter had extended the grant to more than 200,000 acres. A condition of his gift—there are variant wordings and differing interpretations by Governor Baxter and others—is that the area "shall forever be left in its natural wild state, forever be kept as a sanctuary for wild beasts and birds and forever be used for public forest, public park and public recreational purposes." Since 1921, the mountain and most of the neighboring summits have been part of a state game preserve.

KATAHDIN

Katahdin, an irregularly shaped mountain mass, rises abruptly from comparatively flat country to a gently sloping plateau above the treeline. It culminates on its southeastern margin in an irregular series of low summits, of which the southern two are the highest. These peaks are 0.3 mi. apart, and Baxter Peak (5267 ft./1605 m.) to the northwest is the higher of the two. From the southeastern South Peak (5240 ft./1597 m.), a long, curved, serrated ridge of vertically fractured granite, known as the Knife Edge, hooks away to the east and northeast. About 0.7 mi. from South Peak, this ridge ends in a rock pyramid called Chimney Peak. Immediately beyond Chimney Peak, and separated from it by a sharp cleft, is a broader rock peak, Pamola (4902 ft./1494 m.). It is named for the Indian avenging spirit of the mountain. To the north, the broad rock mass of Hamlin Peak (4751 ft./1448 m.) dominates the plateau or tableland, which ends in the series of low North (Howe) Peaks (4734–4612 ft./1443–1406 m.). Refer to the Katahdin map in this guide.

Katahdin was first climbed in 1804 by a party of eleven, including Charles Turner Jr., who wrote an account of the ascent. There may have been unrecorded ascents during the next 15 years, but we know the mountain was climbed again in 1819 and 1820. After this date, ascents became more regular.

The tableland, nearly 4 mi. long, falls away abruptly from 1000 to 2000 ft. on all sides. After that, the slope becomes more gentle. Great arms stretch out to embrace glacial cirques, known locally as basins. The Great Basin, with its branch, the South Basin, is the best known. In the floor of the latter, at an altitude of 2910 ft., Chimney Pond lies flanked by impressive cliffs and bordered by dense spruce forest. It fills about eight acres and is a base for many varied mountain climbs. North of the Great Basin, but still on the eastern side of the mountain, is the North Basin (floor altitude 3100 ft.), whose high, smooth-ledged sides surround a barren, boulder-strewn floor. The nearby Little North Basin has few visitors. On the western side of the tableland, the little-known Northwest Basin lies at about 2800 ft., and farther south, there is a broad valley known as the Klondike. Klondike Pond rests in a small glacial arm of this valley, just below the plateau. At 3435 ft., it is 0.3 mi. long, deep, narrow, and remarkably beautiful.

From the peaks at its northern and southern ends, the tableland slopes gradually toward the center, known as the Saddle. From the eastern escarpment of the Saddle, the land falls off gently toward the dense scrub that carpets the northwestern edge. Many avalanches have scored the walls of the tableland, but only two of these scorings are now climbing routes—the Saddle Slide at the western end of the Great Basin and the Abol Slide on the southwestern flank of the mountain.

Katahdin's isolated position makes for an exceptional view that takes in hundreds of lakes, including Moosehead; the many windings of the Penobscot; and, to the south, the hills of Mt. Desert Island and Camden. Mt. Washington seems to lie in a direct line behind Mt. Abraham and is not visible.

Katahdin is the northern terminus of the Appalachian Trail, which includes the Hunt Trail on Katahdin itself. The great mountain lies on the southeastern side of a scattered group of smaller mountains, many of which offer interesting climbs and good views, particularly of Katahdin. The text describes these mountains following the description of Katahdin and covers them in a clockwise direction—west, north, and then northeast.

West of Katahdin, the following mountains form an elbow-shaped range: the Owl, Barren Mtn., Mt. O-J-I, Mt. Coe, South Brother, North Brother, and Fort Mtn. Sentinel Mtn. and the striking Doubletop Mtn. offer fine views from the western side of Nesowadnehunk Stream. Mullen Mtn. and Wassataquoik Mtn. are in the remote area between Fort Mtn. and Wassataquoik Lake. Sprawling Traveler Mtn. is the principal mountain in the northern section of the park. The South Branch ponds and campground sit at its western base. Turner Mtn. is to the northeast of Katahdin and offers magnificent views of it.

In all, there are at least 46 mountain peaks in the park. Eighteen of them exceed 3500 ft.

Camping facilities that accommodate about seven hundred persons are available at ten different public campgrounds, from which most trails are accessible (see the Katahdin/Baxter map). The campgrounds are: Roaring Brook, Abol, Katahdin Stream, Nesowadnehunk (Sourdnahunk), Kidney Pond, Daicey Pond, South Branch Pond, Trout Brook Farm, Russell Pond, and Chimney Pond. Russell Pond and Chimney Pond are accessible only by trail; park roads serve the other eight. All the campgrounds have lean-tos (except Trout Brook and Kidney Pond) and tentsites (except Chimney Pond and Kidney Pond); some have bunkhouses. Daicey Pond and Kidney Pond have cabins. All these sites offer only the most basic facilities. There are no hot showers, grocery stores, or gasoline stations, and the water is untreated. Campers and visitors supply their own food and cooking utensils.

There are areas for groups of 12 or more at Avalanche Field, Foster Field, Nesowadnehunk Field, and Trout Brook Farm. Backcountry campsites for smaller hiking parties are at Davis Pond, Pogy Pond, Wassataquoik Stream, Wassataquoik Lake Island, Little Wassataquoik Lake, Little East, Webster Stream, Long Pond, Middle Fowler Pond, Lower Fowler Pond, Upper South Branch Pond, Billfish Pond, Center Mtn., Hudson Pond, Littlefield Pond, Matagamon Lake, and Webster Lake. Park headquarters in Millinocket handles all reservations for park facilities. You can rent canoes at the South Branch ponds, Russell Pond, Kidney Pond area, Daicey Pond, and Trout Brook.

In recent years, use of the facilities at BSP has increased considerably. At the same time, park authorities have begun limiting the number of campers in the park. During most of the summer, the campgrounds are completely full. *Reservations are strongly recommended and are the only way to guarantee space. Reservations must be confirmed and paid for in advance; the park accepts no phone reservations.* The address is Reservation Clerk, Baxter State Park, 64 Balsam Dr., Millinocket ME 04462 (207-723-5140). When allotted spaces have been filled, no more overnight campers are allowed in the park. To avoid unnecessary driving and disappointment, campers without reservations should call the reservation clerk before starting a long trip to the park.

If park facilities are filled, you can try a number of private sporting camps and campgrounds in the area around the park. The MFS maintains several campsites in the general area.

The park is open to the public 12 months a year, although roads are not maintained for winter vehicle travel. There is a road fee for non-Maine vehicles. Nearly all of the 186 mi. of trails are blue-blazed. The only exception is the white-blazed Appalachian Trail. Remember that at various points on the tableland of Katahdin, and particularly near its summit, local variation in declination makes the compass somewhat unreliable.

Roads to the park run through Millinocket, Patten, and Greenville. These routes are shown on the official Maine Highway Map (or any other general highway map). Roads in the BSP area are indicated on the Katahdin/Baxter map with this guidebook. To reach the southern and eastern entrances to the park from points to the south, follow I-95 north to the Medway exit, and then go west on ME 157 to Millinocket and the park area; or continue on I-95 to Sherman Mills, and then follow ME 11 to Patten and ME 159 west past Shin Pond to the northern portion of the park. The approach through Greenville to the southern entrance is rougher, longer, and more time consuming than the Millinocket approach, but it is very interesting and offers good views of the Katahdin area.

Currently, the park has two entrances. As they enter or leave the park, all visitors must stop at the entrance gatehouse to register and to pick up or leave passes. You can also find out about the status of hiking trails on the mountains and get other information at the gatehouse.

The southernmost gatehouse is just north of Togue Pond, about 18 mi. from Millinocket. Immediately past the gatehouse, the road forks. The right fork leads 8.1 mi. to the Roaring Brook Campground and trails to Chimney Pond and Russell Pond. The left fork leads to the Abol Campground (5.7 mi.), the Katahdin Stream Campground (7.7 mi.), and the Nesowadnehunk Field and Campground (16.8 mi.).

The second control point is on Matagamon (First Grand) Lake on the approach road to the northeastern part of the park. It is 24 mi. from Patten and ME 11. Follow ME 159 west from Patten past Shin Pond. The Trout Brook Farm Campground is 2.6 mi. to the west on the perimeter road. The South Branch Pond Campground is 9.6 mi. Drive west at first on the perimeter road, and then south about 2.5 mi. on a well-marked turnoff.

You can reach most campgrounds and other facilities in the park from the perimeter road. To meet the terms of former governor Baxter's deeds of trust, the roads are unpaved and relatively unimproved. The perimeter road extends 50.5 mi., from the Togue Pond Gatehouse to the Matagamon Gatehouse. It is a very narrow, winding, dirt or gravel road. Except in a few places, the dense foliage along the road restricts the view. A trip to the park is not really worthwhile unless you plan to hike or camp.

From the Togue Pond Gatehouse, the perimeter road first leads northwest and then generally north. It skirts the southern and western flanks of Katahdin. During the first 5 mi. of the drive, the mountain is briefly visible a few times. After passing the Abol and Katahdin Stream campgrounds, the road reaches Foster Field, where you can see Doubletop, O-J-I, and other mountains in the range west of Katahdin. After that, the views are very restricted all the way to the Matagamon Gatehouse. Most of the perimeter road follows the routes of old logging roads. For clarity and consistency, the older, more colorful road names have been dropped in favor of the term *tote road.*

People planning to camp, hike, and use the facilities in the park should know the rules and regulations, which are revised annually. They can be obtained by writing to Baxter State Park, 64 Balsam Dr., Millinocket ME 04462. The latest versions of the most important rules are summarized below.

Camping is allowed only at authorized campgrounds or campsites. A responsible adult at least 18 years old must accompany groups that include five or more persons under 16 years of age; there must be one adult for each five minors. Larger camping groups may be restricted to authorized group-camping areas. The rules *prohibit bringing pets* into the park and also limit the entry and use of larger recreational vehicles. They also prohibit airplanes, motorboats, motorcycles, trail bikes, and other all-terrain vehicles. Currently, snowmobiles may be operated only on the tote road of the park. They may not be used on South Branch Pond Rd. or Roaring Brook Rd., except by authorized park personnel.

Warning: Increased use of BSP in recent years has resulted in more accidents; several people have died on the mountain. The upper summits are very high and are rugged and bare above the timberline, and the park is fairly far north. As a result, the weather and trail conditions can change very quickly, even in the middle of summer. The weather on Katahdin is similar to that on Mt. Washington, but longer access routes can make conditions even more dangerous in many cases.

Hikers planning to go to higher elevations should take plenty of food, water, and warm clothing. No hired packers serve the park; hikers who do not want to carry their own packs should make needed arrangements before arriving. The trails on many of the routes are among the steepest and most difficult in New England. Hikers should be in good physical condition if they plan to climb the higher and more distant summits; those who are not in good shape should limit their activities accordingly. *Do not* leave the trails (unless bushwhacking is suggested in this guide), particularly on Katahdin or during severe weather or limited visibility.

Hikers entering the park via the Appalachian Trail must register at the first campground, Daicey Pond.

Hunt Trail

The white-blazed Hunt Trail, the route of the Appalachian Trail up Katahdin, climbs the mountain from the southwest. It was first cut in 1900 by Irving O. Hunt, who operated a sporting camp on Sourdnahunk Stream. The trail leaves from the Katahdin Stream Campground. From the treeline to the tableland, this trail is steep and rough. Heed the warnings in the previous paragraphs.

The trail follows the northern side of Katahdin Stream. At 1.1 mi. from the campground, it passes the trail to the Owl on the left, then crosses Katahdin Stream; shortly after that, a trail leaves left to Katahdin Stream Falls. The trail steepens through the spruce and, at 2.7 mi., reaches two large rocks that form a cave, which will shelter four people. There is a *spring,* undependable in dry periods, 50 yd. down the trail from the cave.

The trail passes through a growth of small spruce and, in 0.2 mi., emerges on the bare, steep crest of the southwestern shoulder, called the Camel's Hump. There, cairns mark the trail, which goes on to wind among gigantic boulders. The trail then traverses a broad shelf and climbs steeply 0.5 mi. over broken rock to the open tableland (at 3.7 mi.), where two slabs of rock mark the "Gateway." The trail continues east, following a worn path and paint blazes, until it reaches Thoreau Spring (at 4.2 mi.), where there is *water* except in dry seasons. (At the spring, Baxter Peak Cutoff goes off to the left and reaches the Saddle in 0.9 mi. This trail avoids the summit and is the best route in stormy weather for traveling between Thoreau Spring and the Saddle. To the right, the Abol Trail descends 2.8 mi. to the Abol Campground.) From the spring, the Hunt Trail climbs moderately northeast for 1 mi. to Baxter Peak, with its commanding panoramas and surprising view of the South Basin.

Hunt Trail

Distances from Katahdin Stream Campground

> *to* Owl Trail junction: 1.1 mi., 45 min.

> *to* cave: 2.7 mi., 2 hr. 55 min.

> *to* Gateway: 3.7 mi., 4 hr. 25 min.

> *to* Thoreau Spring and junctions with Abol Trail and Baxter Peak Cutoff: 4.2 mi., 4 hr. 35 min.

> *to* Saddle (via Baxter Peak Cutoff): 5.1 mi., 5 hr. 30 min.

> *to* Baxter Peak: 5.2 mi., 5 hr. 20 min.

> *to* Chimney Pond Campground (via Baxter Peak Cutoff and Saddle Trail): 6.8 mi., 6 hr. 30 min.

> *to* Chimney Pond Campground (via Baxter Peak, Knife Edge, and Dudley Trail): 7.6 mi. (12.2 km.), 7 hr. 45 min.

Abol Trail

The Abol Trail is believed to be the oldest route up the mountain, and evidence exists that the first recorded ascent took place near this trail. It follows a great slide up the southwestern side of Katahdin.

Caution: This trail is *dangerous* because of its steepness and the great amount of loose rock and gravel in the slide. Climb and descend with great care.

The trail leaves the tote road at the Abol Campground. It crosses through the campground and, at 0.2 mi., enters an old tote road and reaches the southern bank of a tributary of Abol Stream. It continues along the southern bank of the stream for 0.6 mi. The trail then bears right (northeast) away from the brook and leads sharply right. It reaches a gravel wash of old Abol Slide (1.3 mi.) and climbs the slide, reaching a more recent slide at 1.9 mi. Beyond this point, the slide is steeper and becomes entirely bare. Huge boulders and increasing steepness mark the latter part of this climb. On the tableland, paint blazes lead 0.1 mi. to Thoreau Spring and the Hunt Trail. Go right on the Hunt Trail and continue northeast up gentle slopes to the summit of Katahdin. Except in dry seasons, there is *water* at Thoreau Spring. It is possible to make a long but rewarding circuit using the Hunt and Abol trails. You can either leave cars at the Abol and Katahdin Stream campgrounds or walk the 2 mi. between them on the tote road. Going up by the Abol Trail is best.

Abol Trail

Distances from Abol Campground

- *to* foot of old Abol Slide: 1.3 mi., 1 hr. 20 min.

- *to* tableland: 2.6 mi., 3 hr. 15 min.

- *to* Thoreau Spring and Hunt Trail junction: 2.8 mi., 3 hr. 20 min.

- *to* Baxter Peak (via Hunt Trail): 3.8 mi. (6 km.), 4 hr. 5 min. (*descending*, 2 hr. 45 min.)

- *to* Katahdin Stream Campground (via Hunt Trail): 9 mi. (14.5 km.), *est.* 9 hr.

Roaring Brook Campground

This campground, at about 1480 ft., is on the southern bank of Roaring Brook at the northern terminus of Roaring Brook Rd. It is about 8.1 mi. from the Togue Pond Gatehouse. Trails to Chimney Pond and Russell Pond start here. Closer by are Sandy Stream Pond (where hikers often see moose) and South Turner Mtn.

Roaring Brook Campground

Distances from Roaring Brook Campground

- *to* Chimney Pond (via Chimney Pond Trail): 3.3 mi. (5.3 km.), 2 hr. 20 min. (*descending*, 1 hr. 40 min.)

- *to* Baxter Peak (via Chimney Pond and Dudley trails and Knife Edge): 5.7 mi. (9.2 km.), 6 hr. 5 min. (*descending*, 4 hr. 40 min.)

- *to* Baxter Peak (via Chimney Pond and Saddle trails): 5.5 mi. (8.9 km.), 4 hr. 35 min. (*descending,* 3 hr. 15 min.)

- *to* Baxter Peak (via Taylor Trail and Knife Edge): 4.3 mi. (6.9 km.), 5 hr. 15 min. (*descending*, 3 hr. 10 min.)

- *to* Hamlin Peak (via Chimney Pond, North Basin Cutoff, and Hamlin Ridge trails): 4.5 mi. (7.2 km.), 4 hr. 15 min.

- *to* North Basin (via Chimney Pond, North Basin Cutoff, and North Basin trails): 3.3 mi. (5.3 km.), 2 hr. 35 min. (*descending*, 1 hr. 50 min.)

- *to* Russell Pond (via Russell Pond Trail): 7 mi. (11.3 km.), 3 hr. 45 min.

- *to* South Turner Mtn. summit (via Russell Pond and South Turner Mtn. trails): 2 mi. (3.2 km.), 1 hr. 50 min.

Helon N. Taylor Trail

A lot of this trail follows the route of the old Leavitt Trail. It provides a direct route from the Roaring Brook Campground to Pamola and follows the exposed Keep Ridge. This route provides the best sustained views of any trail starting from a road in the park, but it also exposes the hiker to the weather. *Be careful.* Avoid this trail in bad weather, particularly if you plan to go all the way to Baxter Peak via the Knife Edge. The Taylor Trail does not have dangerous footing, but it does require almost continuous climbing over rocks and boulders, so it is fairly tiring.

The trail begins on the Chimney Pond Trail 0.1 mi. west of the Roaring Brook Campground. It climbs 0.5 mi. through mixed growth to a ridgecrest. It then levels off for a short period, passing through scrub and a boulder field. After that, it climbs steeply through small birch, enters an old flat burn, and drops to the small Bear Brook, one of the branches of Avalanche Brook. Bear Brook offers the only *water* on the trail.

After Bear Brook, the trail ascends steeply through scrub, a fine stand of conifers, and a boulder field with wide views in all directions. It climbs over and between boulders to Keep Ridge and then along the open ridge—with a spectacular view of the Knife Edge opening up ahead—to the summit of Pamola.

Helon N. Taylor Trail
Distances from Roaring Brook Campground

- *to* start (via Chimney Pond Trail): 0.1 mi., 5 min.
- *to* Pamola summit: 3.2 mi. (5.2 km.), 3 hr. 20 min. (*descending*, 2 hr. 15 min.)
- *to* Baxter Peak (via Knife Edge): 4.3 mi. (6.9 km.), 5 hr. 15 min. (*descending*, 3 hr. 10 min.)
- *to* Chimney Pond Campground (via Knife Edge and Cathedral Trail): 6 mi. (9.7 km.), 4 hr. 55 min.

Chimney Pond Trail

The Chimney Pond Trail begins at the ranger's cabin at the Roaring Brook Campground. Following the old Basin Ponds tote road, it climbs west along the southern bank of Roaring Brook. After 0.6 mi., it bears gradually away from the brook and climbs more steeply. A brook, the outlet of Pamola Pond, crosses at 1 mi. At 1.9 mi., the trail bears left; 50 yd. to the left is the site of the old Basin Ponds Camp, GNP Camp 3, 1921–1936. The trail then bears right and enters an overgrown clearing at 2 mi. At that point, Lower Basin Pond comes into view.

The trail follows the southern end of Lower Basin Pond and continues along its southwestern shore. At 2.2 mi., the trail goes left uphill into the woods. At 2.3 mi., the North Basin Cutoff goes off to the right. Stay left to continue on the Chimney Pond Trail. At 2.7 mi., it follows the side of a depression known as Dry Pond, which holds water in spring and after heavy rains. At 3 mi., the North Basin Trail to Hamlin Ridge and the North Basin leaves on the right, and at 3.2 mi., there is a cabin on the left. The trail then goes downhill slightly to end at the shore of Chimney Pond.

Chimney Pond Trail
Distances from Roaring Brook Campground

- *to* brook crossing: 1 mi., 35 min.
- *to* North Basin Cutoff junction: 2.3 mi., 1 hr. 20 min.
- *to* Dry Pond: 2.7 mi., 1 hr. 55 min.
- *to* North Basin Trail junction: 3 mi., 2 hr. 10 min.
- *to* Chimney Pond Campground: 3.3 mi. (5.3 km.), 2 hr. 20 min.

Chimney Pond Campground

Magnificently located on Chimney Pond (2910 ft.), this campground is an excellent base for climbing to the highest summits and the tableland area. Because of this campground's heavy use and fragile ecology, the park authority enforces several restrictions. No open fires are allowed; campers must use portable stoves. In addition, campers may not set up tents; overnight visitors must sleep in the bunkhouse or lean-tos. Early reservations are a must at this popular site.

Distances from Chimney Pond Campground

- *to* Roaring Brook Campground (via Chimney Pond Trail): 3.3 mi. (5.3 km.), 1 hr. 40 min.

- *to* North Basin (via Chimney Pond and North Basin trails): 1.2 mi. (1.9 km.), 45 min.

- *to* Hamlin Peak (via Chimney Pond, North Basin, and Hamlin Ridge trails): 2 mi. (3.2 km.), 2 hr. 30 min. (*descending*, 1 hr. 45 min.)

- *to* Davis Pond Lean-to (via Saddle and Northwest Basin trails): 4.4 mi. (7.1 km.), 3 hr. 30 min. (*returning,* 3 hr. 45 min.)

- *to* Baxter Peak (via Dudley Trail and Knife Edge): 2.4 mi. (3.9 km.), 3 hr. 45 min. (*returning*, 3 hr.)

- *to* Baxter Peak (via Cathedral Trail): 1.7 mi. (2.7 km.), 2 hr. 30 min. (*descending,* 1 hr. 45 min.)

- *to* Baxter Peak (via Saddle Trail): 2.2 mi. (3.5 km.), 2 hr. 15 min. (*descending,* 1 hr. 35 min.)

- *to* Baxter Peak (via Chimney Pond, North Basin, Hamlin Ridge, and Saddle trails): 4.2 mi. (6.8 km.), 3 hr. 55 min. (*descending,* 3 hr. 5 min.)

- *to* Katahdin Stream Campground (via Saddle Trail, Baxter Peak Cutoff, and Hunt Trail): 6.8 mi. (10.9 km.), 5 hr.

Dudley Trail

The Dudley Trail leads from Chimney Pond to Pamola. It runs from the ranger's cabin east across the outlet of the pond, bears right, climbs over huge boulders, and reenters the woods, where the route is well blazed. On the rocks, cairns mark the trail clearly.

At 0.3 mi. from the pond, a side trail to the left marked Pamola Caves leads past ledges, often streaming with water, and climbs to some caves that are about 0.7 mi. from the Dudley Trail. In the caves, you must worm your way through small winding passages to reach three remarkably straight, spacious corridors. At the junction of the Dudley Trail and the trail to the caves, there is a *spring* 30 ft. straight ahead.

The Dudley Trail continues nearly due east from the junction, reaches a major cleft in the cliffs, and then climbs rapidly south. The soft granite has eroded into curious forms, and the trail becomes more difficult. Emerging above the timberline, the trail is marked by cairns, blue paint blazes on the rocks, and a well-worn path that traverses patches of heath and low spruce. The trail bears slightly right (southwest) nearly to the edge of the South Basin. Then it heads south again and on up the long northern slope of Pamola. The route's boulders rival those on the Hunt Trail, but the constantly changing view of the Great Basin below enhances the climb. After 30 min. among boulders, the going gets smoother and Index Rock (1 mi.) rises ahead. The trail passes just to the right of this landmark and continues less steeply 0.3 mi. to the peak of Pamola (4902 ft.). To reach Baxter Peak and points beyond, continue along the Knife Edge (see below). At Pamola, the Taylor Trail from the Roaring Brook Campground comes in over Keep Ridge from the east.

Descending, the left-hand (western) line of cairns should be followed from the summit of Pamola. Stay near the edge of the South Basin and pass just to the left of Index Rock. At 1 mi. from Pamola, the side trail to Pamola Caves goes to the right and the Dudley Trail descends to the left.

Dudley Trail

Distances from Chimney Pond Campground

to side trail to Pamola Caves: 0.3 mi., 15 min.

to Pamola Caves (via side trail): 0.7 mi., 1 hr.

to Pamola summit: 1.3 mi., 2 hr. (*descending,* 1 hr. 30 min.)

to Baxter Peak (via Knife Edge): 2.4 mi. (3.9 km.), 3 hr. 45 min. (*descending* back to Chimney Pond, 3 hr.)

The Knife Edge

This narrow, serrated ridge tops the southern wall of the South Basin. Cliffs plummet down on the north, and the walls on the south are only slightly less steep. In places, the ridge narrows to only 2 or 3 ft. This is probably the most spectacular mountain trail in the East. The narrowness of the ridge, combined with the dizzying height and sheer cliffs, gives a sense of extreme exposure.

From the summit of Pamola, follow the cairns that lead southwest. The trail drops abruptly into the sharp cleft at the top of the Chimney, then climbs the equally steep rock tower of Chimney Peak. From there, the route is fairly obvious. It traverses the Sawteeth, finally climbing the South Peak and continuing along the rocks of the summit ridge to Baxter Peak. *Caution:* The Knife Edge is *dangerous in a strong wind. Do not leave the trail.* In recent years, several climbers have had accidents while trying to take unmarked "shortcuts" to the bottom.

The Knife Edge

Distance from Pamola summit

   to Baxter Peak: 1.1 mi. (1.8 km.), 1 hr. 45 min.

Cathedral Trail

The three immense Cathedral Rocks extend from the summit ridge and partly separate the South Basin from the Great Basin.

A sign a few feet west of the ranger's cabin at Chimney Pond marks the start of this route to Baxter Peak by way of Cathedral Rocks. The trail climbs through a small, tangled spruce forest and passes into an old evergreen forest. At 0.3 mi., it goes by Cleftrock Pool, on the right. At 0.4 mi., by a large cairn, the trail turns right toward the Cathedrals, crosses a bridge of rock covered with low growth, climbs steeply through boulders to a high point, and from there, continues through low trees.

In 1967, a slide wiped out part of the next section of the trail, but with care you can still follow the route easily. Blazes mark the way around to the right, then up the steep side of the first Cathedral (0.8 mi.). The climb of the second Cathedral (0.9 mi.) is interesting and offers spectacular views of the Chimney and the Knife Edge. The route continues up the ridge to the top of the third Cathedral at 1.1 mi. At 1.2 mi., the trail forks. The right (northwest) fork is the Cathedral Cutoff and leads 0.2 mi. to the Saddle Trail. The Cathedral Trail bears left (southwest) 0.2 mi. over large boulders to the Saddle Trail (1.4 mi.), which it joins 0.8 mi. above the Saddle.

For one of the best circuits of the upper part of Katahdin, go up the Cathedral Trail to Baxter Peak; then either return to Chimney Pond via the Saddle Trail, or take the Knife Edge to Pamola and return to Chimney Pond via the Dudley Trail, or go on to the Roaring Brook Campground via the Taylor Trail.

Cathedral Trail

Distances from Chimney Pond Campground

- *to* second Cathedral: 0.9 mi., 1 hr. 30 min.
- *to* Saddle Trail junction: 1.4 mi., 2 hr. 20 min.
- *to* Baxter Peak (via Saddle Trail): 1.6 mi., 2 hr. 30 min.
- *to* Chimney Pond Campground (via Saddle Trail): 3.9 mi., 4 hr. 5 min.
- *to* Chimney Pond Campground (via Knife Edge and Dudley Trail): 4.1 mi., 4 hr. 15 min.
- *to* Roaring Brook Campground (via Knife Edge and Taylor Trail): 6 mi. (9.7 km.), 5 hr. 40 min.

Saddle Trail

Climbers have taken this general route out of the basin since Saddle Slide occurred in 1899. Before that, they used an older slide just north of the present one.

The Saddle Trail is the easiest route up Katahdin from Chimney Pond. From the ranger's cabin, the worn trail climbs a rocky path through dense softwoods. Beyond this stand, the trail swings to the right (north) and becomes smoother and flatter as it continues through an evergreen forest. It crosses a brook at 0.8 mi., then climbs steeply over large boulders. At 0.9 mi., the trail bears left up Saddle Slide and passes through stunted birches. At 1 mi., it emerges from scrub, and there is a scramble for 0.2 mi. up the loose, open slope of the slide. (Be careful of loose rocks.) At 1.2 mi., the trail suddenly reaches the top of the slide and the level, open tableland at the Saddle between the summits of Baxter Peak and Hamlin Peak. Go left (south) to reach Baxter Peak. The Northwest Basin Trail, to the right, leads to Caribou Spring, the Hamlin Ridge Trail, the North (Howe) Peaks Trail, the Northwest Basin, and all points on the northern end of the mountain. About 250 yd. northwest of the head of the slide, there is *water* (unreliable) at Saddle Spring, which flows among the rocks near the edge of the scrub.

The Saddle Trail to Baxter Peak continues south over gentle slopes. Cairns mark the well-worn path.

At 1.7 mi., the trail passes a large boulder. The northern end of the Cathedral Cutoff, which leads to the Cathedral Trail, is on the left (east); on the right (west) is the eastern end of the Baxter Peak Cutoff, which leads southwest along the base of the summit 0.9 mi. to Thoreau Spring and the Abol and Hunt trails. At 2 mi., the Cathedral Trail from Chimney Pond enters on the left. The Saddle Trail continues on to Baxter Peak at 2.2 mi.

Saddle Trail
Distances from Chimney Pond Campground

- *to* Saddle Slide: 0.9 mi., 40 min.
- *to* Saddle and Northwest Basin Trail junction: 1.2 mi., 1 hr. 25 min.
- *to* Cathedral Trail junction: 2 mi., 1 hr. 55 min.

to Baxter Peak: 2.2 mi., 2 hr. 15 min.

to Chimney Pond Campground (via Cathedral Trail): 3.9 mi., 4 hr.

to Chimney Pond Campground (via Knife Edge and Dudley Trail): 4.6 mi., 4 hr.

to Roaring Brook Campground (via Knife Edge and Taylor Trail): 6.5 mi. (10.5 km.), 5 hr. 25 min.

Baxter Peak Cutoff

This trail makes it possible to go from one side of Katahdin to the other without climbing over the summit, saving 0.7 mi. of distance and about 600 ft. of elevation. It is wise to take this route in bad weather.

The trail leaves the Saddle Trail 1.7 mi. from Chimney Pond. It runs southwest over the open tableland along the base of Baxter Peak and ends at Thoreau Spring, which is on the Hunt Trail, 4.2 mi. from the Katahdin Stream Campground. These two trails form the shortest route between the Chimney Pond and Katahdin Stream Campground (6.8 mi.).

Baxter Peak Cutoff

Distances from Chimney Pond Campground

to start of cutoff (via Saddle Trail): 1.7 mi., 1 hr. 45 min.

to Thoreau Spring (Hunt Trail and Abol Trail junction): 2.6 mi., 2 hr. 15 min.

to Abol Campground (via Abol Trail): 5.3 mi., 5 hr.

to Katahdin Stream Campground (via Hunt Trail): 6.8 mi. (10.9 km.), 5 hr. 30 min.

North Basin Trail

From Chimney Pond, follow the Chimney Pond Trail toward Basin Ponds. At 0.3 mi., the North Basin Trail starts on the left (north; look for sign). The trail runs through spruce forest to a junction with the Hamlin Ridge Trail on the left (west) at 0.7 mi. Then it passes across the foot of Hamlin Ridge to a junction, at 0.9 mi., with the North Basin Cutoff Trail. Signs and a large cairn mark this junction. The North Basin Trail continues to the lip of the North Basin and then reaches Blueberry Knoll, a few feet higher than the floor of the basin, where there is a sweeping view of both the North Basin and the South Basin, as well as the landscape to the east. From Blueberry Knoll, it is possible to bushwhack to the boulder-strewn floor of the North Basin, with its two little ponds. The northern wall is a tremendous sheer cliff.

North Basin Trail

Distances from Chimney Pond Campground

- *to* start (via Chimney Pond Trail): 0.3 mi., 10 min.
- *to* North Basin Cutoff junction: 0.9 mi., 30 min.
- *to* Blueberry Knoll: 1.2 mi., 45 min.
- *to* North Basin Pond (via bushwhack): 1.4 mi., 55 min.
- *to* Roaring Brook Campground (via North Basin Cutoff and Chimney Pond Trail): 3.9 mi. (6.3 km.), 2 hr. 35 min.

North Basin Cutoff

This trail from Basin Ponds to Hamlin Ridge and the North Basin forks right (sign) 2.3 mi. from the Roaring Brook Campground on the Chimney Pond Trail. It traverses an area of second-growth spruce, runs past several active beaver ponds, then climbs steeply through old growth to a junction with the North Basin Trail (0.7 mi.). To reach Hamlin Ridge, turn left (southwest); to reach Blueberry Knoll and North Basin, turn right (northeast).

North Basin Cutoff

Distances from Roaring Brook Campground

- *to* start (via Chimney Pond Trail): 2.3 mi., 1 hr. 20 min.
- *to* North Basin Trail junction: 3 mi., 2 hr. 15 min.
- *to* Blueberry Knoll (via North Basin Trail): 3 mi., 2 hr. 25 min.
- *to* Hamlin Ridge Trail (via North Basin Trail): 3.2 mi., 2 hr. 15 min.
- *to* Chimney Pond Campground (via North Basin and Chimney Pond trails): 3.9 mi. (6.3 km.), 2 hr. 45 min.

Hamlin Ridge Trail

The trail climbs, largely in the open, up Hamlin Ridge, which separates the North and South basins. The views are magnificent. From the Chimney Pond Campground, follow the Chimney Pond Trail 0.3 mi. to the North Basin Trail, then follow the North Basin Trail for 0.4 mi., to the start of the Hamlin Ridge Trail, which reaches the treeline after a climb of about 20 min. Then, after a short stretch of boulder-strewn slope, the trail rises to the backbone of the ridge. It follows the open ridge to Hamlin Peak, and from there it goes on 0.2 mi. west across the open tableland and through a boulder field to Caribou Spring, which usually has *water* in a spring on the right side of the trail near a large cairn. To the right from Hamlin Peak, the North (Howe) Peaks Trail runs along the headwall of North Basin and reaches Howe Peaks in just under a mile.

Hamlin Ridge Trail

Distances from Chimney Pond Campground

- *to* start (via Chimney Pond and North Basin trails): 0.7 mi., 20 min.
- *to* Hamlin Peak: 2 mi., 2 hr. 30 min.
- *to* Caribou Spring: 2.2 mi. (3.5 km.), 2 hr. 40 min.

North (Howe) Peaks Trail

This trail offers a route up the northern slope of Katahdin from the Russell Pond area. It leads first over North (Howe) Peaks. (The official name is Howe Peaks, after Burton Howe, the lumberman who organized a trip that Percival Baxter made to Katahdin in 1920.) The trail continues to Hamlin Peak, from which connecting trails lead to other points on the mountain. The lower end of the North Peaks Trail runs through dense, mixed growth of small trees. The central section follows a brook up into a large ravine between Russell Mtn. on the left (east) and Tip Top on the right (west). Then it climbs the ravine's headwall. Be careful above the treeline when visibility is poor, especially descending. There is plenty of *water* nearly to the treeline and usually at Caribou Spring.

The trail leaves the Northwest Basin Trail 1.2 mi. southwest of the Russell Pond Campground. At 1.5 mi., the trail crosses to the south bank of Wassataquoik Stream. *(Caution:* This crossing can be dangerous or impassable in high water after rain.) It then climbs a short, steep slope to the top of a little horseback ridge at the mouth of a brook. The trail becomes a narrow path through thick, young spruce and reaches a brook at 2.7 mi. It crosses the brook about 90 yd. farther on.

At the foot of a steep rise, the trail bears right (west) away from the western bank of the brook and gradually curves left (south) on a steep climb. At 2.9 mi., it recrosses to the eastern bank of the brook near the foot of a lovely water slide, where the brook runs over sloping ledges. The path parallels the water slide for a short distance before curving to the left away from the brook and climbing through majestic old trees, which become smaller at the top of the headwall. At 4.4 mi., the trail crosses a spring brook—the last place where there is sure to be *water*. At 4.6 mi., the trail becomes a trench in dense scrub, and at 4.9 mi., it reaches the open northern tableland. Cairns lead up to a minor peak (4182 ft./1275 m.), then down its southern slope and across a level stretch covered with scrub. At 5.2 mi., the trail starts its final steep climb to the North Peaks. At 5.6 mi., it reaches the easternmost (4612 ft.) of the high, rocky knobs that make up the summit ridge. (*Caution:* Be careful here in fog. Dangerous cliffs drop off 50 or 60 ft. away, to the southwest [left].) The trail follows the line of the ridge southwest over intervening knobs to a large cairn on the highest peak (4734 ft.), at the southwestern end of the ridge (6.3 mi.). From this point, the views out over the country to the north are spectacular. The trail, well cairned, descends slightly and crosses the tableland.

At 6.5 mi., the trail forks. The North Peaks Trail follows the left (southeast) fork and climbs gradually to Hamlin Peak, where it ends at 6.9 mi. The right fork is the Hamlin Peak Cutoff that leads to Caribou Spring and the Northwest Basin Trail.

North (Howe) Peaks Trail
Distances from Russell Pond Campground

   to   start (via Northwest Basin Trail): 1.2 mi., 35 min.

   to   water slide: 2.9 mi., 2 hr. 5 min.

   to   tableland: 4.9 mi., 4 hr. 5 min.

   to   first (easternmost) North Peak: 5.6 mi., 4 hr. 55 min.

   to   second North Peak: 6.3 mi., 5 hr. 15 min.

   to   Hamlin Peak Cutoff junction: 6.5 mi., 5 hr. 25 min.

   to   Hamlin Peak: 6.9 mi. (11.1 km.), 5 hr. 40 min.

Hamlin Peak Cutoff

Following a good path along the contour, this trail runs from the North Peaks Trail, at a point in the col between North Peaks and Hamlin Peak, to the Northwest Basin Trail at Caribou Spring. By traveling north–south along the tableland, it avoids the climb over Hamlin Peak.

Hamlin Peak Cutoff

Distance from North Peaks Trail junction

   to Northwest Basin Trail junction, Caribou Spring: 0.3 mi. (0.5 km.), 8 min.

Northwest Basin Trail

This route climbs from the Russell Pond area to the Saddle through the wild and secluded Northwest Basin, with its virgin trees, glacial sheepback rocks, five ponds, waterfalls, and interesting central ridge. The lower end of the trail follows the route of the old Wassataquoik Tote Rd.

The trail begins at the Russell Pond Campground. It leads southwest from Russell Pond following the Russell Pond Trail for 0.1 mi. It then diverges right and crosses a dam at the foot of Turner Deadwater at about 0.3 mi. From there it goes on through the woods until it joins the route of the old Wassataquoik Tote Rd., at about 0.5 mi. At 1.2 mi., the North Peaks Trail leaves left. With Wassataquoik Stream on the left, the trail stays on the tote road and climbs gradually, crossing Annis Brook about 2.5 mi. from Russell Pond. The trail crosses a small brook that drains the eastern slope of Fort Mtn. It continues through thick woods and crosses Wassataquoik Stream at 3.6 mi. (*Caution:* Be very careful in high water.)

The trail climbs steadily, soon approaching Northwest Basin Brook. It runs along the brook bed for 300 ft. at about 4.4 mi. (Proceed carefully here; the rocks are very slippery.) Above the junction of the outlets from the first two ponds, Lake Cowles and Davis Pond, the trail leads steeply up to the northern shore of Lake Cowles. It then turns left and crosses the outlet of Lake Cowles at 4.7 mi. Where it climbs to a heath-covered glacial sheepback rock, the path is becoming overgrown with blueberry bushes but is not hard to follow. From the sheepback, there are enjoyable views of the entire basin. The trail continues down to the Davis Pond Lean-to, at 5.1 mi. The shelter, rebuilt in 1987, is located on the northern side of Davis Pond.

From the Davis Pond Lean-to, the Northwest Basin Trail passes the so-called disappearing pond. (The fourth pond is 0.3 mi. below and on the outlet of Davis Pond; the fifth is hidden deep in the woods between the outlets of Lake Cowles and Davis Pond.) The trail first goes southwest and then south as it climbs through a steep and rough area up the basin wall.

The trail emerges from the scrub and, at 6.2 mi., reaches a large cairn that marks a small peak (4401 ft.) near the western end of the Northwest Plateau. The Northwest Plateau reaches toward the west and is a flat extension of the northern tableland. It lies west of North Peaks and separates the Northwest Basin from Klondike Pond Ravine. Its lower slopes push their way far out into the Klondike. The Northwest Basin Trail climbs very gradually across the Northwest Plateau, passing through a belt of scrub at 6.8 mi. Then it continues more to the south across open tableland to Caribou Spring, at 7.3 mi. At the spring, the Hamlin Peak Cutoff leads sharply left to the North Peaks Trail, and the Hamlin Ridge Trail climbs left (east) to Hamlin Peak.

The Northwest Basin Trail descends south toward the Saddle, which it reaches at 8.3 mi. To get to Chimney Pond, descend east on the Saddle Trail.

Keep in mind that poor trail or weather conditions, heavy packs, and different levels of physical conditioning in hiking parties will increase the times given here.

Northwest Basin Trail

Distances from Russell Pond Campground

- *to* North Peaks Trail junction: 1.2 mi., 35 min.

- *to* Annis Brook crossing: 2.5 mi., 1 hr. 30 min.

- *to* Wassataquoik Stream crossing: 3.6 mi., 2 hr. 15 min.

- *to* Davis Pond Lean-to: 5.1 mi., 3 hr. 15 min.

- *to* peak of Northwest Plateau: 6.2 mi., 4 hr. 50 min.

- *to* Hamlin Ridge Trail and Hamlin Peak Cutoff junction, Caribou Spring: 7.3 mi., 5 hr. 35 min.

to Saddle and Saddle Trail junction: 8.3 mi. (13.3 km.), 6 hr.

Russell Pond Trail

This trail runs from the Roaring Brook Campground northward between Katahdin and Turner Mtn. to the Russell Pond Campground. It is the principal approach to the Russell Pond area.

After leaving the Roaring Brook Campground, the trail crosses Roaring Brook. At 0.2 mi., it turns left (northwest; look for sign). To the right, the South Turner Mtn. Trail leads to Sandy Stream Pond and South Turner Mtn. In the next half-mile, the Russell Pond Trail crosses several brooks while gradually climbing the low height-of-land between Sandy Stream Pond and Whidden Pond. The trail descends and passes to the east (right) of the latter, where there is an extensive view of the basins and peaks on the east side of Katahdin. At 1.1 mi., the Sandy Stream Pond Trail comes in on the right. At 1.4 mi., an opening yields good views; after this point, the trail moves into denser forest. Between 2.3 mi. and 3.1 mi., it crosses several brooks, and at 3.3 mi., it reaches a junction on the right with the Wassataquoik Stream Trail, which leads 2.5 mi. to the two Wassataquoik Stream Lean-tos and rejoins the Russell Pond Trail at 3.9 mi. At 3.4 mi., the Russell Pond Trail crosses the Wassataquoik South Branch and soon crosses another brook. There are no bridges here; the crossing is knee-deep in dry weather, dangerous after rain.

The trail, now on the western side of the valley, passes under an overhanging rock at 3.8 mi. Moving away from Wassataquoik Stream, it passes several brooks and springs and climbs gently for nearly 2 mi. to a spruce grove. Then the trail gradually descends, with the impressive, high, forested slopes of Russell Mtn. on the left. At 6.3 mi., it crosses the main branch of Wassataquoik Stream. At 6.5 mi., it crosses the old Wassataquoik Tote Rd. with the abandoned clearing for New City Camps on the right. A trail on the right leads 1.4 mi. to the two lean-tos on Wassataquoik Stream. Immediately beyond the tote road, the Russell Pond Trail crosses Turner Brook (North Branch of the Wassataquoik).

At 6.9 mi., the Northwest Basin Trail to the Saddle leaves on the left (west). Soon after, the trail reaches Russell Pond.

Russell Pond Trail

Distances from Roaring Brook Campground

- *to* Sandy Stream Pond Trail junction: 1.1 mi., 30 min.
- *to* Wassataquoik Stream Trail junction: 3.3 mi., 1 hr. 40 min.
- *to* Wassataquoik Tote Rd. junction: 6.5 mi., 3 hr. 10 min.
- *to* Northwest Basin Trail junction: 6.9 mi., 3 hr. 40 min.
- *to* Russell Pond Campground: 7 mi. (11.3 km.), 3 hr. 45 min.

Wassataquoik Stream Trail

Some once called this old route the Tracy Horse Trail or Wassataquoik South Branch Trail. It runs from the Russell Pond Trail along the South Branch of Wassataquoik Stream to the main branch of Wassataquoik Stream. It leaves the right (east) side of the Russell Pond Trail about 3.3 mi. north of the Roaring Brook Campground, just before that trail crosses the South Branch. It leads to the junction with the main stream and continues along the southern bank of the main stream for about 100 yd.

The park authority maintains two lean-tos at the site of the old Hersey Dam (some remains of the dam are still visible). Reservations for them can be made as for any campsite.

To reach the Russell Pond Campground from the lean-tos, cross to the northern side of Wassataquoik Stream upstream from the lean-tos (no bridge) and look for a blue-blazed trail along the old Wassataquoik Tote Rd. In the downstream direction, this trail leads 1.6 mi. to a junction with the Grand Falls Trail at Inscription Rock. In the upstream direction, it leads 1.4 mi. to a junction with the Russell Pond

Trail just south of the Turner Brook crossing. Turn right on the Russell Pond Trail to reach the campground, which is about 0.4 mi. away.

Wassataquoik Stream Trail

Distances from Roaring Brook Campground

- *to* start of trail to lean-tos (via Russell Pond Trail): 3.3 mi., 1 hr. 40 min.
- *to* lean-tos: 5.8 mi., 3 hr.
- *to* Russell Pond Campground (via Russell Pond Trail): 7.6 mi. (12.2 km.), 3 hr. 45 min.

RUSSELL MOUNTAIN (2801 ft./854 m.)

This mountain is the northernmost extension of Katahdin. Its broad, trailless summit area is devoid of recognizable characteristics and so flat and full of boulders that you have to search for the summit cairn. But the summit offers excellent views in all directions. To reach it, bushwhack west from the Russell Pond Trail about 4.5 mi. north of the Roaring Brook Campground. Since there is no trail to the mountain and conditions change from year to year, check with the ranger at the Russell Pond Campground for the latest information. See also the section on Bushwhacking in the Maine Mountains in this book's introduction.

Russell Pond Campground

On the southwestern shore of Russell Pond (1333 ft.) in the heart of the wilderness north of Katahdin, this campground is a convenient and interesting hiking base. The wildlife in this remote area is especially intriguing. Facilities include tentsites, lean-tos, and a bunkhouse. The Wassataquoik Lake Cabin and the lean-tos on Wassataquoik Stream, Pogy Pond, and Little Wassataquoik Pond are administered from this campground.

Russell Pond Campground

Distances from Russell Pond Campground

- *to* Roaring Brook Campground (via Russell Pond Trail): 7 mi. (11.3 km.), 3 hr. 45 min.

- *to* Hamlin Peak (via North Peaks Trail): 6.9 mi. (11.1 km.), 5 hr. 40 min. (*descending,* 3 hr. 50 min.)

- *to* Davis Pond Lean-to (via Northwest Basin Trail): 5.1 mi. (8.2 km.), 3 hr. 15 min. (*descending*, 2 hr. 45 min.)

- *to* Wassataquoik Lake (via Wassataquoik Lake Trail): 2.4 mi. (3.9 km.), 1 hr. 15 min.

- *to* Little Wassataquoik Lake (via Wassataquoik Lake Trail): 5.2 mi. (8.4 km.), 3 hr. 10 min.

- *to* Nesowadnehunk Campground: 14.3 mi. (relocated 1996)

- *to* Lookout Ledges (via Pogy Notch and Grand Falls trails): 1.3 mi. (2.1 km.), 50 min.

- *to* Grand Falls (via Grand Falls Trail): 2.8 mi. (4.5 km.), 1 hr. 30 min.

- *to* South Branch Pond Campground (via Pogy Notch Trail): 9.7 mi. (15.6 km.), 4 hr. 40 min.

- *to* Wassataquoik Stream Lean-tos (via Wassataquoik Stream Trail): 1.8 mi. (2.9 km.), 1 hr.

Wassataquoik Lake Trail

This trail connects the Russell Pond Campground with the Wassataquoik Lake area and continues on to the west to the tote road and the foot of Nesowadnehunk Lake. Most of the first part of this route was a logging road prior to 1878, and there is evidence it was cut out before 1845. The area was logged several times afterward. The west end of the trail follows a fairly new logging road built after the park was created. The former owners retained cutting rights for a period after they sold the property to Governor Baxter.

The trail leads north off the Pogy Notch Trail opposite Lean-to 4 at the northwestern corner of Russell Pond. At 0.5 mi. from Russell Pond, take the left fork (the right fork leads to Deep Pond). At 1.5 mi., the trail crosses a dam between two of the Six Ponds. It then crosses a brook at 2 mi., and at 2.2 mi., a side trail leads right (north) 300 ft. to a canoe landing for the island campsite on Wassataquoik Lake. The trail, relocated in 1994, parallels the southern shore of the lake. About halfway along, a trail leads left (south) uphill to Green Falls, one of the most beautiful spots in the park.

Near the head of Wassataquoik Lake, at 4.3 mi., the trail joins an old road. After crossing the outlet stream from Little Wassataquoik Lake several times, it reaches the lake itself. It then follows along the northern shore to the lake's western end (about 5.2 mi.). The trail heads west from the lake toward a col between Wassataquoik Mtn. and Lord Mtn. Shortly after leaving the lake, at 4.9 mi., the trail passes the Little Wassataquoik Lake Lean-to. The trail climbs to the col and then descends into the Trout Brook drainage area. From the col, the trail follows an old logging road for about a mile and a half before it leaves the road and turns left at about 6.3 mi. At 7 mi. the trail, relocated in 1996, swings left (south). Wet in places, it crosses a brook several times and, at about 8.2 mi., it crosses the South Branch of Trout Brook. The trail then skirts a series of small hills. At 9.7 mi., it reaches Center Pond, which has fine views of the Brothers. Ford and follow Little Nesowadnehunk Stream to the Nesowadnehunk Campground at 14.3 mi.

Wassataquoik Lake Trail

Distances from Russell Pond Campground

> *to* start (via Pogy Notch Trail): 0.2 mi., 5 min.
>
> *to* Deep Pond side-trail junction: 0.5 mi., 20 min.
>
> *to* dam at Six Ponds: 1.5 mi., 50 min.
>
> *to* side trail to Wassataquoik Lake: 2.2 mi., 1 hr. 10 min.
>
> *to* Green Falls (via side trail): 3.1 mi., 1 hr. 45 min.

- *to* Little Wassataquoik Lake: 4.6 mi., 3 hr. 10 min.
- *to* left turn off old logging road: 6.3 mi., 3 hr. 50 min.
- *to* Center Mtn. Lean-to: 7.9 mi. (12.6 km.)
- *to* South Branch of Trout Brook: 8.2 mi., 4 hr. 30 min.
- *to* Center Pond: 9.7 mi. (15.5 km.), 5 hr. 20 min.
- *to* Nesowadnehunk Campground: 14.3 mi. (22.9 km.), 6 hr. 15 min.

Grand Falls Trail

This trail leads from the Russell Pond Campground to several interesting locations in Wassataquoik Valley. Its first part coincides with the Pogy Notch Trail.

From the campground, follow the Pogy Notch Trail around the western shore of the pond. The Wassataquoik Lake Trail leaves to the left soon after the start of the route. At 0.2 mi., the Pogy Notch Trail continues north (left) at a junction. The Grand Falls Trail takes the right fork, passes the ranger station, and continues to the next junction (0.4 mi.), where the trail to Lookout Ledges leaves to the left (north). The Grand Falls Trail continues ahead on the right through woods and over relatively level ground toward Wassataquoik Stream. As it nears the Wassataquoik, a side trail to the right leads 17 yd. to the bank of the stream and Inscription Rock, a huge boulder with a notice about logging in the area that was inscribed in 1883. A 1.6-mi. segment of the old Wassataquoik Tote Rd., from Inscription Rock to the Wassataquoik Stream Lean-tos, was reopened in 1983, allowing you to loop back to Russell Pond via the Wassataquoik Stream Trail and the Russell Pond Trail. From this junction, the main trail soon reaches the bank of Wassataquoik Stream near the Grand Falls of the Wassataquoik. These falls drop steeply through high granite walls and are impressive, particularly in high water. The ruins of a logging dam lie just upstream.

Grand Falls Trail
Distances from Russell Pond Campground

- *to* Lookout Ledges Trail junction: 0.4 mi., 10 min.
- *to* Inscription Rock (via side trail): *est.* 2.5 mi., 1 hr. 20 min.
- *to* Grand Falls: *est.* 2.8 mi. (4.5 km.), 1 hr. 30 min.

Lookout Ledges Trail

This high outlook (1730 ft./527 m.) offers views from Traveler Mtn. around to Katahdin and is easy to reach from the Russell Pond Campground. Follow the Pogy Notch and Grand Falls trails for 0.4 mi. and turn left at the junction. The trail climbs moderately and steadily for nearly a mile to the ledges.

Lookout Ledges Trail
Distances from Russell Pond Campground

- *to* start (via Pogy Notch and Grand Falls trails): 0.4 mi., 10 min.
- *to* Lookout Ledges: 1.3 mi. (2.1 km.), 50 min.

THE OWL (3736 ft./1139 m.)

This mountain is the first summit in the long, high range that runs west from Katahdin. Its southern face is especially steep.

The Owl Trail

The blue-blazed Owl Trail leaves the Hunt Trail 1.1 mi. from the Katahdin Stream Campground. The trail goes left from the Hunt Trail just before a crossing of Katahdin Stream and then follows the northern bank of a tributary. It turns sharply right (southeast) and crosses the tributary at 1.6 mi. *(last source of water).* The trail climbs gradually through dense spruce and fir and follows the western spur toward the summit. At 2.9 mi., the trail rises steeply through a ravine and then across the upper part of the Owl's prominent cliffs. At 3.2 mi., the trail reaches the first outlook. After a more gradual climb, it reaches the summit at 3.3 mi. Views in all directions are outstanding, especially those into the Klondike and across to the tremendous windrows in Witherle Ravine and on Fort Mtn.

The Owl Trail
Distances from Katahdin Stream Campground

> *to* start (via Hunt Trail): 1.1 mi., 45 min.

> *to* first outlook: 3.2 mi., 2 hr. 35 min.

> *to* the Owl summit: 3.3 mi. (5.3 km.), 2 hr. 40 min.

BARREN MOUNTAIN (3580 ft. and 3681 ft./1091 m. and 1122 m.)

A high, wooded ridge, Barren Mtn. has two well-defined summits and several lower humps. A blowdown that occurred in 1974 eliminated possible approaches from the south and southwest.

One route goes up the southeastern slide of O-J-I, then southeast into the col and up the Barren summit ridge. Scrub growth near the summits of O-J-I and Barren makes this route slow. It is also possible to climb from the Owl-Barren ravine, but blowdowns make this approach very difficult. See the section on Bushwhacking in the Maine Mountains in this book's introduction.

MOUNT O-J-I (3410 ft./1039 m.)

Mt. O-J-I got its name from three slides on its southwestern slope that at one point suggested the three letters. After a major storm in 1932, however, the slides began to enlarge, and the letter shapes have become distorted. A fourth large slide, which can be climbed, came down in 1954; it is south of the so-called south slide.

Two of the other slides, the north and south slides, offer routes up the mountain. They are connected, which allows a circuit of the mountain in either direction. Descending the smooth, steep granite slope on the north slide can be very dangerous, however, particularly in wet weather; it is better to climb up by the north slide and return by the south slide.

The trail leaves the tote road at Foster Field directly opposite the road to Kidney Pond and immediately crosses a brook. At 0.4 mi., the trail forks. Go left to reach the north slide. (The right fork leads to the south slide.) The trail follows an old road and immediately crosses two small brooks. At 1.1 mi., the road ends in a small open area covered with slide gravel and cut by a streambed that is usually dry. (About 45 yd. north of this point, watch for a huge boulder off the trail on the left. The boulder is approximately 73 ft. long, 48 ft. wide, and 25 ft. high.) From the small open area, the trail parallels the streambed without crossing it and leads directly (approximately 200 yd.) to a large open wash at the foot of the north slide and then to the top of the lower ledges. Many sections of this route traverse smooth granite, sometimes covered by gravel; *be careful,* particularly if the rock is wet. Climb to the head of the slide and then go through brush to the summit ridge. There, the trail heads to the western summit, where a trail leads left to Old Jay Eye Rock, a fine observation point. From the summit ridge, a trail leads right to the south slide.

To follow the south-slide route, go right at the fork 0.4 mi. from Foster Field. The route follows an old road and, at 1.8 mi., continues on a narrow trail. As the gravel wash from the slide becomes noticeable on the forest floor, the trail bears right and soon reaches the open wash (2 mi.). Climb to the head of the slide and through brush and scrub to the summit ridge. Then go northwest to the summit (2.9 mi.).

Another route is to approach the mountain by climbing the Mt. Coe slide. The O-J-I Link Trail, cleared in 1983, runs 0.5 mi. from the Mt. Coe slide across the col to a junction with the O-J-I South Slide Trail 0.2 mi. from the summit.

Mount O-J-I

Distances from tote road at Foster Field

- *to* fork in trail: 0.4 mi., 10 min.

- *to* foot of north slide (via left fork): 1.2 mi., 45 min.

- *to* foot of south slide (via right fork): 2 mi., 1 hr. 10 min.

- *to* O-J-I summit (via north slide): 2.7 mi., 3 hr.

- *to* O-J-I summit (via south slide): 2.9 mi., 3 hr. 15 min.

- *to* perimeter road (via north slide–south slide circuit): 5.6 mi. (9 km.), 6 hr.

MOUNT COE (3764 ft./1147 m.)

This peak, just north of Mt. O-J-I, has excellent views into the Klondike and is well worth the challenge of the climb.

Follow the Marston Trail to the sign 1.2 mi. from the tote road. Turn right and follow the trail 0.2 mi. to the bottom of the Mt. Coe slide (it follows a stream). The climb is steady but moderate at first, then steep. At 2.6 mi., the trail bears left and begins to climb the left center of a wide slide area at 2.8 mi. (The O-J-I Link Trail leads right 0.5 mi. to the O-J-I South Slide Trail. It is 0.7 mi. to the summit of O-J-I via this trail.) At 3 mi., the trail enters scrub growth. At 3.3 mi. you will reach the summit.

An extension of the Mt. Coe Trail, cleared in 1983 and further extended in 1987, rejoins the Marston Trail at a point 0.8 mi. from the summit of North Brother.

The trail descends the eastern ridge of Mt. Coe and proceeds toward South Brother. At 4.2 mi., you will pass two clearings with fine views of Mt. Coe. At 4.4 mi., the South Brother Side Trail leads right 0.3 mi. to the summit of South Brother. At 5.1 mi., you will reach the junction with the Marston Trail. Ahead, it is 0.8 mi. to the summit of North Brother. To the left, it is 2.9 mi. to the tote road.

Mount Coe
Distances from tote road at Slide Dam

- *to* start of Mt. Coe Trail (via Marston Trail): 1.2 mi., 50 min.
- *to* foot of Mt. Coe slide: 1.4 mi., 1 hr.
- *to* start of scrub: 3 mi., 3 hr. 45 min.
- *to* Coe summit: 3.3 mi., 4 hr. (*descending*, 2 hr.)
- *to* South Brother Side Trail junction: 4.4 mi., 4 hr. 45 min.
- *to* Marston Trail junction: 5.1 mi. (8.2 km.), 5 hr. 15 min.

THE BROTHERS (North 4143 ft./1263 m.
and South 3930 ft./1198 m.)

North and South Brother are open peaks that offer splendid views in several directions. *Caution:* Early in the season—late May and the first half of June—climbers should expect to find deep snow at high elevations—a distance of 1.5 mi.

Marston Trail

The Marston Trail, the best approach for exploring the Brothers area, was relocated in 1987.

The trail leaves the tote road at the Slide Dam, 5.9 mi. north of the Katahdin Stream Campground and 3.6 mi. south of the Nesowadnehunk Campground. The trail starts from the road, nearly opposite the picnic shelter, and follows the northern bank of Slide Brook to an open, sandy area. At 0.2 mi., the trail bears left into a wooded area and over a slight rise into the drainage area of a second brook. Climbing steadily, the trail follows this brook closely for the next mile. At 0.8 mi., it crosses, and there are several more crossings in the next 0.4 mi. before the trail reaches the junction with the Mt. Coe Trail at 1.3 mi.

The Marston Trail leads to the left and climbs gradually through extensive blowdowns. A small pond with fine views is reached at 2 mi. At 2.1 mi., you will reach the pond's outlet (*last water*). The trail then climbs steeply, passing several viewpoints. It levels off at 2.7 mi. and reaches the upper junction with the Mt. Coe Trail at 2.9 mi. To the left, it is 0.8 mi. to North Brother. To the right, the Mt. Coe Trail leads (1 mi. to South Brother via the South Brother Side Trail) 5.1 mi. to the tote road. After crossing this fairly level valley, it passes a spring at 3.1 mi. and then climbs steeply. At 3.6 mi., the trail leaves the scrub and continues among open boulders, reaching the summit of North Brother at 3.7 mi. Note particularly the view of the western slopes of Katahdin and, in the opposite direction, of the Nesowadnehunk Lake region and the interesting valley of Little Nesowadnehunk Stream.

Marston Trail

Distances from tote road at Slide Dam

   to Mt. Coe Trail, first junction: 1.3 mi., 50 min.

   to pond: 2.1 mi., 1 hr. 10 min.

   to Mt. Coe Trail, second junction: 2.9 mi., 2 hr.

   to North Brother summit: 3.7 mi. (6 km.), 3 hr. (*descending*, 2 hr.)

FORT MOUNTAIN (3861 ft./1177 m.)

This mountain, with its 0.5-mi. summit ridge, is northeast of North Brother. A high saddle connects the two. The best and easiest route to Fort Mtn. is a trail leading left into the bush from the summit of North Brother. This trail is rough, unmarked, and obliterated in sections by blown-down trees; it keeps to the southern side of the North Brother–Fort ridge most of the way. It emerges on the northwestern end of the Fort ridge. The distance is less than 1 mi.

Before trying to take this route, keep in mind that it comes at the end of a very tiring climb to North Brother. See the section on Bushwhacking in the Maine Mountains in this book's introduction.

Fort Mountain

Distances from tote road at Slide Dam

  to North Brother summit (via Marston Trail): 3.7 mi., 3 hr.

  to Fort Mtn. northwestern summit: *est.* 4.7 mi. (7.6 km.), 4 hr.
       (*descending,* 2 hr. 45 min.)

Daicey Pond Campground

When the BSP Authority terminated the private leases still existing in
the park in the late 1960s, it decided to continue operations on a mod-
ified scale at the former Twin Pines Camps at Daicey Pond. There are
ten cabins for rent. Users must provide their own cooking equipment.
Canoes can be rented. To reach Daicey Pond, follow the tote road for
2.7 mi. beyond the Katahdin Stream Campground and turn left
(south). It is 1.5 mi. to the camps, which have beautiful views of the
western side of Katahdin and the mountains to the west. From a canoe
on the pond, you can get an excellent view of Doubletop.

The Appalachian Trail (AT) passes within a short distance of the
campground and skirts the shore opposite the camp for 0.3 mi. Hikers
entering the park from the south along the AT must register at Daicey
Pond. The Katahdin Stream Campground is 1.9 mi. northeast on the
AT. South of Daicey Pond, the AT passes an old dam on Nesowadnehunk Stream and Little and Big Niagara falls. All are worth seeing and
are within 1.3 mi. of the campground. The AT then leads out of the
park to the West Branch of the Penobscot (see the MATC's *Appalachian Trail Guide to Maine* for details).

Daicey Pond is a good starting point for the climb to Sentinel
Mtn. Trails also lead to the Kidney Pond area, and a lovely trail of
about 1 mi. leads from the canoe landing on Daicey Pond, across from
the cabins, to Lost Pond.

Kidney Pond Campground

Formerly a private enterprise, the Kidney Pond Campground reopened
under park management in 1990 for day-use fishing, canoe rental on

some of the surrounding ponds, and cabin rental for family groups and hikers. The campground is reached off the tote road, with day-use parking available.

The Draper Pond Trail runs from the Doubletop Mt. Trail 0.5 mi. to a canoe landing on the pond's southern shore. Rocky Pond Trail (0.6 mi.) to the northwest reaches the pond where park canoes can be rented. A 0.6-mi. trail leads to Little Rocky Pond. From the western shore, the Polly Pond Trail runs 0.9 mi. to just outside the park border. From a canoe landing on the western shore of Kidney Pond, the Celia and Jackson Pond Trail reaches Celia Pond at 0.9 mi. At 1.1 mi., the Little Beaver Pond Trail starts south; it runs 0.7 mi. Jackson Pond, with park canoes, is reached at 1.3 mi.

Kidney Pond is girded east and south by its Outlet Trail (1.8 mi.), which heads east, then south, along Nesowadnehunk Stream and branches, left to the Daicey Pond Campground and right (west) to connect with the Sentinel Mtn. Trail.

South of Kidney Pond, the Lily Pad Pond Trail goes to a canoe landing on a stream, which reaches the pond in 0.25 mi. From Lily Pad Pond's southern landing, the 1-mi. Windy Pitch Pond Trail heads south to the pond, passing Little and Big Niagara falls.

SENTINEL MOUNTAIN (1837 ft./560 m.)

This low mountain rises over the northern bank of the West Branch of the Penobscot River and offers the finest view of the western side of Katahdin. From Kidney Pond Rd., skirt the western side of Kidney Pond, or paddle across it to the canoe landing (Sentinel Landing) on the southern side of the cove on the right (west).

From Daicey Pond, cross Nesowadnehunk Stream. Then branch left (west) from the trail to Kidney Pond at a point 300 yd. from that pond. The trail goes around the southwestern side of the pond to Sentinel Landing, which is about 0.7 mi. from Daicey Pond. (*Caution:* Be careful to avoid several branch trails that are almost as clear as the main trail; some of them lead from a landing the main trail passes before it gets to Sentinel Landing.)

From Sentinel Landing, the blue-blazed trail to Sentinel Mtn. leads southwest. At 0.3 mi. (sign), the trail bears right onto a section that was relocated to avoid beaver flow. At 0.7 mi., you will have to cross Beaver Brook on stepping-stones. The trail climbs the northeastern side of the mountain along a brook, which crosses the trail at 1.1 mi. and furnishes *water* nearly to the open summit ledges. The trail reaches the ledges at 2.2 mi. Follow the ledges to the right (north) to reach the actual summit (2.3 mi.).

From the actual summit at the western end of the summit ridge, the trail continues back along the southern side of the ridge, with an outlook over the West Branch, to form a loop. It rejoins the main trail about halfway between the first ledges and the true summit.

Sentinel Mountain Trail
Distances from Sentinel Landing

   to Beaver Brook crossing: 0.7 mi., 20 min.

   to second brook crossing: 1.1 mi., 40 min.

   to Sentinel summit: 2.3 mi. (3.7 km.), 1 hr. 30 min.

DOUBLETOP MOUNTAIN
(North Peak 3488 ft./1063 m.)

Doubletop's steep, slide-scarred eastern slopes make it easy to identify from many points in the Katahdin region. The views from its two peaks are impressive and are particularly helpful to anyone planning to climb South Brother, Mt. Coe, Mt. O-J-I, or Barren Mtn., or to hike into the Klondike.

Doubletop Mountain Trail, Southern Approach

The Doubletop Mtn. Trail, relocated in 1994, starts at Kidney Pond. At 0.3 mi., it reaches a junction with the Draper Pond Trail; the pond is 0.2 mi. beyond. Cross Slaughter Brook at 0.9 mi.; you will reach Deer Pond at 1.1 mi. At 1.3 mi., bear left on the old Slaughter Pond Tote Rd., which leads to the old Camp 3 clearing.

At the far end of the Camp 3 clearing, the trail to Doubletop forks right (north), leaving the clearing near its northwest corner. *Watch carefully:* This turn is hard to see. Straight ahead (west), an old road continues to Slaughter Pond. Turn right (north) before you reenter the woods or leave the clearing.

The trail follows an old road northwest up a valley, crossing a stream four times. The stream and trail run together for a while, which makes the route extremely wet and muddy. The trail passes close under the cliffs on Squaw's Bosom, the peak west of Doubletop, and then turns northeast at about 2.3 mi. Just after crossing the headwaters of the stream, it reaches uncut spruce woods and passes a spring at 3.1 mi. Turning north again, the trail climbs the saddle west of Doubletop. Then it slabs up a steep, timbered slope on the western side of the mountain to the South Peak (4 mi.), which is above the timberline. The trail continues from the South Peak 0.2 mi. to the North Peak. From the North Peak, the trail descends and leads north to the Nesowadnehunk Campground.

Doubletop Mountain Trail, Southern Approach

Distances from Kidney Pond

- *to* old Camp 3 clearing: 2 mi., 45 min.
- *to* South Peak: 4.6 mi., 3 hr. 20 min.
- *to* North Peak: 4.8 mi., 3 hr. 30 min.
- *to* Nesowadnehunk Campground: 7.9 mi. (12.6 km.), 6 hr. 30 min.

Doubletop Mountain Trail, Northern Approach

The approach from the north leads south from the last lean-to at the Nesowadnehunk Campground. Initially, it parallels Nesowadnehunk Stream, which lies to the east. For the first mile, it follows a fairly level course, and then it turns southwest and ascends gradually in the valley of the brook draining the area between Veto Mtn. on the northwest and Doubletop on the southeast. After about 1.5 mi., the trail swings generally south once more to follow the northern ridge of Doubletop as it climbs more steeply and steadily to the North Peak.

Doubletop Mountain Trail, Northern Approach

Distances from Nesowadnehunk Campground

- *to* North Peak: 3.1 mi., 2 hr. 45 min.
- *to* South Peak: 3.3 mi., 3 hr.
- *to* Kidney Pond Campground road: 7.9 mi. (12.6 km.), 6 hr. 30 min.

Nesowadnehunk Campground

This campground on Nesowadnehunk Stream, although beautiful, is not a major hiking center. It is the base for the approach to Doubletop from the north. It is also a control point for entering the park from the west. Anglers find this campground a convenient base.

MULLEN MOUNTAIN (3450 ft./1052 m.)

This rock-capped peak is north of the Brothers and south of Wassataquoik Mtn. The climb starts in the vicinity of Mullen Pond. Virgin spruce covers the northern slope, and the hiking is smooth. See the section on Bushwhacking in the Maine Mountains in this book's introduction.

The old Mullen Brook Tote Rd., up Mullen Brook to Mullen Pond, provides an approach from the Russell Pond area. (This route is not official—check for permission and trail conditions with the Russell Pond Campground ranger.) The old Mullen Brook Tote Rd. leaves the Northwest Basin Trail on the north, opposite where the Northwest Basin Trail joins the old Wassataquoik Tote Rd., about 0.5 mi. from Russell Pond. The old Mullen Brook Tote Rd. is overgrown and hard to see from the Northwest Basin Trail. Beavers have dammed ponds along the route; where the trail skirts them, it is difficult to follow. Soon after leaving the Northwest Basin Trail, the route follows the edge of a swamp and then turns sharply left, skirts another swamp, crosses a brook, and returns to the old Mullen Brook Tote Rd. This road climbs gradually and then more steeply to Mullen Pond, about 3.5 mi. from the Northwest Basin Trail. To bushwhack to the summit from the eastern shore of the pond, turn left (south) and pass through open spruce woods to a collar of thick dwarf birches just below the open, rocky summit.

Mullen Mountain

Distances from Russell Pond Campground

- *to* old Mullen Brook Tote Rd. junction (via Northwest Basin Trail): 0.5 mi., 25 min.
- *to* Mullen Pond: *est.* 4 mi., 2 hr. 15 min.
- *to* Mullen Mtn. summit: *est.* 5 mi. (8 km.), 4 hr. 30 min.

WASSATAQUOIK MOUNTAIN (2984 ft./910 m.)

Hikers do climb this broad, wooded mountain from the southern shore of Wassataquoik Lake; see the section on Bushwhacking in the Maine Mountains in this book's introduction. (For the approach to the start of the route, see the description of the Wassataquoik Lake Trail.) The trail up Wassataquoik is not officially maintained. It starts west of the outlet brook of Green Falls, crosses the brook, and climbs steeply east of the falls. After several more crossings, it leaves the brook and climbs on up the mountain. Near the top, it is obscured by raspberry bushes and debris from a fire in 1959. From the southern and more precipitous edge of the summit, there is a good view of Mullen Mtn. and the country beyond.

Wassataquoik Mountain

Distances from Russell Pond Campground

- *to* start of trail to Green Falls (via Wassataquoik Lake Trail): *est.* 3.2 mi., 1 hr. 35 min.

- *to* Green Falls: *est.* 3.3 mi., 1 hr. 45 min.

- *to* Wassataquoik summit: *est.* 5 mi. (8 km.), 4 hr.

STRICKLAND MOUNTAIN (2400 ft./732 m.)

It is best to climb this low, wooded summit from Camp Phoenix, on the eastern side of Nesowadnehunk Lake. This camp is an enclave of privately owned land surrounded by BSP and the lake. From the eastern side of the barnyard in the rear of the camps, cross the tote road and follow logging roads over the gentle slope to the point where it starts to get steeper. Beyond, there are no trails, but you can hike through mostly open, pleasant woods to the summit, from which there are good views toward Center Mtn. and the Brothers. Take a compass bearing on Camp Phoenix before descending. See the section on Bushwhacking in the Maine Mountains in this book's introduction.

BURNT MOUNTAIN (1793 ft./547 m.)

There is a firetower on this low summit in the northwestern section of the park. Trees are gradually blocking what were once excellent views from the summit. The Burnt Mountain Trail begins at the Burnt Mtn. picnic area, 13.8 mi. west of the Matagamon Gatehouse or 8.8 mi. north of the Nesowadnehunk Gatehouse.

Burnt Mountain Trail

Distance from Burnt Mtn. picnic area

- *to* Burnt Mtn. summit: 1.3 mi. (2.1 km.), 50 min.

South Branch Pond Campground

This campground is at the eastern end of Lower (northern) South Branch Pond (981 ft.). The South Branch ponds have perhaps the most spectacular surroundings of any in Maine, except the ones near Katahdin. They lie in a deep valley between Traveler Mtn. to the east and South Branch Mtn. (Black Cat Mtn.) to the west. The campground, the usual base for hiking in the Traveler area, has choice views of Traveler's peaks and ridges, of the pond, and of South Branch Mtn. Facilities include open-front shelters, tenting space, a bunkhouse, and rental canoes.

Distances from South Branch Pond Campground

   to Middle Fowler Pond: 4 mi. (6.5 km.), 2 hr. 30 min.

   to North Traveler summit (via North Traveler Trail): 2.5 mi. (4 km.), 2 hr. 20 min.

   to Peak of the Ridges (via Pogy Pond and Center Ridge trails): *est.* 3.5 mi. (5.6 km.), 2 hr. 50 min.

   to southern end of Upper South Branch Pond (via Pogy Notch Trail): 1.9 mi. (3.1 km.), 1 hr.

   to Russell Pond Campground (via Pogy Notch Trail): 9.7 mi. (15.6 km.), 4 hr. 40 min.

Pogy Notch Trail

This trail leads from the South Branch Pond Campground around the eastern shores of the ponds, then south through Pogy Notch. It passes west of Pogy Pond and continues southwest to the Russell Pond Campground. The trail offers fairly easy access to the center of the park and the trails on Katahdin. Nice views enhance the hike.

From the South Branch Pond Campground, enter woods on the trail toward the eastern shore of the pond. The North Traveler Trail diverges left at 0.2 mi. At 1 mi., the trail reaches the delta of Howe Brook and the Howe Brook Trail, which leaves to the west. Soon it enters some woods, where it follows a brook route at first and then bears right (south) away from the brook. At 1.3 mi., the trail climbs over the end of the cliff between Lower and Upper South Branch ponds. The Center Ridge Trail goes left at 1.4 mi. The Pogy Notch Trail descends and passes an old campsite at the southeastern corner of the upper pond. The South Branch Mountain Trail comes in on the right at the old campsite (1.9 mi.). The Pogy Notch Trail continues south, passing through an alder swamp and beaver works at 2.8 mi. It crosses several brooks and rises and falls moderately in the next 0.5 mi. At 3.3 mi., the trail forks. Straight ahead is the old route to Traveler Pond; the Pogy Notch Trail turns right, climbs gradually, and passes through Pogy Notch.

Bear left at 3.9 mi. into a sparsely grown old burn. The trail then crosses a beaver canal and descends into the Pogy Pond watershed. It crosses a brook several times while passing out of the notch area and descending toward Pogy Pond. It then crosses several other brooks and reaches the head of Pogy Pond at 6 mi. (There are clear views of Traveler, Turner, and Katahdin mountains from the shore of the pond.)

The trail bears right, uphill, and at 6.1 mi., a side trail to the left leads 0.2 mi. to the Pogy Pond Lean-to. The main trail descends nearly to the pond (6.2 mi.), then bears right, away from the pond. (Be careful not to take a wrong turn onto a short spur trail to the west. Also, watch carefully for blazes, which are scarce in this area.) The main trail rises gradually, then descends through an old burn, traverses a series of shallow rises, and bears right. At 6.7 mi., it drops into the gully of the western tributary of Pogy Brook, crosses, and climbs up the opposite slope. Then it runs through a swampy hollow, climbs a rocky rise, and descends gradually to cross another brook (7.3 mi.). Immediately after this second brook, the trail bears right and climbs gradually through sparse mixed growth. It crosses a beaver meadow, reaches a rough boulder field at 7.8 mi., and descends through it. The trail descends toward Russell Pond, and at 9.4 mi., the trail to Grand Falls and Lookout Ledges leaves to the left. Just before the Russell Pond Campground, the Wassataquoik Lake Trail leaves to the right.

Pogy Notch Trail
Distances from South Branch Pond Campground

> *to*   North Traveler Trail junction: 0.2 mi., 5 min.

> *to*   Howe Brook Trail junction: 1 mi., 30 min.

> *to*   Center Ridge Trail junction: 1.4 mi., 45 min.

> *to*   South Branch Mountain Trail junction: 1.9 mi., 1 hr.

> *to*   Pogy Pond: 6 mi., 3 hr.

> *to*   Grand Falls Trail junction: 9.3 mi., 4 hr. 30 min.

> *to*   Russell Pond Campground: 9.7 mi. (15.6 km.), 4 hr. 40 min.

SOUTH BRANCH (BLACK CAT) MOUNTAIN
(northern summit 2599 ft./792 m. and southern summit 2585 ft./788 m.)

South Branch Mtn. (Black Cat Mtn. on USGS maps) is across the ponds from Traveler Mtn. It offers extraordinary views of Traveler as well as the region immediately to the west, and the climb can help you pick out routes up Traveler Mtn.

South Branch Mountain Trail

The South Branch Mtn. Trail runs from the South Branch Pond Campground over both summits and down to the Pogy Notch Trail, which it joins at the southern end of the upper pond.

The trail (blue-blazed) starts at the northwestern corner of Lower South Branch Pond, across the outlet brook from the canoe rack (sign). The trail parallels a small brook, staying from 100 to 200 yd. away from it, for 0.3 mi. It then follows a ridge for 0.8 mi. to nearly flat lookouts with vistas of the ponds and the Traveler Range. After contouring for 0.3 mi., the trail turns abruptly right and climbs more steeply to the northern peak.

The southern peak is 0.5 mi. farther—an easy hike along the high saddle connecting the two summits. The trail from the southern peak was relocated in 1983. It descends over gentle meadows and rock fields to open ledges on the southern side of the mountain. At about 3 mi., it swings eastward and descends through mixed forests. There is a short, steep climb of about 0.1 mi., then the trail rejoins the old trail at about 4 mi. At 4.3 mi., it passes a side trail to the upper South Branch Lean-To, and at 4.5 mi., it crosses a brook with beaver works before joining the Pogy Notch Trail at the southern end of the upper pond. Turn left (north) for the South Branch Pond Campground and right (south) for Pogy Notch and Russell Pond Campground.

South Branch Mountain Trail

Distances from South Branch Pond Campground

- *to* lookouts: 1.1 mi., 45 min.
- *to* South Branch Mountain, northern peak: 2 mi., 2 hr.
- *to* South Branch Mountain, southern peak: 2.5 mi., 2 hr. 15 min.
- *to* Pogy Notch Trail junction: 4.5 mi., 4 hr.
- *to* South Branch Pond Campground (via Pogy Notch Trail): *est.* 6.4 mi., 5 hr.

TRAVELER MOUNTAIN (3541 ft./1079 m.)

Traveler Mtn. is a great, starfish-shaped mountain with four high ridges sprawling out south, west, northwest, and north, and four shorter spurs between them.

Fires have ravaged the mountain, the last one in 1902, so that while its lower parts support hardwoods of some size, its upper slopes are mostly bare, and good for climbing. The bareness of these higher slopes makes for a uniform landscape that can be highly confusing in fog or darkness. Although the mountain's altitude is quite a bit lower than Katahdin's, the routes up Traveler from the South Branch Pond Campground are longer, partially without trails, and equally exposed; so treat the mountain with respect, start early, and allow a full day for the climb. Estimate time, distance, and the roughness of the terrain generously.

There are four main routes up Traveler from the South Branch Pond Campground. Three of them follow trails for part of the climb. The following sections describe the routes in order, from north to south.

North Traveler Trail

From the South Branch Pond Campground, follow the Pogy Notch Trail 0.2 mi. to the North Traveler Trail, which diverges left. The North Traveler Trail climbs through open woods to the crest of North Ridge, which it follows over bare ledges in places. The view improves until the trail enters birch woods. After that, the trail passes through lovely alpine meadows and fine old woods that alternate with steep ledges. At about 1.7 mi., in one of the wooded sections, a side trail leaves left to a good *spring*. After emerging from the last section of woods, the trail continues in the open up the ridge to the summit at 3144 ft./958 m. The views are impressive.

North Traveler Trail
Distances from South Branch Pond Campground

- *to* start (via Pogy Notch Trail): 0.2 mi., 5 min.

- *to* side trail to spring: 1.7 mi., 1 hr. 30 min.

- *to* North Traveler summit: 2.5 mi., 2 hr. 20 min.

Howe Brook Trail

The Howe Brook Trail begins at the southeastern corner of Lower South Branch Pond, where the rocky, fanlike delta of Howe Brook merges with the pond. This inlet is 1 mi. south along the Pogy Notch Trail from the campground. The trail follows the route of the brook to the first chutes and potholes. (Howe Brook is noted for its many pools, rock- and water-formed potholes, slides, and chutes, which continue for quite a distance up the valley.) The trail crosses the brook a number of times before it ends at a beautiful waterfall.

Howe Brook Trail

Distances from South Branch Pond Campground

   to   start (via Pogy Notch Trail): 1 mi., 30 min.

   to   waterfall: *est.* 3 mi., 1 hr. 45 min.

Center Ridge Trail

This route starts at the foot of Center Ridge at the northeastern corner of the upper pond, 1.4 mi. south on the Pogy Notch Trail from the South Branch Pond Campground. The Center Ridge Trail runs to the Peak of the Ridges. Diverging left (east) from the Pogy Notch Trail, it climbs steadily through woods and then across open ledges. There are excellent views of Howe Brook Valley and North Traveler. After climbing over many rocky knobs, the trail reaches the Peak of the Ridges (about 3200 ft./975 m.), where it ends. There the route up Pinnacle Ridge comes in on the right.

Center Ridge Trail

Distances from South Branch Pond Campground

   to   start (via Pogy Notch Trail): 1.4 mi., 45 min.

   to   Peak of the Ridges: *est.* 3.6 mi., 2 hr. 50 min.

Loop Route Over Traveler and North Traveler

Only strong parties can make a circuit of Traveler Mtn. Climbers who attempt this trip, which takes at least 12 hours, should be well supplied with food and water and should carry a good compass. It is possible to follow the route by ascending North Traveler first, but this description takes you in the other direction. See the section on Bushwhacking in the Maine Mountains in this book's introduction.

Climb to the Peak of the Ridges on the Center Ridge Trail. To climb Traveler, continue northeast along the ridge from the Peak of the Ridges to the point where you can see clearly down into the meadow in the col on the way to Traveler. From there, you can use binoculars to study carefully the animal yards and rock slides on the way to Traveler summit. There are three animal yards. An almost straight line of animal trails going up the slope (east) connects them to the meadow. You should keep a little to the right of the center of each animal yard to find the path to the next one above. Near the top of the third yard, turn almost 90 degrees to the right (south) and look for an exit out onto the rock slide. At least one is almost completely open. Traverse horizontally and possibly drop down a little to get around the end of the heavy brush. Keep close to the brush and angle up as soon as possible. There are several breaks in the trees through which you can angle up until you come out into the open below one of the western peaks of Traveler. Continue up toward the peak. The rock slope is somewhat loose but stable enough for safe passage. Traveler's summit is about 1.7 mi. from the Peak of the Ridges.

To reach North Traveler from Traveler, first go as far northeast as possible in the open (there is a cairn on the last outcrop). From there, take a compass bearing on the several outcrops visible on the way to North Traveler. Study the areas between these outcrops, and between them and the one you are on. The thick woods make it necessary to follow a compass bearing carefully to come out on the first outcrop. (The strongest member of the party might want to break through the trees, guided by the compass carrier following 5–10 yd. behind.) The trees are so dense that you may not be able to see the next outcrop from the first one. Correct the compass bearing based on your earlier observation and go down into the trees again. Follow the compass to come out on the next outcrop. The next leg of the bushwhack will also have to be on a compass course, but after that, you will be able to stay in the open until you pass over the top of a subsidiary northern peak of Traveler. Then you should take a compass bearing for a spot just above the evergreen growth in the col between there and North Traveler. Lucky climbers may find animal trails that will make hiking easier, but be careful not to go too far to the right (northeast) and get into the evergreen growth. By staying to the left, you will also avoid a deep cut at the bottom of the col.

Hard bushwhacking will continue up the slope of North Traveler. Again, you should watch the compass and, at the same time, take advantage of animal trails. If you are careful not to get too far off course, you will come out into the open and be able to continue to the top of North Traveler. The distance is a very tiring 3 mi. from the Traveler summit.

From North Traveler, descend to the South Branch Pond Campground via the North Traveler Trail.

Loop Route Over Traveler and North Traveler
Distances from South Branch Pond Campground

- *to* Center Ridge Trail (via Pogy Notch Trail): 1.4 mi., 45 min.
- *to* Peak of the Ridges: 3.5 mi., 2 hr. 50 min.
- *to* Traveler summit: *est.* 5.2 mi., 4 hr.
- *to* North Traveler summit: *est.* 8.2 mi., 10 hr.
- *to* South Branch Pond Campground (via North Traveler Trail): *est.* 10.7 mi. (17.2 km.), 12 hr.

Pinnacle Ridge Route

This is the most spectacular of the four routes up Traveler, but there is no trail beyond the Pogy Notch Trail. From the southern end of the south pond, follow the Pogy Notch Trail about 0.8 mi. to a knoll where the slide on Pinnacle is plainly visible. Turn left (east) through pleasant woods and across older slides, and you will reach the Pinnacle slide. Climb up on the left to avoid the cliffs above. From the top of Pinnacle, a steady climb through open brush brings you to the Peak of the Ridges. The distance from the Pogy Notch Trail to the Peak of the Ridges is about 2 mi.

Do not descend Pinnacle Ridge. If you are caught by bad weather as you climb up on the upper slope, there is an emergency way off via the so-called Escape Route down the broad gully between Pinnacle and Center ridges. It gets climbers off the exposed ridge quickly and allows them to follow the little stream and skirt the low cliffs near the bottom to the Pogy Notch Trail near the southern end of the upper pond. See the section on Bushwhacking in the Maine Mountains in this book's introduction.

Pinnacle Ridge Route

Distances from South Branch Pond Campground

> *to* turn off Pogy Notch Trail: *est.* 2.7 mi., 1 hr. 25 min.

> *to* Peak of the Ridges: *est.* 4.7 mi., 3 hr.

> *to* Pogy Notch Trail (via Center Ridge Trail): *est.* 5.8 mi., 3 hr. 35 min.

> *to* South Branch Pond Campground (via Pogy Notch Trail): *est.* 7.2 mi. (11.6 km.), 4 hr. 20 min.

Trout Brook Farm Campground

Trout Brook Farm is on the site of a farm that once served logging operations. The campground is on the northern side of the perimeter road, about 27 mi. west of Patten and 2.6 mi. west of the Matagamon Gatehouse. It is 4.7 mi. east of the Crossing Lunchground, where the perimeter road crosses Trout Brook and where the road to the South Branch Pond Campground leads south. Trout Brook Farm has only tentsites. It is a starting point for many trips in the park, including canoe trips and hikes to Traveler Mtn. and other outlying mountains and hikes along the new trail system in the northern and northeastern sections of the park. Trails north of the Trout Brook Farm Campground are, for the most part, not on the map that accompanies this book. In addition to a handout, *Outlying Campsites,* available from BSP, hikers are referred to *A Guide to Baxter Park and Katahdin,* by

Stephen Clark, and to DeLorme's *Map and Guide of Baxter State Park and Katahdin.*

Wadleigh Brook Trail

This trail, opened in 1997, replaces the Webster Lake Trail. Combined with the Freezeout Trail, this makes a delightful two- or three-day circuit, which is the longest linear backpacking trip in the park. The many tentsites along the route permit flexibility in planning the trip. Although it does not involve mountain travel, it offers streams, ponds, and access to good fishing areas.

The trail leaves the tote road about a mile west of the Trout Brook Crossing Bridge. It follows Wadleigh Brook for a short way then turns northwest. At 1.5 mi., a side trail leads 1 mi. east to an old-growth forest area. At 4.3 mi., the Wadleigh Brook Trail follows the upper side of Wadleigh Bog, then crosses brook leading from Blunder Pond. At 8.4 mi., the trail follows the eastern and northern sides of Hudson Pond, where there is a lean-to, then heads northwest toward Pine Knoll and meets the Freezeout Trail at 10.4 mi., near Hudson Brook. From this junction, the Freezeout Trail goes southwest to the eastern end of Webster Lake, passing the Ice Wagon, Webster Outlet, and Boathouse campsites. In the other direction, the Freezeout Trail heads east-northeast along Webster Stream.

Freezeout Trail

The Freezeout Trail traverses a section of the park known as the Scientific Forest Management Area. This 28,000-acre parcel was specifically designated by Governor Baxter as an area to be managed by the "most modern methods of forest controls," and further as a "showplace for those interested in forestry" and forest management operations.

Caution: Ask at Park Headquarters or any facility in the northern end of the park for locations of the latest timber-harvesting operations. If you run into any equipment working in the woods, do not get too close. Questions and comments are invited; write the Park Forester at Park Headquarters.

The Freezeout Trail parallels the entire length of Webster Stream, which under the right conditions can be a challenging white-water experience (see the *AMC River Guide: Maine*).

The trail generally descends toward Matagamon Lake, paralleling Webster Stream. It sometimes bears away from the stream, but it always returns. At 1.8 mi. east of the junction at Hudson Brook, it passes the Webster Stream Lean-to, and at 5.8 mi., it passes the Little East Branch Lean-to, opposite the confluence of the East Branch of the Penobscot and Webster Stream. (To use lean-tos and tentsites, make arrangements with park officials in Millinocket or at one of the campgrounds.) From there, the trail makes a sharp right turn onto the remains of the old Burma Rd., an improved tote road last used in 1950. Follow it for the remaining 6 mi. to Trout Brook Farm, returning another 5.7 mi. by the tote road to the trailhead.

Wadleigh Brook and Freezeout Trails
Distances from tote road trailhead at Wadleigh Brook

- *to* Freezeout Trail junction: 10.4 mi., 5 hr. 15 min.
- *to* Webster Lake outlet tentsite (via Freezeout Trail): 12.9 mi., 6 hr. 30 min.
- *to* Webster Stream Lean-to: 12.2 mi., 6 hr. 15 min.
- *to* Little East Branch Lean-to: 16.2 mi., 8 hr. 15 min.
- *to* Trout Brook Farm Campground: 22.2 mi., 11 hr. 15 min.

  Complete loop (not visiting Webster Lake): 34 mi., 17 hr.

FOWLER PONDS AREA
In conjunction with the development of the Trout Brook Farm Campground, some new official routes have been opened to several lakes in the area south of the tote road, west of Horse Mtn., and northeast of the South Branch Pond area. Between Barrell Ridge and Billfish Mtn.

are the three Fowler ponds; in the next valley to the northeast are Billfish and Round ponds (which drain to the east) and High and Long ponds (which drain into Fowler Brook). Farther north, at the head of Littlefield Brook, is Littlefield Pond. For years, anglers kept routes to these ponds open from the tote road to the east and north. Official campsites are on the northern shore and outlet of Lower Fowler Pond and at the outlet and southern end of Middle Fowler Pond. See the ranger at the Trout Brook Farm or South Branch Pond campground for camping and trail information. The Clark guide and the BSP handout mentioned above under Trout Brook Farm would be most useful.

The Fowler Brook Trail leads south from the tote road about 2 mi. west of the Trout Brook Farm Campground. It generally follows Fowler Brook and leads to the northern end of Lower Fowler Pond to join the Middle Fowler Pond link mentioned below.

Five Ponds Trail

This trail has two branches leaving the southern side of the tote road at the Trout Brook Farm Campground. The southwest branch forks at about 1.8 mi. The left fork leads between High and Long ponds. It continues past Round Pond and Billfish Pond, then along Littlefield Pond; it then loops back to the Trout Brook Farm Campground as the southeast branch of the Five Ponds Trail. There are tentsites at Littlefield, Billfish, and Long ponds.

After crossing a second brook, the right fork climbs a crest and reaches a second junction. The trail to the left goes to the Middle Fowler Pond outlet and its tentsites; to the right, the link reaches the northeastern shore of Lower Fowler Pond at about 2.5 mi., where it joins the Fowler Brook Trail back to the tote road.

Trout Brook Mountain Trail

This trail also starts at the Trout Brook Farm Campground and climbs through mixed growth and hardwoods to open ledges with excellent views. After reaching the 1767-ft. summit at 1.3 mi., the trail drops between Trout Brook Mtn. and Horse Mtn., then joins the southeastern branch of the Five Ponds Trail to loop back 0.7 mi. to the tote road at the campground.

Fowler Middle Pond Trail

In 1987, a new route was opened from South Branch Pond to Middle Fowler Pond. It is considered to be an extension of the Middle Fowler Pond Trail, connecting the South Branch Pond and Trout Brook Farm campgrounds. The trail leaves the northern end of the South Branch Pond Campground and follows the Ledges Trail for the first 0.3 mi. The trail climbs gradually, following a small brook until open ledges are reached at 1.7 mi. From there, the trail proceeds through the gap between Big Peaked Mtn. and Little Peaked Mtn. It then traverses the northern slope of Traveler Mtn., providing occasional views. At 3 mi., the Barrell Ridge Side Trail leads 0.3 mi. to the open summit of Barrell Ridge. This summit has very fine views, especially of Traveler Mtn. From this point, the trail descends, and it reaches Middle Fowler Pond at 4 mi. (sign). To the left, it is 3.3 mi. to the tote road via the Middle Fowler Pond and Fowler Brook trails. To the right, it is 0.2 mi. to the southern campsite on Middle Fowler Pond.

Fowler Ponds Area
Distances from tote road

Complete Five Ponds Trail loop: est. 5.6 mi.

to Littlefield Pond: *est.* 1.5 mi., 45 min.

to Lower Fowler Pond, northern end (via Fowler Brook Trail): 1.5 mi., 1 hr.

to Lower Fowler Pond, northeastern shore (via High and Long ponds): *est.* 2.5 mi. (4 km.), 1 hr. 15 min.

to Trout Brook Mtn. summit: 1.3 mi.

Complete loop: 3 mi.

Distance from South Branch Pond Campground

to Middle Fowler Pond: 4 mi. (6.4 km.), 2 hr. 30 min.

HORSE MOUNTAIN (1589 ft./484 m.)

In the northeastern corner of BSP, this mountain rises above the western shore of First Grand (Matagamon) Lake. There is an abandoned MFS firetower on the summit, which is easy to reach from the tote road.

The trail leaves the southern side of the tote road 2.5 mi. west of the bridge over the East Branch of the Penobscot and just west of the Matagamon Gatehouse. It rises at an easy rate and, near the top, turns sharply right (west) to the summit and tower.

Horse Mountain
Distance from tote road

   to Horse Mtn. summit: 1.4 mi. (2.3 km.), 1 hr. 5 min.

TURNER MOUNTAIN (northern summit 3323 ft./ 1013 m. and southern summit 3122 ft./952 m.)

This mountain northeast of Katahdin is low compared to the great mountain. Turner offers magnificent views of Katahdin, however, and particularly of the basins. You can approach South Turner from the Roaring Brook Campground. The hike involves a moderate climb up the southwestern slide. North Turner is trailless. The two summits are more than 2 mi. apart and separated by a deep saddle.

South Turner Mountain Trail

This trail starts out across Roaring Brook at the Roaring Brook Campground and coincides with the Russell Pond Trail. (At 0.2 mi., the Russell Pond Trail goes left.) The Sandy Stream Pond Trail goes straight to Sandy Stream Pond. At 0.4 mi., it turns right, crosses the outlets, and continues around the southeastern shore of the pond. (This section is often wet and muddy during rainy seasons.) Along the trail near the southeastern shore of the pond, a number of side paths lead left to the shore. Moose frequent the pond. The trail follows the right fork at 0.7 mi. (The left fork is the Sandy Stream Pond Trail, which leads northwest 0.9 mi. to Whidden Pond and a junction with the Russell Pond Trail 1.1 mi. north of the Roaring Brook Campground.) The South Turner Mtn. Trail enters a small boulder field at 0.9 mi. and follows cairns and paint blazes on the rocks as it climbs. At 1.1 mi., it turns left and rises steeply. At 1.5 mi., it passes a side trail right to a *spring*, bears left, and continues. At 1.8 mi., the trail leaves the scrub and starts over open ledges. It follows cairns and paint blazes to the summit at 2 mi.

South Turner Mountain Trail

Distances from Roaring Brook Campground

- *to* start (via Russell Pond Trail): 0.2 mi., 5 min.

- *to* Whidden Pond Trail junction: 0.7 mi., 20 min.

- *to* South Turner summit: 2 mi. (3.2 km.), 1 hr. 50 min.

Section 2

Aroostook

Aroostook County, with an area of 6453 square mi., sprawls along Maine's northern and northeastern boundary. It is larger in area than Connecticut and Rhode Island combined. Aroostook's greatest north–south dimension is about 120 mi., and its greatest east–west dimension is 104 mi.

The mountains of Aroostook County are widely scattered. There are no ranges or compact mountain areas except two small clusters of hills—the Deboullie Mtn. region west of Eagle Lake and east of the Allagash territory, and the hills west of Bridgewater and around Number Nine Lake. Solitary Mars Hill (1660 ft.), which rises from almost level country near the county's eastern boundary, is probably the best-known mountain. Peaked Mtn. (2260 ft./689 m.), a trailless summit in the wilderness west of Ashland, is the county's highest.

See page xvii in the introduction to this guide for information on North Maine Woods and its control policies in the western part of Aroostook County.

NUMBER NINE MOUNTAIN (1638 ft./499 m.)

This peak is west of Bridgewater in the small group of mountains around Number Nine Lake. The lake has an interesting MFS campsite. Refer to the USGS Howe Brook quadrangle, 15-min. series, or the Number Nine Lake quadrangle, 7.5-min. series.

At the southern end of Bridgewater, turn west off US 1 onto Boutford Rd. (West Rd.), which leaves in front of the Bridgewater Grammar School. This road runs west, northwest, and then west again into a wilderness area. At about 11 mi., take the left fork (south) toward

Number Nine Lake (1084 ft.), which is less than 1 mi. farther. The road, partly paved, turns left across the outlet, follows the southern side of a logged area, and climbs 1.5 mi. to the summit, where there is a helipad and an abandoned radar installation with antennae. A few steps are missing, but the tower gives a grand 360-degree view.

Number Nine Mountain

Distance from US 1 in Bridgewater

   to Number Nine Lake: *est.* 12 mi. (19.2 km.)

Distance from lake outlet

   to Number Nine summit: 1.5 mi. (2.4 km.), 1 hr. 15 min.

MARS HILL (1660 ft./506 m.)

This monadnock rises abruptly from an almost level area of farms and woodland in the eastern section of the town of the same name. Refer to the USGS Mars Hill quadrangle, 15-min. series or 7.5-min. series.

The mountain runs north–south for 3 mi. and parallels the Canadian border, which is about 1 mi. to the east. The southern peak is the highest and is being developed as a recreation area (with picnicking and tenting) by the Mars Hill Junior Chamber of Commerce. There is also a ski area on the mountain. A rough road climbs this peak, rising slightly more than 1000 ft. in 1.6 mi. The views from the summit extend across the potato fields in all directions to other mountains in the county, and on to Katahdin to the southwest and across the St. John River Valley into New Brunswick to the east.

From Mars Hill Village, take US 1A north for 0.4 mi. Then turn right (east) onto Boynton Rd. The pavement ends 1.7 mi. from US 1A. Turn right and then take the first left (toward Mars Hill and the ski area). For the southern (highest) peak, turn right and then take the first left to the ski area. The trail goes up the left side of the main ski slope. For the northern peak, turn left instead. Drive 1.7 mi., passing the country club. The posted road at utility pole S 23/20 heads up the mountain.

Mars Hill

Distance from start of access road

  to Mars summit: 1.6 mi. (2.6 km.), 1 hr. 15 min.

QUAGGY JO (1213 ft./370 m.)

Quaggy Jo (also called Quoggy Joe and Quaquajo) dominates Aroostook State Park from the southwestern corner of Presque Isle. The 1700-acre state park offers swimming, boating, camping, and picnicking. A side road runs west to the park from US 1 (sign) 4 mi. south of Presque Isle and 10.5 mi. north of Mars Hill village. Refer to the USGS Presque Isle quadrangle, 15-min. series, or the Echo Lake quadrangle, 7.5-min. series.

    The mountain, which rises 600 ft. above Echo Lake, has two peaks. On the higher, southern peak there are four radio transmitters and an aircraft beacon. The slightly lower, northern peak has better views to the northwest and east.

    The trail to the summit starts just south of the playground area and soon joins the Quaquajo Trail to climb quickly to the northern peak. From the northern peak, a trail leads south to the true summit on the southern peak.

Quaggy Jo

Distances from parking area

  to summit of northern peak: 0.8 mi., 40 min.

  to summit of southern peak: 1.5 mi. (2.4 km.), 1 hr. 5 min.

DEBOULLIE MOUNTAIN (1981 ft./604 m.)

Deboullie Mtn. is the highest of a small cluster of mountains in the wilderness south of St. Francis and southwest of Eagle Lake. Refer to the USGS Fish River Lake quadrangle, 15-min. series, and the Gardner Pond and Deboullie Pond quadrangles, 7.5-min. series.

The views, only available from the unmanned MFS firetower on Deboullie's summit, take in Long, Eagle, and Square lakes. From one spot, Quebec Province can be seen beyond the strip of New Brunswick that runs north of Fort Kent. Other mountains in the area include Black Mtn. (1901 ft.) to the east, and Gardner Mtn. (1817 ft.) and Whitman Mtn. (1810 ft.) to the south. Interspersed between the mountains are small but picturesque lakes and ponds. There are also a warden's cabin, unused since 1984, and a helipad on the summit.

In 1975, the state of Maine, through a land exchange, took ownership of 15,000 acres on and around the mountain. The Bureau of Public Lands plans to manage the land as a protected area with primitive recreation.

The present access to the township is from St. Francis Rd. and checkpoint (fee), which turns left off ME 161 about 6.5 mi. southwest of St. Francis and soon heads south and then east for some 20 mi., ending at a parking area at Pushineer Pond. The hiking trail starts west, skirts the northern edge of Deboullie Pond (1128 ft.), crosses an intermittent rockslide, and, at its western end, heads steeply up to the summit.

Deboullie Mountain

Distance from end of auto road at Pushineer Pond

   to Deboullie summit: 2.5 mi. (4 km.), 1 hr. 35 min.

HEDGEHOG MOUNTAIN (1594 ft./486 m.)

This mountain is in T 15 R 6 just off ME 11 between Winterville and Portage. (*T* and *R* stand for "township" and "range." The state of Maine uses this system to designate unincorporated areas.) The mountain, which runs north–south, falls off steeply on its eastern side. Refer to the USGS Winterville quadrangle, 15-min. series or 7.5-min. series.

The trail up Hedgehog starts on the western side of ME 11, 3.5 mi. south of Winterville and 12.8 mi. north of Portage. There are also a picnic site, a campsite, a good *spring,* and a parking area at the start. The trail begins at the picnic area. The summit has a radio antenna but no views.

Hedgehog Mountain
Distance from warden's cabin

   to Hedgehog summit (via left fork): 0.6 mi. (1 km.), 30 min.

ROUND MOUNTAIN (2174 ft./654 m.)

This mountain is west of Ashland and south of American Realty Rd., which serves as an access road. Peaked Mtn. (2260 ft.), 2 mi. to the southwest, is the highest point in Aroostook County, but there is no trail up it. Refer to the USGS Mooseleuk Lake quadrangle, 15-min. series, or the Round Mountain quadrangle, 7.5-min. series.

   At the western end of the bridge over the Aroostook River in Ashland, turn west off ME 11 onto a paved road. In 0.6 mi., go straight ahead on American Realty Rd., which is private but open to the public for a fee paid at a tollgate about 6 mi. west of Ashland. The road runs west and, about 14 mi. from ME 11, goes over a pass (1280 ft.) between Greenlaw Mtn. and Orcutt Mtn. Then it descends and crosses the Machias (Aroostook) River in another 2 mi. It reaches the start of the trail to Round Mtn. about 22 mi. from ME 11 and about 0.3 mi. west of the line between T 11 R 8 and T 11 R 9.

   The trail starts out southward, crosses the outlet of Rowe Lake, and runs along the southwestern shore. Beyond, it passes to the west of Round Mtn. Pond and skirts the northwestern base of the mountain, then climbs steadily to the summit where there is a radio shack and helipad.

Round Mountain
Distances from American Realty Rd.

   to warden's camp: *est.* 3.3 mi., 1 hr. 40 min.

   to Round Mtn. summit: 4 mi. (6.4 km.), 2 hr. 20 min.

HORSESHOE MOUNTAIN (2084 ft./635 m.)

Horseshoe Mtn. is part of the Rocky Brook Range, which has some surprisingly rugged terrain for this part of the state. Refer to the USGS Mooseleuk Lake quadrangle, 15-min. series, or 7.5-min. series.

The road to the trail leaves the left side of American Realty Rd. (see the preceding description) about 41 mi. west of Ashland and 2.5 mi. before the Upper McNally Pond Campsite. About 1 mi. from American Realty Rd., the road to the trail turns sharply left up over a hill. The trail begins on the right at this corner, where there is a small sign on a tree.

At first, the trail is an obscure road that leads in about 0.3 mi. to a firewarden's cabin. The trail then passes directly behind the cabin, and after another 200 yd., it reaches a side trail on the right. (The side trail goes 0.8 mi. to the very picturesque Horseshoe Pond.) About 0.5 mi. from the cabin, the main trail gets increasingly steeper; and in another 0.5 mi., it reaches the summit, which is flat. The Katahdin area is 40 mi. to the south.

Horseshoe Mountain

Distances from road

 to firewarden's cabin: 0.3 mi., *est.* 20 min.

 to Horseshoe summit: 1.3 mi. (2.1 km.), 1 hr. 10 min.

PRIESTLY MOUNTAIN (1900 ft./579 m.)

Priestly Mtn., in northern Piscataquis County, near the Aroostook boundary, rises west of the Allagash River about 60 mi. west of Ashland. Its summit bears a steel firetower, a cabin, a helipad, and an Allagash Wilderness Waterway repeater.

Drive to a point on Churchill Dam Rd. about 7.5 mi. before American Realty Rd. (see the section on Round Mtn.), 67 mi. west of Ashland and west and south of Umsaskis Lake. Refer to the USGS Umsaskis Lake quadrangle, 15-min. series, or the Umsaskis Lake West quadrangle, 7.5-min. series.

The trail (small sign on a tree) leaves the west side of Churchill Dam Rd. (left when going northwest from the Churchill Dam) on a hill. At first it is an old road and flat. It runs generally southwest for 1.6 mi. and crosses Drake Brook, the outlet of Priestly Lake. The trail turns south near the northwestern side of Priestly Lake. About 1.6 mi. from the brook, it reaches a firewarden's cabin, where it turns abruptly right (west) uphill to the right of the cabin. It then rises moderately for 0.5 mi. to the summit. The firetower has a long stretch of excellent views, particularly of the Allagash Wilderness Waterway.

Priestly Mountain

Distances from Churchill Dam Rd.

   to firewarden's cabin: 1.6 mi.

   to Priestly summit: 2 mi. (3.2 km.), 1 hr. 25 min.

MOUNT CHASE (2440 ft./849 m.)

This mountain, north of Patten and just west of the Aroostook County border, has an abandoned MFS firetower. There are extensive views from the summit. Looking northeast of Katahdin, you will see Mt. Chase as the very prominent mountain in the distance. Refer to the USGS Mt. Chase quadrangle, 7.5-min. series.

The approach road diverges left (west) from ME 11 6.5 mi. north of Patten, 1.5 mi. north of the Penobscot/Aroostook border, and 9.5 mi. south of Knowles Corner. Follow the approach road for 2.3 mi. There is parking space.

The trail, well marked at first with signs and red painted arrows, leaves the right (northern) side of the road and proceeds first west, then almost due north, following a jeep road to the warden's cabin, which it reaches in about 0.8 mi. Beyond the cabin, the trail climbs steadily north to the summit. There is *no water* on the trail. The firetower cab has been removed.

Mount Chase

Distances from trailhead parking

   to firewarden's cabin: *est.* 0.8 mi., 40 min.

   to Mt. Chase summit: *est.* 1.5 mi. (6.1 km.), 1 hr. 25 min.

Section 3

Piscataquis Mountains

This section includes the mountains of Piscataquis County west and southwest of the Katahdin area. Moosehead Lake, about 34 mi. long with an area of 117 square mi., is the state's largest lake. The approach to most of the mountains in this section is through Greenville, a convenient climbing center at the southern end of the lake. Big Squaw Mtn. (3196 ft.), west of Greenville, and Mt. Kineo (1806 ft.), reached by water through Rockwood, are the most frequently climbed and best-known peaks in the area. The Appalachian Trail (AT) crosses White Cap Mtn. (3644 ft.), the highest peak in the section. The AT, in its northeast–southwest course, also passes over the Barren-Chairback Range and close to the interesting and striking Borestone Mtn. (1947 ft.).

Lily Bay State Park is on the eastern shore of Moosehead Lake, 8 mi. north of Greenville on Greenville-Ripogenus Rd. This area of 576 acres offers picnicking, camping, boat launching, and swimming. (In 1974, the Scott Paper Company donated the Squaw Mountain ski area and considerable land on that mountain to the state for a park. In 1976, the state added the Little Squaw unit by exchanging land with another paper company.)

An expanding network of private roads, open to the public, serves the wilderness country north of Rockwood. (See the section, Policies of Landowners in Northern Maine in the introduction to this guide, which discusses the North Maine Woods association.)

BIG SQUAW MOUNTAIN (3196 ft./974 m.)

Big Squaw Mtn. dominates the country to the southwest of Moosehead Lake. It is located west of Greenville and is known for its exceptional views of the lake area. An abandoned firetower (reconditioned in 1985, but now run down) marks the site of the first fire lookout in the state, established in 1905. There is a major state-owned ski area on the mountain's eastern slope. This area is north of the hiking trail; refer to the USGS Greenville quadrangle, 15-min. series.

From ME 15, turn left (west) on the paper-company road just north of the bridge over Middle Squaw Brook and 5.3 mi. north of Greenville (signs for Maine Public Lands and Big and Little Squaw). Drive up this road for about 1 mi. to where the firewarden's trail leaves the right side of the road (sign reading Big Squaw Mountain Trail). Parking space is on the left.

The trail is easy to follow and leads 2.5 mi. to the warden's cabin. There is *water* near the cabin and also a few hundred yards above. From the cabin, the trail heads straight up the steep slope, with many rocks placed as stepping-stones. Reaching the narrow crest of the ridge, it turns right (north) and climbs another 0.5 mi. to the summit, which is cluttered by three small antennae and their buildings.

From the tower, a short trail leads north to a ledge with a view down over Mirror Lake, an isolated pond on the northeastern spur of the mountain.

A trail also has been cut from the top of the ski lifts and trails to the summit.

Big Squaw Mountain Trail
Distances from paper-company road

to   cabin: 2.5 mi.

to   Squaw summit: 3.3 mi. (5.3 km.), 2 hr. 45 min.

LITTLE SQUAW MOUNTAIN (2126 ft./648 m.)

The hiking-trail system of Little Squaw Mtn. focuses on the Loop Trail around Big and Little Squaw ponds. Hiking it clockwise gives you the best view build-up and is easiest on the terrain. The area can be reached from the Mountain Rd. trailhead. To reach this, go past the parking area on the Big Squaw access road, taking the left fork about 1.8 mi. from ME 16 and continuing for a total of 3 mi. to the trailhead.

The right fork follows North Rd., which in the future will be improved almost to Indian Pond for carry-in boating. From there, an old angler's trail connects Indian Pond with Little Notch Pond.

From the Mountain Rd. trailhead, go southeast 0.5 mi. over log walks to Big Squaw Pond and another 0.5 mi. to Little Squaw Pond. The Loop Trail (signed) presents varied terrain and several delightful outlooks over ponds and surrounding mountains. At a high point on the loop, a sign points to the Notch Ponds Trail, heading westerly. This trail follows the sidehill and, shortly after crossing an old road, branches right a quarter-mile to an overlook. It then drops through a notch down to the ponds.

Little Squaw Mountain

Distances from parking area

- *to* Little Squaw Pond: 3.5 mi., 2 hr.
- *to* Big Squaw Pond: 4 mi., 2 hr. 30 min.
- *to* Mountain Rd. parking: 4.5 mi. (7.2 km.), 3 hr.

MOUNT KINEO (1806 ft./550 m.)

Mt. Kineo, with its sheer southeastern face, rises spectacularly 800 ft. above Moosehead Lake on a peninsula jutting from the eastern shore of the lake to within 1 mi. of the western shore at Rockwood. The view over the lake from the vacant refurbished MFS firetower on the summit is quite remarkable. Refer to the USGS Moosehead Lake quadrangle, 15-min. series, or the Mt. Kineo quadrangle, 7.5-min. series.

To reach the mountain, take the shuttle boat from Rockwood, hire a boat locally, or bring your own. There are two trails up the mountain. The Bridle Trail and the Indian Trail run northwest from the Kineo House (food) for 0.8 mi. along a shore carriage road under spectacular cliffs of Kineo flint. At the northwestern end of these cliffs, the Indian Trail diverges sharply right (sign) and rises along the top of the cliffs, rejoining the Bridle Trail for the last 0.4 mi. to the summit. The Bridle Trail continues along the shore 0.3 mi. farther before starting to climb. It has no views and is longer, but it has easier grades. The Indian Trail is the more interesting and affords the best views. There is *no water* on either trail.

Mount Kineo
Distances from dock at Kineo Cove

> *to* Bridle Trail and Indian Trail junction: 0.8 mi.

> *to* Kineo summit (via Indian Trail): 1.6 mi. (2.6 km.), 1 hr. 10 min.

> *to* Kineo summit (via Bridle Trail): 2 mi. (3.2 km.), 1 hr. 20 min.

GREEN MOUNTAIN (2395 ft./730 m.)

This mountain is northwest of Pittston Farm and northeast of Boundary Bald Mtn. There is a MFS firetower on the highest of its several summits. Refer to the USGS Penobscot Lake quadrangle, 15-min. series, or the Foley Pond quadrangle, 7.5-min. series.

Take the Great Northern Paper Company gravel road for 20 mi. north from Rockwood to the tollgate ($4.00 per car). From the tollgate, continue left through Pittston Farm. Beyond Pittston Farm, Boundary Rd. to Green Mtn. forks left from North Branch Rd. The trail leaves the right (north) side of the road about 7 mi. beyond this fork.

The trail starts as a steep driveway to the warden's cabin, which it passes in 0.3 mi. It then rises gradually, with several short dips, to the summit. The trail is well worn and easy to follow.

Green Mountain
Distances from North Branch Rd.

> *to* cabin: 0.3 mi.

> *to* Green Mtn. summit: 1.5 mi. (2.4 km.), 1 hr. 15 min.

LITTLE RUSSELL MOUNTAIN (2400 ft./730 m.)

Little Russell Mtn. is close to the Piscataquis County line in T 5 R 16, Somerset County. (*T* and *R* stand for "township" and "range," and identify unincorporated areas in Maine.) An abandoned MFS firetower is on the summit. Refer to the USGS St. John Pond quadrangle, 15-min. series, and the Russell Mtn. quadrangle, 7.5-min. series.

Take the Great Northern Paper Company road for 20 mi. north from Rockwood to the tollgate (free for Maine cars; $8.00 per out-of-state car). Take the road right to the Seboomook Dam, and then drive north on the road toward Caucomgomoc Lake. The trail (sign) leaves the right (east) side of the road about 19 mi. north of the Seboomook Dam and about 1.3 mi. north of Lost Pond, which is in the saddle (about 1975 ft.) between Russell Mtn. and Little Russell Mtn. (There is a MFS campsite at Lost Pond, 0.3 mi. from the road.)

The trail ascends gradually. In its upper half, it gets steeper, with expanding views to the north. The trail is wide, well worn, and easy to follow.

Little Russell Mountain

Distance from road

   to Little Russell summit: 1.3 mi. (2.1 km.), 55 min.

SOUBUNGE MOUNTAIN (2104 ft./641 m.)

This mountain is north of the Ripogenus Dam and northwest of Doubletop Mtn. An abandoned MFS firetower is on the summit. Refer to the USGS Harrington Lake quadrangle, 15-min. series, or the Doubletop Mtn. quadrangle, 7.5-min. series.

The trail leaves the northern side of Telos Rd. about 8 mi. north of the Ripogenus Dam. It runs generally northwest across level country for 1 mi., then climbs north to the tower.

Soubunge Mountain
Distance from road

  to Soubunge summit: *est.* 2 mi. (3.2 km.), 1 hr. 30 min.

BIG SPENCER MOUNTAIN (3240 ft./988 m.)

Rising sharply from the countryside north of the tiny hamlet of Kokadjo, Big and Little Spencer mountains, near First Roach Pond, are prominent landmarks from many points in the Moosehead area. Big Spencer has a MFS firetower on the northeastern end of its 2-mi. summit ridge (3230 ft.). The summit is about 0.3 mi. southwest of the tower. The unrestricted views in all directions are beautiful. Refer to the USGS Ragged Lake quadrangle, 15-min. series, or the Big Spencer Mtn. quadrangle, 7.5-min. series.

To reach the trail to the firetower, turn northwest (left) from Greenville-Ripogenus Rd. on a side road about 8.3 mi. northeast of Kokadjo, 2 mi. southwest of Grant Farm, and about 3 mi. north of the Sias Hill checkpoint ($4.00 per Maine car; $8.00 per out-of-state). Drive 6 mi. on this road. The trail leaves on the left (south) side of the road (sign) and climbs to the right (north) of the mountain's nose. In its upper part, beyond the warden's cabin, the trail is quite steep: It gains more than 1000 vertical feet in the last 0.7 mi. to the summit. The *last water* is at the warden's cabin.

Big Spencer Mountain
Distance from road

  to Big Spencer summit: *est.* 2 mi. (3.2 km.), 2 hr. 15 min.

LITTLE SPENCER MOUNTAIN (3040 ft./927 m.)

Like its partner, Big Spencer, the elongated mass of Little Spencer forms a prominent landmark in the Moosehead area. For years, its trail was just a flagged herd path used mostly by people staying at a local camp near Spencer Pond. The challenging trail starts out on a wooded easy grade but soon climbs steeply, crosses several sloping rock-piles, and ascends through a narrow chimney. There are great views of the Moosehead Lake area from several rock outlooks and the summit. Refer to the USGS Lobster Mtn. quadrangle, 7.5-min. series, and maps 41 and 49 in the DeLorme *Maine Atlas and Gazetteer.*

To reach the trail, head north from the Kokadjo General Store and take the left fork at 1.3 mi. Travel northwest on the gravel road and turn right at about 8.3 mi., where a small sign reads Spencer Pond Camps. Little Spencer is now a very clear mountain profile ahead. Continue on the road, watching for a Little Spencer Mountain Trail sign on the right at 10.3 mi., 80 yds. beyond a small brook culvert, near an old logging road.

Caution: Use care when climbing through the steep chimney section. Hikers up ahead can dislodge loose rocks to injure climbers below. Send one person through at a time.

A herd path leads to the middle and lower summits.

Little Spencer Mountain
Distance from road

   to Little Spencer summit: *est.* 2 mi. (3.2 km.), 2 hr. 15 min.

NESUNTABUNT MOUNTAIN (1550 ft./472 m.)

This mountain, part of the Maine Public Reserve Land, is found in T 1 R 11. Its summit offers some of the best views of the Katahdin Range from the south as well as views over Nahmakanta Lake. The Wadleigh Stream Lean-to on the Appalachian Trail is about 2 mi. away. Refer to the USGS Rainbow Lake West quadrangle, 7.5-min. series, and map 1 of the MATC's *Appalachian Trail Guide to Maine.*

From ME 11, take the road northwest at Bear Brook, about 16 mi. northeast of Brownville Junction. Follow it for about 25 mi. toward the northwestern end of Nahmakanta Lake. There is a checkpoint with fee just off ME 11 at the Jo-Mary Campground. Where the Appalachian Trail crosses this road, follow it south to the northern summit. A 250-ft. side trail leads to splendid views.

Nesuntabunt Mountain
Distance from Appalachian Trail crossing

   to northern summit: 1.2 mi. (1.9 km.), 45 min.

NUMBER FOUR MOUNTAIN (2890 ft./881 m.)

This summit, with a vacant MFS firetower, is at the northern end of the jumbled mountain mass lying between Kokadjo on the north, Lily Bay on the west, and Big Lyford and the West Branch ponds on the east. Baker Mtn. (3520 ft.) and Lily Bay Mtn. (3228 ft.), other major peaks in this mass, are higher but have no trails. Refer to the USGS First Roach Pond quadrangle, 15-min. series, or the Number Four Mtn. quadrangle, 7.5-min. series.

   Turn east off Greenville-Ripogenus Rd. (Lily Bay Rd.) onto Frenchtown Rd., which is about 8.5 mi. northeast of Lily Bay and 1.4 mi. south of Kokadjo. The trail, marked by signs put up by SAPPI Warren Paper Company, leaves the southern side of Frenchtown Rd. about 3.5 mi. from the intersection. The trail runs southwest, with little change in grade, for more than 2 mi. Then, 0.75 mi. after crossing Lagoon Brook *(last water),* you will find a cairn on the left and a sign that reads No. 4 MT on a tree. From this point, the trail climbs, first gradually and finally more steeply, through white birch and spruce to the summit ridge. The tower is locked.

Number Four Mountain
Distances from Frenchtown Rd.

   to cabin site: 2.3 mi., 1 hr. 20 min.

   to firetower: 3.8 mi. (6.1 km.), 2 hr. 30 min.

WHITE CAP MOUNTAIN (3644 ft./1111 m.)

White Cap Mtn. is the highest point on the Appalachian Trail between Katahdin and Bigelow, and also the highest mountain in this section. There are outstanding views from its summit. Refer to the USGS First

Roach Pond and Jo-Mary Mountain quadrangles, 15-min. series; the Big Shanty Mountain, and Hay Mountain quadrangles, 7.5-min. series; or map 2 in the MATC's *Appalachian Trail Guide to Maine.*

White Brook Trail

The AT in the Gulf Hagas–White Cap area has been relocated; it now leads from the Pleasant River past the Hermitage and then turns northeast to parallel Gulf Hagas Brook to Gulf Hagas Mtn., West Peak, and Hay Mtn. To reach the White Brook Trail—the former route of the AT, and still maintained by the MATC—turn left (northwest) off ME 11 5.5 mi. north of Brownville Junction. The sign (Katahdin Iron Works) at the turnoff marks the start of a 6.8-mi. drive on a gravel road from ME 11 to a gate at the Iron Works, a very interesting state historical memorial with a blast furnace and a beehive charcoal burner. Register at the gate and pay a fee to the caretaker. Bear right after driving through the gate and cross the West Branch of the Pleasant River. At about 3 mi., fork right. About 5.8 mi. from the Iron Works, the road crosses the high, narrow bridge over White Brook. At the next junction, continue straight ahead up the western side of White Brook. (The left fork leads to Hay Brook and Gulf Hagas.) Follow the major gravel road for 3.8 mi., taking the main branch at each fork, and park well off the road where it crosses two brooks. The trail follows an old logging road for 1 mi. to a large wood yard. The White Cap–Hay Mountain sag is clearly visible from this yard. Depending on logging operations, this road may be impassable.

A blue-blazed trail leaves the left side of the road and climbs the southern slope toward the sag through a heavily logged area.

At 0.4 mi., the trail crosses White Brook near the ruins of the warden's cabin. From there, it climbs more steeply and reaches the junction with the AT at 1 mi. Turn right and climb the last steep stretch to the summit at 2.1 mi. There are panoramic views from the open ledge. They take in Saddleback (2998 ft.), Little Spruce (3274 ft.), Baker (3520 ft.), Big Squaw (3196 ft.), Hay (3244 ft.), and Big Spencer (3240 ft.) mountains, along with the vast lake country to the north, rising to the Katahdin Range. The view is one of the finest in the state.

White Brook Trail
Distances from road at wood yard

  to White Brook crossing: 0.5 mi.

  to AT junction: 1 mi.

  to White Cap summit (via the AT): 2.1 mi. (3.4 km.), 1 hr. 30 min.

GULF HAGAS

Just off the Appalachian Trail between the Barren-Chairback Range and White Cap Mtn., Gulf Hagas is a unique scenic area consisting of a deep, narrow, slate canyon about 4 mi. long on the West Branch of the Pleasant River in northern Piscataquis County. The West Branch falls about 400 ft. in the 4 mi., and in many places, the canyon's vertical slate walls force the river into very narrow channels that form a series of waterfalls, rapids, chutes, and pools. The falls are particularly spectacular in late spring during peak runoff. During winter, ice builds up on the walls and, because the sun rarely reaches certain faces, often lasts into late June.

The successors to the St. Regis and Great Northern paper companies own the property. In 1969, the canyon was designated a registered natural landmark, and the owners agreed to set aside five hundred acres, including all of the canyon, for the public's enjoyment. While retaining ownership, the paper companies have agreed not to harvest wood on the reserved land as long as the area is designated a landmark.

Loggers first harvested the area more than a century ago, when Pleasant River Rd., the approach from both ends of the canyon, was built. Trails were cut to the rim of the canyon in the last century but fell into disuse. The last extensive logging took place during the 1930s, when new trails were cut. The trails are still well marked and well maintained. The trail system runs near the rim of the canyon, with frequent side trails to viewpoints and falls. By using the old Pleasant River Rd., hikers can make a circuit from the south. Refer to the USGS First Roach Pond, Sebec Lake, and Sebec quadrangles, 15-min. series; the Barren Mountain East quadrangle, 7.5-min. series; or map 2 in the MATC's *Appalachian Trail Guide to Maine*.

See the preceding description of the approach to White Cap Mtn. After crossing the high bridge 5.8 mi. from the Katahdin Iron Works, go left off the major gravel road at the first junction. Follow this logging road for about 1.8 mi. to Hay Brook, which is about 7.5 mi. from the Iron Works. The approach road is rocky and rough but generally passable. A campground with tentsites lies along the West Branch of the Pleasant River. Reservations can be made (fee) at the control gate at Katahdin Iron Works.

From the parking area, cross Hay Brook and follow Pleasant River Rd., past Pugwash Pond, for 0.7 mi. There, the AT comes in from the left. Continue straight ahead. The trail shortly reaches the Hermitage, a beautiful stand of tall white pine now owned by The Nature Conservancy (a log cabin and other buildings have been removed). From the Hermitage area, follow the white-blazed AT northwest along Pleasant River Rd. for 0.9 mi. to Gulf Hagas Brook, where the relocated AT turns sharply right to follow the brook. Continue straight ahead and cross Gulf Hagas Brook (no bridge and dangerous in high water). Immediately after the crossing, the Screw Auger Falls Trail leaves left and descends steeply along the rim of the canyon to Gulf Hagas Brook, where it passes a series of spectacular waterfalls visible from viewpoints to the left of the falls trail.

A new rim-trail section continues west, and at 0.7 mi., a side trail leads left to Hammond Street Pitch, a point high above the canyon that offers a fine view of the gorge. Return to the rim trail and turn left (at 0.9 mi., a connector road leads 0.2 mi. back to Pleasant River Rd.). Continuing along the rim, at 1.2 mi. from Pleasant River Rd., is a series of side paths leading to views of the Jaws, where the river squeezes around a slate spur and narrows in many places. Back on the rim trail, at 1.8 mi. from Pleasant River Rd., a spur trail leads to a viewpoint below Buttermilk Falls. After that, the canyon gradually becomes shallower, and at times the trail approaches the banks of the West Branch. At 1.9 mi. from Pleasant River Rd., the trail passes Stair Falls; at 2.8 mi., it reaches the ledge above Billings Falls, where the narrowed river drops into a large pool. In another 0.1 mi., the trail bears sharply away from the river. (At this point, a short side trail leads left to the edge of the river near a rocky island called Head of the Gulf, where there are some interesting logging artifacts.) The trail rejoins Pleasant River Rd. in another 0.2 mi. Turn right (southeast) to follow the road along the side of the mountain high above Gulf Hagas back to Screw Auger Falls, the Hermitage, and Hay Brook. Although it is often very marshy and wet, the road offers a quicker return than the rim trail.

Gulf Hagas Circuit

Distances from campground

- *to* AT junction: 0.7 mi., 20 min.
- *to* Screw Auger Falls Trail junction: 1.6 mi., 45 min.
- *to* rim-trail junction: 2.1 mi., 1 hr.
- *to* spur trail to Hammond Street Pitch (via rim trail): *est.* 2.4 mi., 1 hr. 10 min.
- *to* side paths to Jaws outlook: 2.9 mi., 1 hr. 30 min.
- *to* side trail to Buttermilk Falls: 3.5 mi., 1 hr. 45 min.
- *to* Stair Falls: 4.1 mi., 2 hr.
- *to* ledge above Billings Falls: 4.5 mi., 2 hr. 15 min.
- *to* side trail to Head of the Gulf: 4.6 mi., 2 hr. 20 min.
- *to* Pleasant River Rd.: 4.7 mi., 2 hr. 25 min.
- *to* rim-trail junction (via Pleasant Valley Rd.): 6.7 mi., 3 hr. 20 min.
- *to* Gulf Hagas Brook: 7.1 mi., 3 hr. 35 min.
- *to* campground: 8.8 mi. (14.2 km.), 4 hr. 40 min.

CHAIRBACK MOUNTAIN (2219 ft./676 m.)

This interesting, open peak is at the eastern end of the Barren-Chairback Range. It is a day hike from a logging road south of the West Branch of the Pleasant River. Refer to the USGS Sebec and Sebec Lake quadrangles, 15-min. series; the Silver Lake and Barren Mtn. East quadrangles, 7.5-min. series; or map 3 in the MATC's *Appalachian Trail Guide to Maine.*

From Katahdin Iron Works, follow the gravel paper-company road. At about 3 mi., take the left fork at the LLPC (Little Lyford Pond Camps) sign. (The right fork leads to Gulf Hagas.)

Park at 6.7 mi. from the Iron Works, short of where the Appalachian Trail crosses the road. Then descend 0.2 mi. to the AT. Follow it south as it climbs a short way on a hauling road, then turns sharply left. At 1.7 mi., the AT reaches the top of a ridge, and a side trail leads right 0.2 mi. to East Chairback Pond. Continue over a series of ridges. The last half-mile of the climb rises over a very steep talus slope to reach the summit, with its outstanding views.

Chairback Mountain
Distances from parking (via AT)

  to side trail to East Chairback Pond: 1.7 mi., 1 hr. 20 min.

  to Chairback summit (via AT): 4.1 mi. (6.6 km.), 2 hr. 35 min.

BARREN MOUNTAIN (2660 ft./811 m.)

At the western end of the Barren-Chairback Range, Barren Mtn. is the highest and most accessible peak. It is in Elliotsville Plantation (USGS Sebec Lake quadrangle, 15-min. series, and Barren Mtn. West and Barren Mtn. East quadrangles, 7.5-min. series). There are interesting outlooks from Barren Slide and Barren Ledges over Bodfish Intervale, Lake Onawa, and Borestone Mtn. The summit tower is now closed to hikers and scheduled for removal.

To climb Barren Mtn. via the Appalachian Trail, drive from Monson on Elliotsville Rd. 11.8 mi. to Bodfish Farm. Follow the Long

Pond tote road 1.6 mi. to the junction with the AT. Then drive 1.6 mi. on the tote road and park. The AT follows the road for 50 yd. and leaves southeast.

Leave the road right (north) on the AT and descend 0.1 mi. Cross Long Pond Stream at the normally knee-deep ford. The trail turns east, passing Slugundy Gorge. At 0.9 mi., it reaches a blue-blazed side trail leading 150 yd. to the Long Pond Stream Lean-to.

After the junction, the main trail climbs the northwestern slope of Barren Mtn. At 1.8 mi., another blue-blazed side trail leads south to the head of Barren Slide, an interesting mass of boulders with a view west. A little farther, the main trail crosses the head of Barren Ledges, from which there is a striking view. The route then bears left and winds along the northern slope of the range over rough terrain to the base of the cone. From there, it climbs steeply through boulders for a short distance to the summit.

(The AT continues northeast over the remaining peaks of the range to the valley of the West Branch of the Pleasant River. This hike is a camping trip of several days over rough terrain. See the 1992 edition of the MATC's *Appalachian Trail Guide to Maine* if you plan to take the trip across the range.)

Barren Mountain

Distances from Long Pond tote road (via AT)

   to   side trail to Long Pond Stream Lean-to: 0.9 mi.

   to   side trail to Barren Slide: 1.8 mi., 1 hr. 30 min.

   to   Barren Mtn. summit: 3.9 mi. (6.3 km.), 3 hr.

LITTLE WILSON FALLS

A worthwhile side trip in this area is to Little Wilson Falls, a striking 57-ft. waterfall in the canyon gouged through slate by Little Wilson Stream. Driving from Monson on Elliotsville Rd., park just before you cross the Big Wilson Bridge. Go left on a faint dirt road (formerly the Appalachian Trail). At 0.8 mi., pass the MFS Little Wilson Campsite and cross Little Wilson Stream. At 2 mi., turn left onto the relocated Appalachian Trail, and at 2.1 mi., cross Little Wilson Stream. At 2.4 mi., you will reach the rim of a ledge with an outstanding view of the 57-ft. falls and a deep slate canyon.

Little Wilson Falls

Distances from Big Wilson Bridge

to MFS Little Wilson Campsite: 0.8 mi.

to Little Wilson Falls: 2.4 mi. (3.7 km.), 1 hr. 25 min.

BORESTONE MOUNTAIN (1947 ft./593 m.)

Spelled Boarstone on USGS and other maps, this small but rugged mountain, complete with two peaks and three small ponds well up on its southwestern slope, rises above Lake Onawa. The views from the bare summits are excellent. The National Audubon Society sanctuary established there welcomes hikers year-round on the Moore's Ponds Route. It is open dawn to dusk. From June 1 through October 31, nature programs, a self-guided tour, and a staffed interpretive center halfway up are available. Fees are $1.50 for adults and $1.00 for students; group rates with prearrangement. No dogs or guns are allowed in the sanctuary. Refer to the USGS Sebec Lake quadrangle, 15-min. series, or the Barren Mtn. West quadrangle, 7.5-min. series.

Moore's Ponds Route

From Monson, follow Elliotsville Rd. After crossing the Big Wilson Bridge at 9 mi., bear left and cross the Canadian Pacific Railroad tracks in another 0.7 mi. The route to Borestone leads right 0.1 mi. beyond the railroad, following a private road through a gate. The road climbs steadily through switchbacks and then runs along a shelf to Sunrise Pond, the lowest of the three Moore's ponds, where it ends. The other two ponds are known as Midday and Sunset. Follow the trail, blazed with green triangles, around the southeastern end of Sunrise Pond and cross the outlet. After that, the trail, turning north and then east, climbs steeply up the main cone to the open western peak. It descends slightly into the saddle and then rises to the higher eastern peak.

Moore's Ponds Route
Distances from Elliotsville Rd.

   to   Sunrise Pond: 1 mi., 40 min.

   to   Borestone, western peak: 1.8 mi., 1 hr. 20 min.

   to   Borestone, eastern peak: 2 mi. (3.2 km.), 1 hr. 30 min.

HIGH CUT HILL (955 ft./291 m.)

High Cut Hill is in Garland, just south of the Penobscot/Piscataquis county line. There is a magnificent 360-degree view. Refer to the USGS Dover-Foxcroft quadrangle, 15-min. series or 7.5-min. series.

Approach by turning west off ME 15 onto ME 94 at the West Charleston four corners. Drive 3.2 mi. to a dirt road on the right. (From Garland, go north 1 mi. and east 1.6 mi.) The trail ascends north through open pasture to the summit. The first 0.5 mi. is drivable, but parking is limited.

High Cut Hill
Distances from paved road

   to   High Cut Hill summit: 1.3 mi. (2.1 km.), 55 min.

Section 4

East of the Penobscot

This section describes the mainland area east of the Penobscot River and south of Aroostook County, between the Penobscot River plain on the west and the coastal rivers, including the Union, Narraguagus, Machias, and St. Croix, on the south and east. In this region, the country rolls up into low, mostly widely scattered mountains. Lead Mtn. (1475 ft.) and Passadumkeag Mtn. (1463 ft.) are the highest, and several others are over 1000 ft. In general, extensive views characterize these mountains, some of which have attractive open summits and ledges. This section first describes the mountains to the south and west first, and then those to the north and east.

TUNK MOUNTAIN (1157 ft./353 m.)

This mountain is located in T 10 S D (*T* stands for "township" and *S D* for "Southern Division"). It is northeast of Schoodic Mtn. There is no trail on Tunk's upper part, but bushwhacking is fairly easy. Refer to the USGS Tunk Lake quadrangle, 15-min. series, and the Tunk Mountain quadrangle, 7.5-min. series.

Take US 1 east from Ellsworth for 6 mi. and bear left on ME 182. At about 7.5 mi. east of ME 200 in Franklin, park at the entrance of a road on the left that is 0.2 mi. east of the eastern end of Fox Pond and 2.7 mi. west of the outlet of Tunk Lake.

The trail leads north through gentle terrain that rises gradually to Salmon Pond. It continues on to Mud Pond as a footpath, identifiable only by its worn treadway. Once the trail crosses by the western end of the pond, it rises sharply and becomes much less distinct as it passes through spruce forest. Eventually, it breaks onto open ledges on the slopes of the five-peaked summit ridge. The whole southern face of the mountain consists of cliffs and steep ledges. Views are limited but interesting, particularly those of Spring River Lake and the Black Hills.

Tunk Mountain

Distance from entrance of road off ME 182

    to Tunk summit: 1.5 mi. (2.4 km.), 1 hr. 30 min.

SCHOODIC MOUNTAIN (1069 ft./326 m.)

Schoodic is one of a small group of mountains northeast of the head of Frenchman's Bay, and it is very popular for climbing. It is located in T 9 S D. Refer to the USGS Tunk Lake quadrangle, 15-min. series, and the Sullivan quadrangle, 7.5-min. series.

    A good trail to the abandoned firetower on the summit starts 2.2 mi. south of Franklin Village and 4 mi. north of Sullivan. It leaves the eastern side of ME 200 between two bridges at the foot of a steep hill in East Franklin. Park in the space just north of the northern bridge. Take the paved road east and follow the right fork up a hill. At about 0.5 mi., the road (which can sometimes be driven to this point) crosses a large brook, the last sure source of *water* on the trail. At about 1 mi., the road crosses some railroad tracks. Turn right and follow the road beside the tracks for a short distance until it swings away to the left. Pass through a logged area, keeping straight at the next left fork. About 20 min. farther, take the well-worn path to the left (cairn). The trail then climbs steeply but presents no difficulties. The top of the mountain is bare and flat and offers views in all directions. Those of Mount Desert Island and Frenchman's Bay are very scenic.

    Another easier approach to the mountain is by the trail that leaves from the southern (near) end of the Schoodic Beach parking lot. (See the directions to the parking lot in the Black Mtn. description, below.) Follow blue blazes through woods up the mountain until you reach open ledges where the trail from Schoodic Beach joins from the right at a large stone cairn. Continue following stone cairns up ledges to the top.

The trail from Schoodic Beach up Schoodic Mtn. leaves from the western end of the beach, following an old road for a short distance then ascending left.

Schoodic Mountain

Distances from ME 200

  to large-brook crossing: *est.* 0.5 mi., 15 min.

  to railroad tracks: 1 mi., 30 min.

  to warden's cabin site: 2 mi., 1 hr.

  to Schoodic summit: 2.8 mi. (4.5 km.), 1 hr. 40 min.

Distances from Schoodic Beach parking lot

  to Schoodic summit: 0.8 mi. (1.4 km.), 45 min.

  to Schoodic Beach: 0.5 mi.,15 min.

  to Schoodic summit via beach: 0.6 mi., 45 min.

BLACK MOUNTAIN

The point from which most hikers access Black Mtn. is US 1 in East Sullivan. Turn onto ME 183 and proceed about 4.5 miles, following the main tarred road. About 150 yd. after you cross some abandoned railroad tracks, take the first gravel road to the left (look for a blue-and-white Public Lands sign). Follow the gravel road about 0.3 mi. to a Y. At this point, the Schoodic Beach Rd. bears to the left down a hill and another gravel road, known as Black Mtn. Rd., continues up the hill straight ahead. The left branch heads to Schoodic Mtn., Schoodic Beach, campsites on Donnell Pond, and Black Mtn. Cliffs. The right branch heads to the Black summit, Wizard Pond (Big Chief Trail), Rainbow Pond, and Caribou Mtn.

Black Mountain Cliffs Loop

To reach the Schoodic Mtn. and Black Mtn. Cliffs trailhead, bear left at the first Y and continue about 1 mi. to a second Y. Continue straight ahead, avoiding Flanders Pond Rd. to the left, for about 1 mi., to the Donnell Pond public parking lot at the end of the road. The trail up to Black Mtn. Cliffs leaves from the northern (far) end of the parking lot. Bear right just past the small brook and follow blue blazes through the woods, crossing several old logging roads up to the base of Black Mtn. Blazes and rock cairns continue up over interesting cliffs and ledges to the top of the ridge. At a junction here, a trail bears right (northerly) toward Wizard Pond, Black Mtn. Bald, various other longer trail loops, and the trailhead on Black Mtn. Rd. To reach the cliffs, continue straight ahead along the ridgeline, through the spruce forest. The trail goes past several small overlooks to reach a junction from which a side trail heads downslope over open ledges to the left to cliffs overlooking Donnell Pond. This overlook is a good spot for observing the large turkey vultures and eagles flying in the area. Continuing straight on the main trail, you will gradually descend through hardwood forest to Schoodic Beach. This hike is of moderate difficulty.

Black Mountain Cliffs Loop

Distance from Schoodic Beach parking lot

- *to* Black Mtn. base: 0.8 mi., 40 min.
- *to* junction with Wizard Pond/Black Mt. Bald trail: 1.2 mi., 90 min.
- *to* Donnell Pond overlook: 1.5 mi., 1 hr 50 min.
- *to* Schoodic Beach: 2.1 mi., 2 hrs. 30 min.
- *Complete* Black Mtn. Cliffs loop: 2.7 mi., 3 hrs.

Black Mountain Ridge

To reach the Black Mtn. Ridge trailhead, take Black Mtn. Rd. 2 mi. from its intersection with Schoodic Beach Rd. Just beyond a three-car parking area, currently marked with blue blazes and a stone cairn, the trail leaves left. It follows the approximate route of the old Big Chief Trail. It is well worn and easily followed as it passes beautiful granite cliff faces. It is marked with blue paint blazes until it breaks out onto the open granite ledges. At the junction here, follow rock cairns around the southeastern face of the middle peak of Black Mtn. (continuing straight ahead would lead you to a Wizard Pond overlook). There are spectacular views across the adjacent lakes and the entire Downeast coast.

When you reach the cliff between the middle and eastern peaks of Black Mtn., you will find a trail junction. Bear right to drop down to Wizard Brook (Wizard Pond is just upstream), then proceed up the slopes of the easternmost and highest peak of Black Mtn. Known locally as Bald Peak, it has beautiful 360-degree views of Downeast Maine. From the junction, your first viewpoint (of Wizard Pond) lies about 200 yd. ahead. The trail continues, connecting with another trail on Black Mtn.'s ridgeline along with various long and short hikes including a loop around Caribou Mtn. This hike is easy to moderate.

Black Mountain Ridge
Distance from trailhead

- *to* middle peak ledges: 0.4 mi., 35 min.
- *to* Wizard Pond overlook: 0.6 mi., 45 min.
- *to* Wizard Brook: 0.8 mi., 55 min.
- *to* Bald Peak: 1 mi. (1.6 km.), 1 hr. 5 min.

BLUE HILL (934 ft./285 m.)

This isolated mountain rises just north of the town of the same name. There is a MFS firetower as well as a microwave tower on the summit. Refer to the USGS Blue Hill quadrangle, 15-min. series or 7.5-min. series.

Opposite the Blue Hill Fair Grounds, 13 mi. from Ellsworth on ME 172, go right onto a road that heads west. An excellent MFS trail leaves this road on the right (north), 0.8 mi. from ME 172. (You can also reach the start of the trail by turning east from ME 15, 1 mi. north of Blue Hill Village and 11 mi. south of the junction with US 1 between Orland and East Orland. The trail is on the left [north], 0.5 mi. from ME 15.) Not far from the start, it branches right and runs through a fine stand of spruce to the summit. Extensive views take in the Mt. Desert Island mountains and Blue Hill Bay. See *A Hiker's Guide to Blue Hill Mountain,* by Alison Dibble, sponsored by the Blue Hill Heritage Trust. This pamphlet is available in local stores and inns for a $2.00 donation.

Blue Hill

Distance from road between ME 172 and ME 15

   to   Blue Hill Summit: 1 mi. (1.6 km.), 45 min.

GREAT HILL (1038 ft./316 m.)

Great Hill appears on the USGS Orland quadrangle, 7.5-min. series. It is also called Great Pond Mtn., and is known locally as Old Baldy. It is in the town of Orland, northeast of Alamoosook Lake.

Leave US 1 in East Orland 6 mi. east of Bucksport and 14 mi. west of Ellsworth at Toddy Pond Outlet (sign reading Craig Brook National Fish Hatchery). Take Hatchery Rd. to the north for 1.4 mi. Bear right onto the Don Fish Trail at brick gateposts. Park at 0.8 mi. Take the trail up to the left (sign reading Mt. Trail and tan register box). The trail climbs up and down through woods. Joining a ledgy jeep road up, it soon emerges onto spacious open ledges from which you can see from Mt. Desert Island to Penobscot Bay. The wooded summit, about 100 ft. higher with an open ledge, offers views to the northeast and east.

Be careful to note where the trail leaves the woods, so that you can find this spot again on the way down; there are no markers on the ledges.

Great Hill

Distance from parking area

   to   Great Hill summit: 1.8 mi. (2.9 km.), 1 hr. 15 min.

BALD MOUNTAIN (1234 ft./376 m.)

This interesting mountain (also known as Dedham Bald Mtn.) is in the town of Dedham, and a MFS trail in good condition leads to a tower and radio towers on the summit. The Bald Mtn. ski area used to occupy the western side of the mountain. After it closed, the lifts and other equipment were removed. Refer to the USGS Green Lake quadrangle, 7.5-min. series.

From US 1A in East Holden, 9 mi. from Bangor and 18 mi. from Ellsworth, turn south onto paved Upper Dedham Rd.; do not take ME 46. In 2.8 mi., take a left at the fire station. Then, 6.5 mi. from US 1A, where the road bears right, continue straight on FR 62 for 100 yd. and park on ledges to the left. The trail starts at the parking area and is easy to follow. It leads through open fields and over ledges to the tower, which the MFS maintains for communication. From the tower, you can see to the north and northwest from Katahdin to Bigelow, and the nearby ledges on the northern side of the mountain look out over beautiful Phillips Lake, now known as Lucerne-in-Maine. The eastern side offers views of the Mt. Desert Island mountains.

An alternative route follows the old ski trail, which is easy to see from the approach road. The ski trail intersects Upper Dedham Rd. 0.3 mi. before (north of) the firetower trail at the parking area.

Bald Mountain

Distance from parking area

   to   Bald Mtn. firetower: 0.5 mi. (0.8 km.), 30 min.

RIDER BLUFF (813 ft./248 m.)

This bluff in Holden is in the first line of hills east of the Penobscot River plain. It makes a good outlook from which to view the Bangor-Brewer area and the mountains from Katahdin to Bigelow, Sugarloaf, and Abraham. Most people hike up the service road for the WLBZ-TV tower on the summit. (During dry weather, cars can usually make it up this road, too.) Refer to the USGS Brewer Lake quadrangle, 7.5-min. series.

From US 1A, turn southwest on paved South Rd., 8 mi. from Bangor and 1.4 mi. northwest of East Holden. The turn is just southeast of the Holden Town Hall and Grange. In 1.3 mi., the blacktop road makes a sharp left turn. Go straight ahead on the private access road. It descends slightly, crosses a small brook, then turns right (west) and climbs toward the col between Rider Bluff and Hog Hill. About 0.7 mi. from the blacktop road, it turns and climbs more steeply to the summit.

Rider Bluff

Distance from blacktop road

   to Rider summit: *est.* 1 mi. (1.6 km.), 40 min.

BLACKCAP MOUNTAIN (1022 ft./312 m.)

Five radio and TV masts top Blackcap Mountain, which is in Eddington. Vegetation blocks views, except to the east. Refer to the USGS Orono and Orland quadrangles, 15-min. series, and the Chemo Pond quadrangle, 7.5-min. series.

To reach the summit, take ME 46 northeast from US 1A at East Holden. Drive 4.3 mi. and turn right onto Blackcap Rd. (sign reading Katahdin Area Council Boy Scout Camp). The road to the scout camp goes left from the summit road, 0.5 mi. from ME 46. Stay right at that and all other junctions. Continue 1.9 mi. to the end of the road. If the road is washed out, a four-wheel-drive vehicle will be necessary.

Roberts Trail

Hikers can pick up the Roberts Trail either at the summit of Blackcap (at the southern end of the road), to the right of the southernmost tower, or on the scout camp road at the outlet of Fitts Pond, which is opposite a gravel bank near the entrance of the camp 1.5 mi. from the summit road. Other trails also diverge from this point and lead to Burnt Pond and Little Burnt Pond. Blue and white paint blazes and directional arrows mark the Roberts Trail, which crosses the pond outlet on a tripod bridge and climbs steeply to the cluster of radio and TV masts. It continues along the summit ridge over open ledges and through patches of trees to the southern end of the ridge. Then it drops steeply east and northeast to the southern end of Fitts Pond. It crosses a swampy patch to the eastern shore of the pond and runs along the shore. At first, it stays close to the shore. Then it goes up on the bluff and returns to the entrance of the Boy Scout camp. At the southern end of the pond, be careful not to take a wrong turn onto a jeep road that diverges east.

Roberts Trail

Distances from scout camp entrance

   to radio and TV masts: 0.6 mi., 45 min.

   to southern end of Blackcap summit ridge: 1.4 mi., 1 hr. 10 min.

   to southern end of Fitts Pond: 2.3 mi., 2 hr.

   to scout camp entrance: 3.8 mi. (6.1 km.), 3 hr.

EAGLE BLUFF (790 ft./241 m.)

With one of the more open and scenic views in eastern Maine, this sheer cliff overlooks Mountainy Pond and almost unbroken wilderness. A tote road rises gradually to within 0.8 mi. of the summit, which is bare. The sheer southern side is good for rappelling, friction climbing, and rock climbing. The granite is stable, but not many climbers take advantage of it. Refer to the USGS Orono and Orland quadrangles, 15-min. series, and the Green Lake quadrangle, 7.5-min. series.

The trail begins at the Katahdin Scout Camp. (See the preceding section for approach routes.) Park in the lot at the reservation.

From behind the mess hall (the largest building), the trail follows the road, which rises quickly at first. At about 2.8 mi., turn sharply right into a hunting camp. To the left of the camp, an orange-blazed trail climbs steeply, levels off, and then pitches quickly to the summit.

Eagle Bluff
Distance from scout camp

   to   Eagle Bluff summit: 3 mi. (4.8 km.), 2 hr.

WOODCHUCK HILL (SNOWSHOE MOUNTAIN) (834 ft./254 m.)

An easy hike in the area northeast of Blackcap Mtn., Woodchuck Hill offers good campsites at both its summit and its base. Refer to the USGS Orono quadrangle, 15-min. series, and the Chemo Pond quadrangle, 7.5-min. series.

The approach by road is the same as for Blackcap Mtn. Park in the lot at Camp Roosevelt (a scout camp). Follow the unmarked road through the camp then turn left on the blue- and yellow-blazed trail. This passes through a campsite beyond Snowshoe Pond and comes out onto the Bangor Water District road (paved). Cross the road to utility pole 68, then follow well-marked blue and yellow blazes and arrows up over cliffs to the open summit with views.

Woodchuck Hill
Distance from scout camp

   to   Woodchuck summit: *est.* 1.3 mi. (2.1 km.), 45 min.

PEAKED (1160 ft./354 m.) AND LITTLE PEAKED

MOUNTAINS

These two summits make a particularly rewarding snowshoeing trip in winter. It is easy to complete the circuit in an afternoon from many points in the surrounding area.

Peaked Mountain

Peaked Mtn., commonly called Chick Hill, straddles the Clifton/Amherst line. A well-marked and popular MFS trail leads to the summit. Refer to the USGS Great Pond quadrangle, 15-min. series, and the Hopkins Pond quadrangle, 7.5-min. series.

About 18 mi. from Bangor and 3.5 mi. east of the junction of ME 9 and ME 180, leave ME 9 on the northern (left) side onto a gravel road 1.1 mi. east of the Parks Pond Campground. In about 0.7 mi., after passing a small group of houses, park. Follow an old discontinued "Airline" road to the firewarden's campsite (0.2 mi.). There is a dependable *spring* behind the campsite. Continue on the old road and, at about 0.6 mi., as the road levels off, turn right onto a clearly blazed trail. At about 0.9 mi., the trail rises more steeply; from the lower ledge, you can see nearby Little Peaked Mtn. to the west. Occasional cairns mark the way to the summit, which offers vistas in all directions and is particularly colorful in fall. The view includes five lakes, the Penobscot River, the Mt. Desert Island mountains to the southeast, and Mt. Katahdin to the northwest.

Peaked Mountain

Distance from parking area

> *to* Peaked Mtn. summit: 1.3 mi. (2.1 km.), 50 min.

Little Peaked Mountain

The views from Little Peaked Mtn. (Little Chick Hill) are also good, except to the north. To reach Little Peaked Mtn., take the trail to the right at the parking area.

Another easy route is to take the trail up Peaked Mtn. Just before beginning the climb up the steeper part of the peak, turn right, descend briefly to the col, and bushwhack to Little Peaked.

For a third route, start up the Peaked Mtn. Trail. At 0.4 mi., go right onto a cairned road closed with a cable for 0.2 mi. Turn right at the cairn and climb directly to the summit.

LEAD MOUNTAIN (HUMPBACK) (1475 ft./450 m.)

Lead Mtn. is in T 28 M D in Hancock County, just west of the Washington County line. The trail appears on the USGS Lead Mtn. quadrangle, 7.5-min. series.

Take the newly bulldozed road left at the rear of the yard of the MFS station (94 yd.) in Beddington. The station is 0.1 mi. west of the ME 9 bridge over the Narraguagus River and 1.1 mi. east of the ME 9 and ME 193 junction. Park at the turnaround 1.7 mi. from the station. The trail follows the gated road for 10 min., then turns right up into the woods just before the University of Maine acid-rain project structures and heads for the summit (blue-blazed). At 1.3 mi., a side path leads 200 yd. left to Bear Pond. At 1.5 mi., the trail divides. The left fork goes close to a reliable *spring* 100 ft. to the left of the main trail (sign). Then it rejoins the main trail. At 2.5 mi., you will reach the warden's cabin in a col below the summit. The trail continues straight on past the cabin and then bears left (west) to the site of the firetower, which is on a flat summit several acres in area. The ledges 200 yd. southwest of the summit are a good lookout.

Descending, remember that where the trail divides, the right fork leads past the *spring.*

Lead Mountain
Distances from MFS station

> *to* side trail to Bear Pond: 1.3 mi., 40 min.

> *to* warden's cabin: 2.5 mi., 1 hr. 45 min.

to Lead summit: 3 mi. (4.8 km.), 2 hr.

PEAKED MOUNTAIN (938 ft./286 m.)

Peaked Mtn. is in T 30 in Washington County, north of ME 9 and less than 30 mi. east of the mountain near Clifton with the same name. Refer to the USGS Tug Mtn. quadrangle, 15-min. series, and the Peaked Mtn. quadrangle, 7.5-min. series.

A good MFS trail leaves the northern side of ME 9 at an MFS sign (09-67-0), found about 9.8 mi. east of the Narraguagus River and about 14.8 mi. west of Wesley. You will pass the cabin Mayor Haven at 0.2 mi. Take the right fork at 0.3 mi., and park at 0.6 mi. (hiker sign). Follow the tote road a short distance to the former firewarden's cabin (private, name of Pelton). Between buildings, take the trail, which rises gently to an open ledge with some views. The MFS firetower has been removed. Extensive wilderness spreads out below in all directions.

Peaked Mountain

Distance from parking area on tote road

to Peaked Mtn. summit: 1.3 mi. (2.1 km.), 45 min.

WASHINGTON BALD MOUNTAIN (983 ft./300 m.)

This mountain's MFS firetower was abandoned in 1970. The mountain is in T 42 M D. Refer to the USGS Fletcher Peak quadrangle, 7.5-min. series.

A paper company maintains the gravel road that leaves the northern side of ME 9, 14 mi. east of the Narraguagus River in Beddington and 10.5 mi. west of Wesley. Take the road north to its end (13.1 mi.), where there is room for four or five cars to park. From this point, logging operations have obscured the trail. A map-and-compass bushwhack is recommended. (See p. xxii for more information on bushwhacking.) Climb the last steep pitch to a tower, which was erected in

1935. There is a *well* sunk in the granite near the warden's cabin (now privately leased).

Trails lead to Third, Fourth, and Fifth Machias lakes from the summit but are not recommended. You can see First, Second, Third, and Fourth Machias lakes and many mountains from the 65-ft. tower.

Washington Bald Mountain

Distance from end of paper-company road

   to Washington Bald firetower (via right fork): 2.2 mi. (3.5 km.), 1 hr. 30 min.

PASSADUMKEAG MOUNTAIN (1465 ft./446 m.)

Passadumkeag Mtn. is southeast of Enfield. It runs in a gradual east–west arc for some 5 mi. and rises well above the surrounding countryside, which is particularly flat to the west and southwest. Until 1970, the MFS staffed the firetower on the highest summit and maintained a good logging road to it. Refer to the USGS Saponac quadrangle, 15-min. series, and the Burlington and Saponac quadrangles, 7.5-min. series.

Leave West Enfield on ME 155, heading east from its junction with US 2. After 2.5 mi., turn right onto ME 188, and follow it to the Saponac four corners (green buildings), about 19 mi. from US 2. Turn sharply right onto a gravel road and cross the Passadumkeag River. At 0.4 mi., turn right at the head of a gravel pit. Pass the blue house (a former ranger station) and continue on the increasingly rough road. From this road, where logging has obliterated the trail, the climb becomes a bushwhack to the 30-ft. firetower. The tower can also be reached by following Greenfield Rd. from the south, starting from US 2 in Costigan. This becomes a rough jeep trail. From the tower, you can see Brandy Pond to the southeast in T 39 M D, Saponac Lake to the north, West lakes and Nicatous Lake to the east, and many mountains, including Katahdin.

Passadumkeag Mountain
Distances from parking area

   to   private cabin: 4 mi., 2 hr.

   to   Passadumkeag firetower: 4.5 mi. (7.2 km.), 2 hr. 30 min.

POCOMOONSHINE MOUNTAIN (605 ft./184 m.)

Located in Princeton, this mountain rises nearly 500 ft. above Poco-moonshine Lake. Before abandoning it in 1970, the MFS built a road on the back side of the mountain to the tower (the first trail described below). Refer to the USGS Big Lake quadrangle, 15-min. series, and the Princeton quadrangle, 7.5-min. series.

From US 1, 2.3 mi. south of Princeton, turn southwest onto South Princeton Rd. At 0.9 mi., turn right onto a gravel road (sign reading Pokey Mt. Scenic Area). Travel 4.1 mi. to a fork. The right fork leads to a parking area with view of Pocomoonshine Lake. A blue-blazed trail ascends to the summit and tower foundation following the old firewarden's road. The left fork leads 0.2 mi. to a second parking area. From there depart two blue-blazed trails, the left leading 0.1 mi. to a tent platform, the right meandering gradually up the mountain, joining the firewarden's road 0.1 mi. from the summit. There is no view from the site of the former firetower, but a blue-blazed trail loops around the summit area to some outcrops, which offer views in various directions.

Another trail to the summit leaves US 1 to the right at 3.8 mi.

Pocomoonshine Mountain
Distance from parking area

   to   Pocomoonshine summit: 0.5 mi. (0.8 km.), 30 min.

Section 5

Camden Hills

The Camden Hills, a compact and attractive group of mountains, rise above the western shore of Penobscot Bay in the towns of Camden, Lincolnville, and Rockport. They share many characteristics with the Mt. Desert Island mountains 40 mi. to the east—fine softwood forests, bold cliffs and ledges, and wide vistas of water and mountains. Mt. Megunticook (1380 ft.) is the highest of the group and, with the exception of Cadillac Mtn., is the highest point along the Atlantic seaboard in the United States. A chain of lower summits continues northeast for several miles; Bald Rock Mtn. (1100 ft.) is the most conspicuous. Cameron Mtn. (811 ft.) is west of Bald Rock and northeast of Maiden Cliff. The Cameron summit is private property, a commercial blueberry field. Mt. Battie (800 ft.) lies to the south of Megunticook and is only 0.5 mi. by trail from Megunticook St. in Camden. The Megunticook River and Lake separate the main peaks of the group from the hills running to the southwest, which are, from northeast to southwest, Bald Mtn. (1272 ft.), Ragged Mtn. (1300 ft.), Spruce Mtn. (960 ft.), Pleasant Mtn. (1064 ft.), and Meadow Mtn. (660 ft.). Refer to the USGS Camden, Lincolnville, and West Rockport quadrangles, 7.5-min. series, as well as the map included with this guide.

Camden Hills State Park (5500 acres) embraces much of the Mt. Megunticook Range, plus a large area to the north and northeast and a short stretch on Penobscot Bay north of Camden on US 1. Park facilities include picnic and camping areas. An automobile road (toll) runs to the summit of Mt. Battie from the park headquarters. *The water supply is not reliable* in many parts of the park, so carry water if you hike there. Most trails are blazed with white paint.

Not in the Camden Hills, but included in this section of the guide, are several outlying mountains to the west of the Penobscot River, south of US 2, and east of the Kennebec River. This section also covers the offshore island of Monhegan.

MOUNT BATTIE (800 ft./243 m.)

This mountain lies to the south of Mt. Megunticook. For climbing, it is the most popular of the Camden Hills, because its open ledges offer outstanding views and it is close to Camden. For several years after 1897, there was a hotel on the summit. The stone viewing tower there now was erected as a war memorial in 1921.

A toll road for cars runs to the summit. Starting at the Camden Hills State Park Headquarters on US 1, it climbs gradually to the Battie-Megunticook col, turns southwest, and finally curves southeast to the top (1.4 mi.).

Mount Battie Trail

This trail, marked with white blazes and cairns, rises steeply over the rocky nose of Mt. Battie. Take ME 52 (Mountain St.) from its junction with US 1 in Camden. Then take the fourth right, and then the first left onto Megunticook St. Continue steeply uphill, where there is a small parking area. The trail first climbs northwest and then rises more steeply north through thinning woods. It soon emerges on the open ledges and runs to the summit tower.

Mount Battie Trail
Distance from parking area on Megunticook St.

   to Battie summit: 0.5 mi. (0.8 km.), 30 min.

Carriage Road Trail

This trail climbs along the more gradual western and northwestern slopes of Mt. Battie, via the route of the old carriage road up the mountain, and leaves the right (northeastern) side of ME 52 about 1.3 mi. from the US 1 and ME 52 junction. The road runs north 0.3 mi. to where the Carriage Road Trail forks right, while the Carriage Trail, leading to the Tableland Trail, continues.

The Carriage Road Trail rises gently on the old carriage road, which is washed out in many places. The trail joins the toll road near the summit parking area.

Carriage Road Trail
Distance from ME 52

>   *to*   Battie summit: 1.1 mi. (1.8 km.), 35 min.

Carriage Trail

In conjunction with the Tableland Trail, this trail provides a route up Mt. Megunticook from the southwest. To approach the trail, see the Carriage Road Trail, above.

The trail climbs very gradually. It reaches the Tableland Trail near the Battie-Megunticook col. To reach Ocean Lookout and, beyond that, the true summit of Mt. Megunticook, go left on the Tableland Trail. (To the right, the Tableland Trail leads to the Mt. Battie summit.)

Carriage Trail
Distances from ME 52

>   *to*   Tableland Trail junction: 1 mi., 30 min.

>   *to*   Ocean Lookout (via Tableland Trail): 1.7 mi., 1 hr. 20 min.

>   *to*   Megunticook summit (via Tableland and Ridge trails): 2.2 mi. (3.5 km.), 1 hr. 35 min.

Nature Trail

The Nature Trail is a 1.2-mi. link between the lower part of the Megunticook Trail and the Tableland Trail. It provides access to both Mt. Battie (via the Tableland Trail) and Mt. Megunticook (via either the Megunticook or Tableland Trail and the Ridge Trail). The Nature Trail is accessed from the Mt. Battie hiker's parking lot, about 0.25 mi. up the road (state park entrance fee) on the right. From the parking lot, turn left (northwest) to reach the Tableland Trail; turn right (north-northeast) to reach the Megunticook Trail. It is possible to make a nice loop of approximately 3.4 mi. over Ocean Lookout: Take the Nature Trail to the Megunticook Trail up to Ocean Lookout, then return via the Tableland Trail and the northwestern end of the Nature Trail.

Nature Trail
Distances from Mt. Battie Rd. hiker's parking lot

- *to* Tableland Trail junction: 0.9 mi. (1.5 km.), 30 min.

- *to* Battie summit (via Tableland Trail): 1.7 mi. (2.7 km.), 45 min.

- *to* Ocean Lookout (via Megunticook Trail): 1.3 mi. (2.1 km.), 1 hr. 15 min.

- *to* Ocean Lookout (via Tableland Trail): 1.7 mi. (2.7 km.), 1 hr. 25 min.

MOUNT MEGUNTICOOK (1380 ft./420 m.)

Mt. Megunticook is the highest of the Camden Hills. A ridge forms the mountain and runs northwest–southeast for approximately 3 mi. The true summit has no view, but Ocean Lookout, 0.4 mi. to the southeast, takes in the expanse of Penobscot Bay. Several outlooks on the Ridge Trail offer views to the northwest over Megunticook Lake. Maiden Cliff is a prominent bluff near the northwestern end of the mountain.

Mount Megunticook Trail

This trail climbs the eastern slope of the mountain from the northeastern end of the Nature Trail to Ocean Lookout. Parking is available at the Mt. Battie Rd. hiker's parking lot, approximately 0.25 mi. up Mt. Battie Rd. (state-park entrance fee) on the right. The trail starts from the park camping area and climbs first gradually, then steeply. At 1.4 mi., it reaches Ocean Lookout, where the Tableland Trail from Mt. Battie comes up from the left (south). From Ocean Lookout, follow the Ridge Trail to the right about 0.4 mi. to the Mt. Megunticook summit.

The 5-mi. long Snowmobile Trail has been cut along the eastern side of Mt. Megunticook. It leaves the right side of the Mt. Megunticook Trail just after camping area, leading around the eastern side of Mt. Megunticook before turning east to the Youngtown Rd. trailhead (found just northwest of the intersection of Youngtown Rd. and ME 173). Hikers can complete a loop trip over Mt. Megunticook via the Mt. Megunticook Trail, the Ridge Trail, the Slope Trail, and the Snowmobile Trail.

Mount Megunticook Trail
Distances from park camping area

- *to* Ocean Lookout: 1.4 mi., 1 hr.
- *to* Megunticook summit and Slope Trail junction (via Ridge Trail): 1.9 mi. (3 km.), 1 hr. 20 min.
- *to* Snowmobile Trail (via Slope Trail): 3.4 mi., 2 hr. 10 min.
- *to* park camping area (via Slope and Snowmobile trails): 5.4 mi. (8.6 km.), 3 hr. 20 min.

Tableland Trail

This trail starts from the summit of Mt. Battie. It crosses the parking area, runs to the northeast, and gradually descends—crossing the toll road at 0.5 mi.—to the Battie-Megunticook col. At 0.7 mi., you will pass the Nature Trail on the right and, at 0.8 mi., the Carriage Trail on the left. Starting the ascent of the Mt. Megunticook mass, the Tableland Trail keeps to the right (east) of two lines of cliffs and, again swinging to the northwest, climbs steeply to Ocean Lookout. The true summit is another 0.5 mi. to the northwest along the Ridge Trail.

Tableland Trail
Distance from Battie summit

to Ocean Lookout: 1.5 mi. (2.4 km.), 1 hr.

Jack Williams Trail

This woodland trail leaves the Tableland Trail below its intersection with the Ridge Trail and follows the plateau area below Megunticook Ridge before rising to meet the Ridge Trail approximately halfway between the junctions of the Ridge and Zeke's trails and the Ridge and Scenic trails. The Jack Williams Trail offers views of the rising cliffs along Megunticook Ridge, along with mature hardwood stands. The trail is named to honor a local trail volunteer.

Jack Williams Trail
Distance from Tableland Trail

to Ridge Trail: 1.6 mi. (2.6 km.), 1 hr. 30 min.

Adam's Lookout Trail

This trail connects the Megunticook and Tableland trails while providing an excellent eastern-facing lookout over Penobscot Bay. An approximately 2.25-mi. loop can be made from the Mt. Battie Rd. hiker's parking lot by following the Nature Trail north to the Megunticook Trail, then taking the Adam's Lookout Trail to the Tableland Trail. Return to the parking lot via the western end of the Nature Trail.

Adam's Lookout Trail
Distance from Megunticook Trail

to Tableland Trail: 0.3 mi. (0.5 km.), 10 min.

Maiden Cliff Trail

Maiden Cliff (800 ft./243 m.) rises abruptly above Megunticook Lake. A steel cross stands near the spot where Elenora French, a young girl, fell to her death in 1864. The trail starts from the northeastern side of ME 52 at a parking area about 2.9 mi. north of the junction of ME 52 and US 1 in Camden, where the highway approaches a cove of Megunticook Lake. The trail climbs north, at first following a washed-out logging road along a small brook. At about 0.5 mi., the Ridge Trail to Mt. Megunticook continues ahead. The Maiden Cliff Trail branches left then climbs more steeply to open ledges and the cross. For a rewarding alternative route to Maiden Cliff, go straight on the Ridge Trail. Then, in about 0.25 mi., go left (north) on the Scenic Trail. After crossing several open ledges with fine views of the lake, the Scenic Trail reaches Maiden Cliff in another 0.5 mi.

Maiden Cliff Trail

Distances from ME 52

- *to* Ridge Trail junction: *est.* 0.5 mi., 30 min.
- *to* Maiden Cliff: 0.9 mi., 50 min.
- *to* Maiden Cliff (via Ridge and Scenic trails): 1.2 mi. (1.9 km.), 1 hr. 10 min.

Scenic Trail

This trail forks right (east) from the Maiden Cliff Trail near Maiden Cliff. It climbs over very open ledges with many views, then descends slightly to a junction with the Ridge Trail (approx. 0.7 mi. from ME 52 via the Maiden Cliff and Ridge trails).

Scenic Trail

Distance from Maiden Cliff

- *to* Ridge Trail junction: 0.5 mi. (0.8 km.), 30 min.

Ridge Trail

This trail leaves the Maiden Cliff Trail 0.5 mi. from ME 52 and runs along the main ridge of Mt. Megunticook, over the wooded summit

(1380 ft.), and on to Ocean Lookout with its fine views of Penobscot Bay. From the Maiden Cliff Trail junction, hike up to the right. In about 0.25 mi., the Scenic Trail to Maiden Cliff diverges left. The Ridge Trail continues to climb, after a brief descent, with occasional lookouts over Megunticook Lake. About 0.9 mi. from the junction with the Scenic Trail, Zeke's Trail comes in from the left (sign). In another 0.2 mi., the Ridge Trail crosses over a subsidiary summit (1290 ft.), descends slightly, and then climbs gradually to the true summit, which is wooded. Just beyond the summit, the Slope Trail diverges left (north). In another 0.2 mi., the Ridge Trail descends to end at Ocean Lookout.

Ridge Trail
Distances from ME 52

- *to* start (via Maiden Cliff Trail): 0.5 mi., 30 min.
- *to* Scenic Trail junction: 0.7 mi., 40 min.
- *to* Zeke's Trail junction: 1.6 mi., 1 hr. 5 min.
- *to* Megunticook summit and Slope Trail junction: 2.5 mi., 1 hr. 45 min.
- *to* Ocean Lookout: 2.9 mi. (4.7 km.), 2 hr.

Megunticook Traverse

This traverse is probably the nicest walk in the Camden Hills area. It offers a series of marvelous views and a lot of ridge walking. Climb the Mt. Battie Trail from Camden. Then follow the Tableland Trail to Ocean Lookout. Continue over Mt. Megunticook on the Ridge Trail to the Scenic Trail, which leads to Maiden Cliff. Then descend the Maiden Cliff Trail to ME 52. This route is equally good in the opposite direction. Either way, you will need a car spot.

Megunticook Traverse

Distance from parking area on Megunticook St. (Mt. Battie trailhead)

   to ME 52 (Maiden Cliff trailhead): 5.8 mi. (9.3 km.), 3 hr. 30
   min.

MOUNT MEGUNTICOOK FROM THE NORTH

Hikers can approach Mt. Megunticook and its subsidiary summits
from the north via a network of trails that for the most part branch
from the Snowmobile Trail. These trails are not as heavily used as
those on the southern and western slopes of the mountain. The woods
have suffered logging and extensive blowdowns in the past, so be particularly careful not to wander off the routes described. Since *water
supplies in the northern hills are not always dependable,* always carry
a supply of water.

Snowmobile Trail

This trail serves as the chief approach to the trails up Mt. Megunticook
from the north. It also is the approach for Cameron Mtn. and Bald
Rock Mtn. The southern end of the trail meets the lower end of the
Megunticook Trail near the camping area. A summer bypass cuts out
several low, wet areas of the trail.

   To reach the Snowmobile Trail, take ME 173 from Lincolnville
Beach. After 2.3 mi., turn left onto Youngtown Rd., and within less
than 100 yd. turn left into a small parking area at the trailhead (town
sign says Bald Rock Road). In about 1.3 mi., the Bald Rock Trail goes
up to left and the Cameron Mtn. Trail goes down to right (no signs).
In another 0.3 mi., the Sky Blue Trail diverges right, leading to the
Cameron Mtn. Trail, which in turn provides access to the upper part
of Zeke's Trail. At 2.5 mi. along the trail, Zeke's Trail diverges right
and climbs to the Ridge Trail. At 3 mi , you will reach a junction with
the Slope Trail at the site of a former ski lodge. The Slope Trail climbs
up to the Ridge Trail near the true summit of Mt. Megunticook. At 0.2

mi. beyond this junction with the Ridge Trail, the Spring Brook Trail (not part of the park) bears left and down to US 1.

Snowmobile Trail
Distances from Youngtown Road

- *to* Bald Rock Mtn. Trail and Cameron Mtn. Trail: 1.3 mi., 50 min.
- *to* Sky Blue Trail junction: 1.6 mi., 1 hr.
- *to* Zeke's Trail junction: 2.5 mi., 1 hr. 30 min.
- *to* junction with lower end of Megunticook Trail: 5 mi. (8 km.), 3 hrs.

BALD ROCK MOUNTAIN (1100 ft./335 m.)

About 2.5 mi. northeast of Mt. Megunticook, this mountain offers fine views from its ledgy summit. The Bald Rock Mountain Trail no longer leads from US 1 to the summit, due to logging activity in the area; it is only accessible via the Snowmobile Trail. There is *no dependable water* on the upper part of this route.

From the Snowmobile Trail, the Bald Rock Mountain Trail diverges left (east) 1.3 mi. from Youngtown Road. The trail, a well-worn path, climbs to the summit, passing an old shelter just below it.

Bald Rock Mountain Trail
Distance from Snowmobile Trail

to Bald Rock summit: 0.8 mi. (1.3 km.), 30 min.

Cameron Mountain Trail

This interesting trail diverges right (west) from the Snowmobile Trail about 1.3 mi. from the Youngtown Rd. trailhead opposite the Bald Rock Mtn. Trail. At about 0.1 mi., it turns left (avoid the first left), following an old town road. It crosses Black Brook and rises gradually past abandoned farmland, old cellar holes, and apple trees. The trail then follows the boundary of Camden Hills State Park and passes the summit of Cameron Mtn. This is private property; please do not trespass. The trail then descends a bit before turning left (south) and starting to climb (ignore Ski Lodge sign). About 0.8 mi. from the turn, the Sky Blue Trail diverges left. In another 67 yd. the Cameron Mtn. Trail ends at Zeke's Trail.

Cameron Mountain Trail
Distances from Snowmobile Trail

> *to* Cameron Mtn., south of summit: *est.* 1 mi., 35 min.

> *to* Sky Blue Trail and Zeke's Trail junctions: 1.9 mi., 1 hr. 25 min.

> *to* Megunticook summit (via Zeke's and Ridge trails): 3.7 mi. (5.9 km.), 2 hr. 25 min.

Sky Blue Trail

This trail has been cleared and its cairns rebuilt. Although it offers few long views, it makes a very pretty walk in the woods, with mature beech and maple forest, some large black spruce trees, and open blueberry clearings. The Sky Blue Trail leaves the Snowmobile Trail about 0.3 mi. beyond the start of the Cameron Mtn. Trail. It follows a course parallel to the Cameron Mtn. Trail. At about 1.5 mi., it reaches the Cameron Mtn. Trail. At this junction, go left to reach Zeke's Trail or right to reach Cameron Mtn.

Sky Blue Trail
Distance from Snowmobile Trail

> *to* Cameron Mtn. Trail junction: 1.5 mi. (3.2 km.), 1 hr. 30 min.

Zeke's Trail

This trail diverges right (west) from the Snowmobile Trail about 2.5 mi. from the Youngtown Rd. trailhead. The Cameron Mtn. Trail diverges right (north) at 0.8 mi., soon reaches a junction with the Sky blue Trail, and loops back east, past Cameron Mtn. to the Snowmobile Trail. At 1.3 mi., a trail (sign) leads right to Zeke's Lookout (1190 ft.) which, after a short, steep climb, offers good views of Bald Rock Mtn. and Upper Penobscot Bay. Zeke's Trail ends at its junction with the Ridge Trail, about 1 mi. northwest of the summit of Mt. Megunticook.

Zeke's Trail
Distances from Snowmobile Trail

> *to* Cameron Mtn. Trail junction: 0.8 mi. (1.3 km.), 40 min.

> *to* Zeke's Lookout Trail: 1.3 mi. (2.1 km.), 1 hr.

> *to* Ridge Trail junction: 1.3 mi. (2.1 km.), 1 hr.

Slope Trail

This trail goes from the Snowmobile Trail east across the bridge over Spring Brook to the summit of Mt. Megunticook. The trail climbs steeply and reaches the Ridge Trail close to the true summit of Mt. Megunticook.

Slope Trail
Distance from Snowmobile Trail

> *to* Megunticook summit: 1.5 mi. (2.4 km.), 1 hr. 15 min.

Camden Hills North Circuit

This is an interesting and scenic circuit hike. Starting at Youngtown Rd., take the Snowmobile Trail to the Bald Rock Trail and climb Bald Rock Mtn. Return to Snowmobile Trail, then continue to the Sky Blue Trail, Zeke's Trail, and Zeke's Lookout. Backtrack to the Cameron Mtn. Trail and return to the Snowmobile Trail and Youngtown Road.

RAGGED MOUNTAIN (1300 ft./396 m.)

This mountain, 4 mi. west of Camden, is the highest of the hills to the southwest of the Megunticook River and Lake. Its summit offers views comparable with those on the main Megunticook Range. There is a radio tower on the summit.

To approach from Camden, follow US 1 south to John St. on the right (sign reading Snow Bowl). Follow signs to the Snow Bowl.

Park at the Snow Bowl and follow the longest (T-bar) ski lift as far as it goes. Then enter the woods, continuing in the same direction on a trail that generally follows a power line, to climb to the summit.

Ragged Mountain

Distance from Snow Bowl

   to Ragged summit: *est.* 1.1 mi. (1.8 km.), 1 hr. 10 min.

FRYE MOUNTAIN (1139 ft./347 m.)

Frye Mtn. is in Montville. There is a MFS firetower on its summit. Refer to the USGS Morrill quadrangle, 7.5-min. series.

A dirt road that is good enough for cars passes within 0.3 mi. of the top. From the south and west, take ME 220 north from ME 3 near Liberty for 6 mi. (You will pass the road to Center Montville at about 5 mi.) Turn right (east) onto a dirt road at the sign reading Frye Mountain, Game Management Area, State of Maine. At 0.6 mi., turn right (south). At 0.4 mi., you will cross a stream. After another 0.5 mi., turn left (east). Drive 1.1 mi. (total 2.6 mi.) to the start of the short trail (right) to the summit (sign reading Firetower and Scenic View). You can find an alternative route to the mountain about 5 mi. south of Fosters Corner (in Knox) on ME 220.

The trail climbs southeast to the summit. The firetower views are excellent.

Frye Mountain

Distance from dirt road

   to Frye summit: 0.3 mi. (0.5 km.), 15 min.

MOUNT HARRIS (1233 ft./376 m.)

The highest of the cluster of hills in Dixmont, Mt. Harris has a fire-tower (locked) on its heavily wooded summit. This trail offers a pleasant woods-road walk, but no views in summer. The mountain is nearly halfway between Waterville and Bangor. Refer to the USGS Brooks quadrangle, 15-min. series, or the Dixmont quadrangle, 7.5-min. series.

    The trail, unmarked, begins on the left side of ME 7, 1.6 mi. south of Dixmont Corner at utility pole 43. Park by the side of the road.

    The lower portion of the trail is a well-graded jeep road rising gently in an almost straight line to the east. The road turns to the left above the first building it reaches, a hunting camp, but returns to the straight line. After it reaches a brown lean-to (enclosed and locked), the road rises more sharply to an intersection at the crest of the col. The trail to the tower leaves to the left. It rises steeply at first, and then more gently, to the large, wooden tower on the summit. The warden's cabin and another outbuilding (locked) are nearby.

    There is *water* at a public spring at the side of ME 7, 0.1 mi. south of Dixmont Corner.

Mount Harris

Distance from ME 7

   to firetower: 1.3 mi. (2.1 km.), 1 hr.

MOUNT WALDO (1064 ft./324 m.)

This attractive mountain, with its many open ledges, is in Frankfort. It is best known for the granite quarries on its eastern side. Refer to the

USGS Bucksport quadrangle, 15-min. series, or the Mt. Waldo quadrangle, 7.5-min. series.

The trail approach is via US 1A in Frankfort. Turn west onto Old Belfast Road 0.15 mi. south of the Frankfort Town Office Building. Go under a railroad overpass and up the hill. At 0.2 mi., turn right onto Tyler Ln. and go to a fork; take the unpaved left branch for a total of 1.8 mi. from the town office. Leave your car there and walk up the partially gated cart road that heads off to the left across open fields and ledges to the top of Mt. Waldo, with its microwave tower. Long views to the west are visible all the way up the trail, and on top, the view takes in an area from the Penobscot River Valley to Penobscot Bay.

Mount Waldo

Distance from parking place

 to Waldo summit: 1 mi. (1.6 km.), 45 min.

MONHEGAN ISLAND

This rugged island, with its spectacular sea cliffs and pleasant hiking trails, is 12 mi. off the coast of Maine. In summer, visitors can get to the island either by excursion boat from Boothbay Harbor, by the *Hardy Boat* from New Harbor, or by mail boat from Port Clyde. The village of Monhegan clusters around the harbor, while the rest of the island is still in its natural state. The size of the island is about three-quarters of a mile by one and a half miles.

A hiking trail goes around the shore of the island, and many trails connect this shore path with the village. The southwestern section of the shore path gets more use and is easier to follow than the northeastern part. The most popular connecting trail goes from the end of the road in back of the lighthouse to Whitehead, the highest sea cliff on the island. Another popular trail goes through Cathedral Woods, a lovely stand of tall spruce.

Camping is not allowed on the island. There are several small hotels and guest houses, and visitors can buy maps of hiking trails at stores on the island.

Section 6

Southwestern Maine

This section includes the mountains of York and Cumberland counties and those of Oxford County south of and near US 302. The mountains and hills of southwestern Maine are low, and woods cover many of them all the way to the top. Those summits that are open provide fine views of the surrounding country northwest toward the White Mountains and east and southeast to the coast. Because they are close to summer camps and population centers, many of the mountains in this section are popular hiking areas. Pleasant Mtn. (2006 ft.) is the highest. Most of the others are around 1000 ft. or lower.

Camping facilities are available at Bradbury Mtn. and Sebago Lake state parks, as well as at many privately operated camping areas.

BRADBURY MOUNTAIN (484 ft./147 m.)

This summit in Pownal is only partly wooded and offers good views of the countryside. Refer to the USGS Freeport quadrangle, 15-min. series, and the North Pownal quadrangle, 7.5-min. series.

To reach Bradbury Mtn., drive west from I-95 on ME 136 in Freeport and immediately turn left onto Pownal Rd. Drive 4 mi. to Pownal center and turn right (northeast) onto ME 9. Drive 0.8 mi. to Bradbury Mtn. State Park, which has parking, picnic tables, playgrounds, and camping areas. A trail (sign reading Summit) leads 0.3 mi. from the northwestern corner of the picnic area to the ledgy southern summit of Bradbury. Near the top, another trail leads right to an outlook toward the north. From the summit, a series of short, well-marked trails interconnect to cover the whole park area. A pleasant loop, the Knight's Woods Trail, lies on the opposite side of ME 9. Like the Tote Road Trail on the mountain, it lends itself to cross-country skiing in winter. A map and information are available at the entrance from the ranger.

Bradbury Mountain
Distance from state-park picnic area

   to Bradbury, southern summit: 0.3 mi. (0.5 km.), 15 min.

RATTLESNAKE MOUNTAIN (1035 ft./315 m.)

This summit in the southwestern part of Casco is a favorite climb for camp groups in the vicinity. Refer to the USGS Gray quadrangle, 15-min. series, or the Raymond quadrangle, 7.5-min. series.

   In 1992, flagrant incidents of public misuse of the area caused the Friends of Nubble Pond to shut off the southern access off Plains Rd. near Camp Hinds—we hope temporarily. The mountain can still be enjoyed from the Sheep Pasture and Northern Approach trails.

Sheep Pasture Trail

This trail, near the northern end of Rattlesnake Mtn., has been maintained by the owning family. Hikers are welcome, but please observe the rules shown on a sign. Park off ME 85 in a small space 0.9 mi. south of the junction with ME 11 at Webb's Mills.

Sheep Pasture Trail
Distance from ME 85

   to Northern Approach Trail junction: 0.5 mi., 25 min.

   to Rattlesnake main summit: 1 mi. (1.6 km.), 40 min.

Northern Approach

On ME 11, drive 0.2 mi west of its junction with ME 85 at Webb's Mills. Turn left onto a paved road; at a Y continue to bear left. The trail begins on the right (across from a barn) at about 0.4 mi. Blue-blazed and somewhat overgrown, it parallels a gravel road much of the way up, climbing gradually to reach the Sheep Pasture Trail junction and the northern ledge (view) beyond. It continues along the ledges to the summit, the southern ledges, and a trail that leads westward down to a col then up to the southwestern peak. Another trail descends steeply southward down the rocks to a woods road, which rejoins ME 85 by staying well north of Nubble Pond.

Northern Approach
Distances from trailhead

to   Sheep Pasture Trail junction: 1.2 mi., 40 min.

to   northern ledges: 1.3 mi., 40 min.

to   Rattlesnake main summit: 1.9 mi. (3 km.), 1 hr.

MOUNT AGAMENTICUS (691 ft./210 m.)

This 691-ft. monadnock rises above the coastal plain of southern York County. Because it was so conspicuous, it was an important landmark for the early European explorers who sailed along the New England coast. According to legend, it was also the burial place of either St. Aspinquid or Passaconaway. There is a firetower at the top, which was the site of a radar observation post during World War II. There is an unused ski development on the northern slope of the mountain. Refer to the USGS York Harbor quadrangle, 7.5-min. series.

The best approach route from the south is the Maine Turnpike. Take the York exit right just before the tollgate; turn left across the turnpike and take the second right, onto Chase Pond Rd. (Go past Chase Pond on the left.) Turn left onto Mountain Rd. and bear left at a small village. From this point, it is 1.6 mi. to the Big A summit road. From the north, follow US 1 through Ogunquit. Turn right onto Clay Hill Rd. Cross I-95 at 2.4 mi. from US 1, and at 4.1 mi., turn right onto Mountain Rd. At 5.7 mi., you will reach the summit road.

The blacktop summit road turns right and goes uphill 0.7 mi. to the summit. The dirt road straight ahead leads around the mountain to an approach to the base of the former ski lifts.

The road to the summit, which has two hairpin turns, should be driven with care. At the summit is a parking area, a closed ski lodge, and a riding stable.

The trail (now a jeep road) from the base starts from the northeastern corner of the clearing and climbs around the northern and eastern sides of the mountain, joining the blacktop road near the top. Many paths, some maintained as bridle trails, lead through woods to the open summit. A wooden sign at the summit maps some of these trails, albeit inaccurately.

Mount Agamenticus
Distance from ski-area base

   to Agamenticus summit: 0.5 mi. (0.8 km.), 30 min.

OSSIPEE HILL (1058 ft./322 m.)

Ossipee Hill (also called Ossipee Mtn.) is located in Waterboro. There are several radio towers, buildings, and a MFS firetower on its summit. From the firetower, there are good views of the Presidential Range in New Hampshire; to the east, you can see over the flat Saco River Valley and on to Portland Harbor and Casco Bay. A forest fire in 1947 burned off much of the mountain. Refer to the USGS Buxton quadrangle, 15-min. series, or the Waterboro quadrangle, 7.5-min. series.

From ME 5 at Waterboro Center, take the crossroad (Ossipee Hill Rd.) southwest and immediately turn sharply right onto paved McLucas Rd. beyond the fire station. This road changes to dirt and, in winter, is plowed for only about 0.25 mi. It is starting to see residential development. The road rises gradually west-northwest about 2 mi. to a saddle. In dry conditions, most cars find it passable to this saddle, where limited parking is available at the roadside. At the saddle, turn left (south) off McLucas Rd. and climb steeply for about 0.25 mi. before the road levels out. Along this stretch there are several old stone foundations and a small *spring* on the eastern side of the road. Turn right at a large gate to climb toward the summit. The towers are just southeast of the true summit, which does not have a trail but can be reached by a short bushwhack.

Ossipee Hill
Distances from ME 5

   to saddle: 2 mi.

   to Ossipee summit: 2.6 mi. (4.2 km.), 1 hr. 40 min.

DOUGLAS MOUNTAIN (1416 ft./430 m.)

This small mountain in Douglas Hill, west of Sebago Lake, offers excellent views of the Presidentials, Pleasant Mtn., and the Atlantic Ocean. It is the highest of the Saddleback Hills. Refer to the USGS Sebago Lake quadrangle, 15-min. series, or the Steep Falls quadrangle, 7.5-min. series.

Turn west from ME 107 onto Douglas Mtn. Rd. There is no sign, but the intersection is 0.5 mi. north of the junction of ME 107 and Macks Hill Rd., and 1 mi. south of Sebago. After 0.9 mi., take a sharp left turn at the top of a hill and go 0.5 mi. farther to a loop-shaped parking area with a Nature Conservancy sign. The path starts between two stone pillars and is easy to follow straight up ledges to the top. A second, even easier path through the woods splits off right soon after the trailhead. The two trails meet at the top, where there is a stone observation tower and a large rock inscribed *Non sibi sed omnibus* (Not just for myself, but for all). An orange-blazed nature trail makes a 0.75-mi. loop from the summit.

Douglas Mountain
Distance from parking area

   to Douglas summit: 0.3 mi. (0.5 km.), 15 min.

MOUNT CUTLER (1232 ft./375 m.)

The open ledges of this summit in Hiram offer good views of the White Mountains to the northwest. Refer to the USGS Cornish and Hiram quadrangles, 7.5-min. series.

At the junction of ME 5 and ME 117 in Hiram, cross the cement bridge to the western bank of the Saco River. Drive to the left of a former store and continue west on Mountain View Rd. to the site of a former railroad station, where there is ample parking. The red-blazed trail starts across the tracks. In 100 yd., it turns right into a picnic area that holds some abandoned ells once used by the railroad. The trail up the mountain continues straight ahead from the upper left end of the picnic area. It climbs the first ledge, and soon it turns sharply left. At this turn, a faint trail to the right leads 60 yd. to an overlook above the ledges facing the bridge. The main trail soon reaches the long, open ridge of Mt. Cutler, where south-facing ledges look down on the Saco River. The trail turns right (west) to the eastern summit, descends to cross a woods road, then climbs to the main summit as an open bushwhack. There are ledges and good views.

Mount Cutler

Distances from railroad-station site

- *to* overlook: 0.4 mi., 20 min.

- *to* Cutler, eastern summit: 0.7 mi., 40 min.

- *to* Cutler, main summit: 1.3 mi. (2.1 km.), 1 hr. 5 min.

PLEASANT MOUNTAIN (2006 ft./610 m.)

This mountain on the Denmark/Bridgton town line rises abruptly from the comparatively flat surrounding countryside. It is an isolated mountain mass that stretches about 4 mi. on a north–south line. The ledgy, open main summit, where there is a MFS firetower, was once known as House Peak because there was a hotel there from 1873 to 1907. At least six other summits along the ridge also have names. The mountain was burned over in about 1860, and the forest and ledges are open enough for many views.

The views from the main summit and from Big Bald Peak are outstanding. The southeastern face of Mt. Washington, 29 mi. to the northwest, is particularly noticeable. The Shawnee Peak ski area is on the northern slope of the northern peak. Refer to the USGS Pleasant Mtn. quadrangle, 7.5-min. series, as well as the map included with this guide.

Firewarden's Trail (Old Carriage Road)

Although not the most scenic route up Pleasant Mtn., this trail is the most popular one. It climbs to the main summit from the west. From US 302, turn south onto Warren Rd. 2.6 mi. west of the access road to the ski area and 7 mi. east of Fryeburg. On the side road, stay right at all road junctions. There is a farmhouse on the left 1.2 mi. from US 302 with free parking and trail signs.

For its first half, the trail is actually a truck road. It crosses a brook and climbs easily along the north bank. It recrosses the brook at the warden's cabin, where there is an approved campsite with a shelter. The trail then narrows to a rough jeep road (not open to private cars), swings right (southeast), and climbs steadily to the summit ridge. In the final 0.2 mi., the Bald Peak Trail (blue-blazed) comes in on the left (sign); there is a storm shelter to the right.

Firewarden's Trail

Distances from parking area at farmhouse

- *to* warden's cabin and campsite: 1.3 mi., 50 min.
- *to* Bald Peak Trail junction: 2.3 mi., 1 hr. 50 min.
- *to* Pleasant Mtn. main summit: 2.5 mi. (4 km.), 2 hr.

MacKay Pasture Trail (Southwest Ridge Trail)

This attractive scenic trail is being used by hikers, local camp groups, and snowmobilers. It leaves the northeastern side of Lake Rd. 3.5 mi. from the Moose Pond Dam on ME 160 in Denmark, or 3.4 mi. along either Warren Rd. or Denmark Rd. from US 302 in East Fryeburg. It begins at a logging yard opposite FR 78 (which leads to Long Pond).

The trail follows a woods road, marked by cairns, generally northeast through mixed hardwoods; it then becomes steeper through pine forest. At approximately 0.4 mi., the trail turns sharply right (southeast), slabs across the hill, turns left, and reaches the open ledges at 0.6 mi. The trail ascends the mostly open ridge, northeasterly, marked by cairns to the southwestern summit (1900 ft.) at 1.6 mi., with almost constant views over Moose and Beaver ponds, as well as back to Long Pond. The trail, keeping to the ridge, descends over a short saddle and ascends to the open middle summit (1904 ft.) at 2 mi., where a new cell tower and access road have been built. You can view Moose Pond from blueberry ledges west of the tower; then return to the trail west of the tower, drop down to the road, and pick up the trail again. It soon swings east at approximately 2.4 mi., climbs to the ridge, and ends at the Ledges Trail (blue-blazed) at 2.7 mi.

MacKay Pasture Trail
Distances from Lake Rd.

- *to* southwestern summit: 1.6 mi., 1 hr. 20 min.
- *to* middle summit: 2 mi., 1 hr. 35 min.
- *to* Ledges Trail: 2.7 mi., 2 hr.
- *to* Pleasant Mtn. main summit: 2.9 mi. (4.7 km.), 2 hr. 15 min.

Ledges Trail (Formerly Called Moose Trail)

The trail leaves the western side of the paved road along the western side of Moose Pond 3.3 mi. south of US 302, 1.5 mi. south of the Bald Peak Trail, and 0.6 mi. north of the Walker's (narrows) Bridge, which separates the two sections of Moose Pond. You can park beside the road.

The trail, blue-blazed, begins on a logging road (sign) and gradually climbs through overgrown hardwoods. At 0.5 mi., cross two often dry streambeds. Climb steeply for 0.3 mi. to open ledges with views south and southeast.

The trail follows the ledges, with the southwestern summit visible ahead on the left. At 1.6 mi., the MacKay Pasture Trail comes in on the left. It climbs through oak scrub and blueberry bushes to the main summit tower. Views to the west, including Fryeburg and the Saco River Basin and ponds, are outstanding.

Descending, the trail enters the woods on a southeasterly bearing from the tower.

Ledges Trail
Distances from paved road

to streambeds: *est.* 0.5 mi., 25 min.

to lower end of ledges: 1 mi., 1 hr.

to MacKay Pasture Trail junction: 1.6 mi., 1 hr. 30 min.

to Pleasant Mtn. main summit: 1.8 mi. (2.9 km.), 1 hr. 40 min.

Bald Peak Trail

This trail climbs the eastern side of Pleasant Mtn. to Big Bald Peak, and then runs south along the ridge to join the Firewarden's Trail just below the main summit.

When combined with the Ledges Trail and a 1.5-mi. walk on the road, the Bald Peak Trail forms an enjoyable circuit. The ski trail described below also allows a circuit. There is *no sure water* on this trail during dry periods.

To reach the trail, follow the second paved road along the western shore of Moose Pond to a point about 1.8 mi. south of the road's junction with US 302, and about 1.3 mi. south of the Shawnee Peak ski area. Just south of Shawnee Peak East, and 0.1 mi. south of the entrance to East Pinnacle Condominiums, you will find the trailhead on the right between utility poles 49 and 50 (sign). Park there. The trail starts westward, crosses a brook, and climbs steeply. At 0.2 mi., turn left and follow the northern bank of the brook. At 0.4 mi., a short spur trail (sign) leads left to the Needle's Eye, a brook cascading through a cleft in the ledge. At 0.7 mi., just before the second of two small brooks, turn left (Sue's Way turns right). Climb steeply through a stand of hemlock, then come out of some scrub onto the ledges (cairn); turn left to reach, in 100 yd., Big Bald Peak (1940 ft.) at 1.1 mi. There are excellent views in all directions.

At the sign, the blue-blazed North Ridge Trail comes in on the right from the top of the ski area via the northern peak. *Descending,* note that the trail to the ski area continues straight ahead (north); the Bald Peak Trail bears right (east-northeast).

From Big Bald Peak, the Bald Peak Trail follows the crest of the ridge, first south and then southwest over two humps toward the main summit. At 2.2 mi. from the start, the trail joins the Firewarden's Trail, which leads left (south) past the storm shelter to the Pleasant Mtn. main summit and the firetower.

Descending, the Bald Peak Trail diverges right from the Firewarden's Trail (sign) about 0.2 mi. north of the tower.

Bald Peak Trail
Distances from road

- *to* Needle's Eye Trail: 0.4 mi., 35 min.

- *to* brook crossing and Sue's Way junction: 0.7 mi., 50 min.

- *to* Big Bald summit: 1.1 mi., 1 hr. 20 min.

- *to* Firewarden's Trail junction: 2.2 mi., 1 hr. 50 min.

- *to* Pleasant Mtn. main summit (via Firewarden's Trail): 2.4 mi. (3.9 km.), 1 hr. 55 min.

Sue's Way

This blue-blazed trail, named in memory of Sue W. Blood, runs from a point 0.7 mi. up the Bald Peak Trail to the North Ridge Trail near the North Peak. It allows an interesting loop hike over these two peaks. There is a *spring* one-third of the way up the trail.

Sue's Way
Distance from Bald Peak Trail

- *to* North Ridge Trail: *est.* 0.5 mi. (0.8 km.), 25 min.

North Ridge Trail

This trail begins at the base of the Shawnee Peak ski area. From the base lodge (which is open all year), the trail follows the chairlift directly up the mountain for 1 mi. to the warming hut at the North Peak. The views are extensive. The North Ridge Trail leads south from the warming hut past the chairlift from Shawnee Peak East. Descend 100 yd. on the upper edge of the southernmost ski trail. At the first turn, enter the woods on the right. Sue's Way (blue-blazed) enters from the gully on the left. The trail turns due west, stays level for a bit, and then goes slightly downhill. At 1.2 mi., it turns left and slabs around the western side of the North Peak through open red pine to a low peak about 0.5 mi. from the warming hut. The trail bears right to cross an open ledge with a view of Big Bald Peak and Pleasant Mtn.'s main summit, then drops steeply into a col before heading up to Big Bald Peak. Just before the final climb up the cone, the Bald Peak Trail comes in from the left.

North Ridge Trail

Distances from ski-area base lodge

- *to* warming hut: 1 mi., 1 hr.
- *to* Sue's Way junction: 1.1 mi., 1 hr. 5 min.
- *to* Big Bald summit (via Bald Peak Trail): 2 mi. (3.2 km.), 1 hr. 45 min.

BURNT MEADOW MOUNTAIN (northern peak 1575 ft./479 m.)

Located in Brownfield, this mass consists of three summits of nearly equal height. Deep cols separate the middle peak, Stone Mtn. (1624 ft.), from the northern and southern peaks (1575 ft. and 1592 ft., respectively). Fire swept the entire mountain in 1947, and the trails that existed then disappeared. Trail development by snowmobilers and the construction of a ski area, now abandoned, have opened up new routes. Refer to the USGS Kezar Falls quadrangle, 15-min. series, and the Brownfield quadrangle, 7.5-min. series.

One approach is the eastern spur of the northern peak. This trail was reopened in 1984. From the junction of ME 113/5 and ME 160 in East Brownfield, drive west and south on ME 160 through Brownfield and past Burnt Meadow Pond. Park where the prominent eastern spur of the northern peak comes down to the highway. This point is 3.1 mi. from the junction with ME 113/5 and 0.4 mi. south of Burnt Meadow Pond. The cairned, blue-blazed trail heads west up the slope, staying on the southern edge of the ridge. At 0.4 mi., it passes over a small hump and drops slightly into a shallow col. Beyond the col, continue west up the crest of the spur, which becomes steeper and more open, with a sharp drop-off on the left, as it rises to the summit. There is *no water* on the trail.

A snowmobile trail leads north from the summit along the ridge to the top of the old ski area, with partial views.

Burnt Meadow Mountain

Distance from ME 160 (via eastern spur)

   to northern peak summit: 1.2 mi. (1.9 km.), 1 hr. 30 min.

PEARY MOUNTAIN (958 ft./292 m.)

The open ledges of this little mountain in Brownfield afford good views of the White Mountains and the mountains of western Maine. Refer to the USGS Brownfield quadrangle, 7.5-min. series.

At the junction of ME 160 and ME 113 in East Brownfield, proceed north on ME 113 for 2.2 mi. to Farnsworth Rd. (5 mi. south of the US 302 and ME 113 junction in Fryeburg). Turn west onto Farnsworth Rd. and drive 1.4 mi. to the bridge crossing the Little Saco River. The trail (snowmobile trail), not marked, begins at the east side of the stream. It heads south first on the level, and then at a gradual grade, to a col in a small clearing at 0.8 mi., with a fireplace on the right. Turn left (southeast) off the trail, passing an old foundation at this point, and go through open woods and ledges 0.2 mi. to the southern summit. There are good views in all directions. The main summit is 0.4 mi. northeast across open ledges and scrub without a trail. Views are to the east and north.

The col can also be approached from the south. Drive across the bridge over the Shepards River and follow the road straight ahead, parking where it turns sharply right.

Peary Mountain
Distances from trailhead

> *to* col: 0.8 mi., 35 min.

> *to* Peary, southern summit: 1 mi., 45 min.

> *to* Peary, main summit: 1.4 mi. (2.3 km.), 1 hr.

JOCKEY CAP (600 ft./182 m.)

This ledge near Fryeburg ME rises perpendicularly about 200 ft. above the valley, and offers an excellent view in all directions. At the top, there is a bronze profile of the surrounding summits, a monument to Robert E. Peary. Refer to the USGS Fryeburg quadrangle, 7.5-min. series.

A trail leaves the northern side of US 302, 1 mi. east of Fryeburg, through a gateway between a store and the Jockey Cap Cabins. It soon reaches Molly Lockett's cave, named for the last of the Pequawket Indians; she is said to have used it for a shelter. The trail then divides. The left branch continues ahead, circling to the west; the right branch turns abruptly right and climbs steeply, hugging the eastern side of the ledge. *Descending*, be alert, since there are many side paths that do not lead back to the cabins. (Round-trip by either route: 25 min.)

Jockey Cap
Distance from US 302

> *to* Jockey Cap summit: 0.2 mi. (3 km.), 15 min.

Section 7

Oxford Hills

This section describes the part of Oxford County that lies between US 302 on the south and the Androscoggin River on the north. The summits in the eastern part of the Oxford Hills are scattered. They include, among others, Streaked Mtn. (1770 ft.) near South Paris; Speckled Mtn. (2183 ft.) in the secluded Shagg Pond area; Mt. Zircon (2240 ft.) south of Rumford; Mt. Abram (1960 ft.), with its ski slope, near Locke Mills; and Mt. Tire'm (1104 ft.), a good viewpoint in Waterford.

Farther west, the hills build up into the continuous mountainous areas of the Evans Notch–Chatham region, which is along the Maine/New Hampshire border. Most of these mountains lie within the White Mountain National Forest (WMNF), where the network of trails is more complete and signs and maintenance are usually better. This guide describes those summits that lie in Maine, plus West Royce, just over the line in New Hampshire. For a description of the other New Hampshire summits, see the *AMC White Mountain Guide.* Most of the western Oxford Hills appear on the Carter-Mahoosuc map in this guide.

The minerals of the Oxford Hills are interesting, especially in the Mt. Mica Mine near Paris Hill and the Bumpus Mine between Bethel and Lynchville.

There are four small WMNF campgrounds in the region covered here. One is Crocker Pond, which you can reach from US 2 at West Bethel or from ME 5 south of Bethel. Hastings Campground is on Evans Notch Rd. just south of its junction with Wild River Rd. The Cold River and Basin campgrounds are 0.3 mi. west of the Maine/New Hampshire border and just south of Evans Notch.

STREAKED MOUNTAIN (1770 ft./539 m.)

Streaked Mtn., in Hebron and Buckfield, is a conspicuous, rounded summit with open ledges commanding fine views in all directions. It is easy to reach, and there is a MFS firetower on the summit as well as several antenna arrays. Refer to the USGS West Sumner quadrangle, 7.5-min. series.

Turn southeast from ME 117 onto paved Streaked Mtn. Rd. about 5 mi. northeast of ME 26 in South Paris and 5.3 mi. southwest of Buckfield. At 0.5 mi., the trail starts left by the brook, soon enters the woods, and climbs steeply onto the ledges. After that, it is an open climb to the top, as the trail slabs along the ledges to the left and joins the power line. *Descending,* leave the power line at the second pole, and slab left down the ledges. Be careful not to go too far south and miss the point where the trail enters the woods.

From the Buckfield side, the climb to the summit is longer but more gradual. Turn south off ME 117 onto Sodom Rd., about 1 mi. west of the center of Buckfield and 3.5 mi. east of the Buckfield/Paris line. Keep straight on paved and gravel road for 2.1 mi. (you can park here). The trail begins right on a gravel road, crossing Bicknell Brook several times. At 1.4 mi. (you can also park here, out of trucks' way), take the woods road left across a brook, just before reaching a logging yard. Go right of the triangular piece where the road from Kings Hill comes in from the left. (See the snowmobile signs to Streaked Mtn.) The road widens as it passes through logging operations, then reenters woods. Bear left at the next fork. Turn left at the intersection with Whitman School Rd. (unmarked here). After passing a house on the left, the road swings around right, and goes west and southwest up ledges to the summit.

This same approach can be reached from McAlister Rd., which leaves ME 117 at 1.1 mi above Sodom Rd. The rough road turns right at 0.6 mi., and joins the woods road above at 1.5 mi. from ME 117. Turn right and continue until you reach Whitman School Rd.

Streaked Mountain

Distance from Streaked Mtn. Rd. on South Paris side

   to   Streaked Mtn. summit: 0.5 mi. (0.8 km.), 30 min.

Distance from Sodom Rd. on Buckfield side

   to   Streaked Mtn. summit: 4 mi. (6.4 km.), 2 hr.

SINGEPOLE RIDGE (1420 ft./433 m.)

Across the valley southwest of Streaked Mtn., this open ridge offers broad views to the west and southwest. Brett Hill Rd. climbs south off ME 117, 3.1 mi. west of the Buckfield/Paris line for 0.4 mi. and turns west. The trail begins straight ahead (south) on a gravel road much used for logging and recreational vehicles. Take the left fork at 0.4 mi., where the trail levels out. At 1.1 mi., take the right fork up the ledge, or bear right at the next fork soon thereafter. The open-ledge summit at 1.3 mi. continues to an outlook at 1.4 mi. Back down 0.1 mi., a road leads north by a quarry and down to rejoin the trail.

Singepole Ridge
Distance from Brett Hill Rd. turn

   to   Singepole summit: 1.3 mi. (2.1 km.), 40 min.

CROCKER HILL (1374 ft./419 km.)

Crocker Hill, locally called Brown Mtn., in Paris, site of George L. Vose's 1868 panorama of the White Mountains, also offers views of the surrounding countryside and other mountains. Refer to the USGS West Sumner quadrangle, 7.5-min. series.

Leave Paris Hill between two houses on a rise at the eastern end of Lincoln St. and continue east (Mt. Mica Rd.) for 0.8 mi. Take the dirt road left 0.8 mi. to a left turn and park. The Old Crocker Hill carriage road leaves straight ahead. Take the left fork where the old carriage road divides. Look for an old stamping mill on the left soon after the trail forks. The trail ascends gradually, then veers sharply right just above the mill. A few yards after the switchback, on the left, is the old mine shaft. Farther on, after a switchback left, the trail leaves the road and proceeds right up over ledges.

At the first summit clearing, continue east to another clearing for an overlook of other hills and villages.

Crocker Hill

Distance from parking place

> *to* Crocker summit: 0.5 mi. (0.8 km.), 30 min.

BEAR MOUNTAIN (1208 ft./367 m.)

Southerly access to Bear Mtn. in Hartford is via Old County Rd. This road used to serve a firetower (now dismantled) and logging operations. It is no longer good enough for passenger cars. Refer to the USGS Buckfield quadrangle, 7.5-min. series. From the north, access is from ME 108 in Livermore; see the description below.

From ME 4 at North Turner, turn west onto ME 219. At 0.4 mi., turn right onto Bean St. across the outlet of Bear Pond. Then take an immediate (0.1 mi.) left along the northern shore of the pond. Follow the blacktop road 2.3 mi. to a crossroad, turn right, and drive 0.1 mi. to the last house on the left. Ask the owner for permission to park in the farmyard. Follow the road past a brook (often dry) immediately beyond the farm and, still following the road, gradually climb the ridge. As the road levels out, a trail to the right leads to the western summit of Bear Mtn. (Stay to the right at all intersecting logging roads.) There is a good view to the southwest.

The main road continues straight ahead toward the height-of-land. After passing a road on the left, it swings around to the right (south). Note the view to the south across Bear Pond.

Bear Mountain

Distances from farmyard

> *to* side trail to western summit: *est.* 0.8 mi., 35 min.

> *to* Bear main summit: 2 mi. (3.2 km.), 1 hr. 25 min.

Route from the North

Refer to the USGS Canton quadrangle, 7.5-min. series. From ME 108 in Livermore, 0.4 mi. from ME 4, turn south onto Bear Mtn. Rd. just past a gravel operation. There is minimal parking at 0.6 mi. The trail is the old road, which dips to a brook then climbs steadily, eventually leveling off. Turn left at the junction with the road from the south, go by open fields, and scramble up to the open summit ledges and views.

Bear Mountain from the North

Distances from trailhead

> to junction: *est.* 1.3 mi.
>
> to Bear main summit: *est.* 2 mi. (3.2 km.), 1 hr. 25 min.

BLACK MOUNTAIN (2133 ft./650 m.)

A broad, flat mass, this mountain lies in Sumner and Peru, east of adjacent Speckled Mtn. There are about five more or less definite summits, running roughly east–west. A trail with no signs climbs to the easternmost summit (2080 ft.) from the Sumner side. Refer to the USGS Worthley Pond quadrangle, 7.5-min. series.

Turn north off ME 219 onto Valley Rd., 1.6 mi. west of Hartford/Sumner Elementary School or 4 mi. east of the west Paris line. Follow this road for 1.5 mi., then turn left onto Labrador Pond Rd. Pass the pond with good views of Speckled Mtn. and Black Mtn. Go 1.2 mi. to a fork. Take Black Mtn. Rd. left, go 0.8 mi., then bear right at another fork. Go another 1.5 mi. and park where a dirt road bears left.

Follow this dirt road for 0.4 mi., turning right onto a woods road. Just before a logging yard, fork left across a brook on a stone culvert and take the right trail up the mountain (approximately 20-degrees mag.). The road levels out in 0.5 mi. and crosses the brook. Beyond the brook, pass a cairn soon thereafter and bear left (northeast) onto the trail at the next turn. The trail leaves right, partly eroded, narrow, and poorly marked. It climbs steadily northeast to ledges and the eastern summit. The view to the east and south is only partly open. Woods cover the main summit, 0.5 mi. to the west-northwest, and there is no trail. Exploration of the ledges will reveal a small but beautiful pond as well as additional views.

Black Mountain

Distance from parking place

   to   Black Mtn., eastern summit: 1.3 mi. (2.1 km.), 1 hr. 20 min.

BALD MOUNTAIN (1692 ft./516 m.)

This mountain is in the northeastern corner of Woodstock near Shagg Pond. Together with neighboring Speckled Mtn., just to the east, it offers interesting hiking in a little-known, secluded area. It is easiest to reach by approaching Shagg Pond through Sumner from ME 219. Refer to the USGS Mt. Zircon quadrangle, 7.5-min. series.

From the public landing at Shagg Pond, continue along the road for 0.5 mi. to a parking area left at the top of the hill. (You can also reach the parking area by driving southeast from Abbotts Mill.) Take FR 1010 across the road. It leads to Little Concord Pond, which comes into sight in 0.4 mi. The trail up Bald Mtn. leads right just before the road reaches the pond. The trail starts at the top of a 20-ft. ledge (cairn). To reach it, climb the crack of the ledge to the right. At the top, locate the cairn; from there, hike up the ridge to the summit. From the ledges south of the summit is a fine view of the Shagg Pond area. See below for a description of how to reach Speckled Mtn. from the Bald Mtn. ledges.

Bald Mountain

Distances from parking area

   to   Little Concord Pond: 0.4 mi.

   to   Bald Mtn. summit: 1 mi. (1.6 km.), 1 hr.

SPECKLED MOUNTAIN (2183 ft./665 m.)

Speckled Mtn. is to the east of Bald Mtn. in Peru. The route to it from the summit of Bald Mtn. drops into a col and follows the ridge to the

Speckled summit. This mountain's outstanding feature is its rugged southern face—a line of nearly sheer cliffs. The views from the summit are extensive in all directions. Refer to the USGS Mt. Zircon quadrangle, 7.5-min. series.

Route from Bald Mountain

From the ledge viewpoint on Bald Mountain, follow the open ledge southeast to find a steep blue-blazed trail north to the col. Cross a snowmobile trail, then climb generally east to the ridge and summit of Speckled Mtn. The trail has been obscure in some areas.

Route from Bald Mountain
Distance from Bald Mtn. ledges

to Speckled Mtn. summit: 1.3 mi. (2.1 km.), 1 hr. 10 min.

Speckled Mountain Pasture Trail

The Speckled Mtn. Pasture Trail offers a direct approach to the mountain in addition to the traverse from Bald Mtn. Views are open to the north.

From ME 108 in West Peru, drive southwest past a school for about 4.8 mi. The trail starts as a very rough jeep road to the left (south) at the top of a rise. There has been substantial logging in the area, and the trail is obscure.

From the main road, go 1 mi. to an old wood yard and a fork in the road. Take the right fork (the left fork is a snowmobile trail, which crosses the brook) and follow the road, passing an old camp on the right, for another mile to a large and obvious stone wall. Turn left and follow the line of the wall. After the wall ends in about 0.3 mi., cross a gravel logging road and follow the trail more steeply up the mountain. From this point, you can follow the blazes, cairns, and yellow flagging to the summit. The trail is intermittently marked; be careful of the confusing cairns near the summit, where several routes leave in different directions.

Speckled Mountain Pasture Trail
Distance from paved road

  to Speckled summit (via ridge): 3 mi. (4.8 km.), 2 hr.

MOUNT ZIRCON (2240 ft./683 m.)

This mountain is in the towns of Milton and Peru. The view is well worth the climb. To reach Mt. Zircon, take the highway between Rumford and Abbotts Mill on the southern bank of the Androscoggin. Refer to the USGS Mt. Zircon quadrangle, 7.5-min. series.

A rebuilt private road with a locked gate, 13.1 mi. from ME 26 at box 2131, leaves the highway just west of the former Mt. Zircon Spring Water Company bottling plant. Take the left fork at 1 mi., passing a springhouse on the left at 1.5 mi. The trail leaves the eastern side of the road about 2 mi. south of the highway. It climbs steadily, with a short scramble just below the rocky summit. There has been extensive logging in the area, and the trail has been disrupted in recent years. You can get water just south of the foot of the trail, near the site of the former warden's cabin.

Alternatively, the trailhead can be reached from the other end of the same woods road. Take Abbotts Mill Rd. off ME 232. Bear left at 1.7 mi. A woods road leaves left 0.2 mi. farther on; park there.

Mount Zircon
Distances from South Rumford Rd.

  to start of trail (via truck road): 2 mi., 1 hr. 10 min.

  to Zircon summit: 2.8 mi. (4.5 km.), 1 hr. 55 min.

Distance from parking by Abbotts Mill Rd.

  to start of trail: 2.4 mi.

  to Zircon summit: 3.1 mi. (5 km.), 2 hr. 12 min.

MOUNT ABRAM (1960 ft./597 m.)

Mt. Abram, in Greenwood, offers interesting views to the north and west from high pastures and ledges. There is a ski area on the northeastern slope of the mountain, but it does not affect the route described here. A chairlift runs to the summit, however. Refer to the USGS Bryant Pond and Greenwood quadrangles, 7.5-min. series.

Take the paved Irish Neighborhood Rd., which goes east from ME 35 about 3 mi. south of Bethel and about 0.3 mi. north of the Albany/Greenwood town line. About 1 mi. from the turn, take the left fork to the former B. L. Harrington farm high on the western slope of the mountain. A dirt road bears right just before the farm and continues for 0.4 mi. up to the renovated Harrington homestead. From the northern end of this building, walk north, then turn right across an open field. The trail starts up the slope in about 0.1 mi., crossing a small brook at the edge of the woods. At 0.3 mi., take the right fork uphill in an easterly direction. (The left fork is a gently undulating snowmobile trail that heads, through woods, around the mountain. It crosses a field to a large red house, reaching Howe Hill Rd. 0.6 mi. from the junction.) Continue up the trail and cross a faint clearing, avoiding a more obvious sharp L turn. Then head straight up steeply, reaching a hedgerow with snowmaking pipes at 0.7 mi. Clamber across, noting the location for your return, and turn right up a wide ski trail to the summit and a Ski Patrol hut. The best views are to the west, reached by an open path to a field a bit below the summit. The ski trail can be rejoined from the field's lower right corner.

Alternatively, you can leave ME 26 on a road leading south in Greenwood. At about 1.4 mi., the road bears southwest, and soon after that, a road leads left to the base of the ski area. From there, you can follow ski trails to the summit.

Mount Abram

Distance from old Harrington homestead

   to Abram summit: 1.1 mi. (1.8 km.), 1 hr.

MOUNT TIRE'M (1104 ft./336 m.)

Mt. Tire'm in the town of Waterford yields a good view, with little effort, of the Long Lake region. Refer to the USGS Norway quadrangle, 15-min. series, or the Waterford Flat quadrangle, 7.5 min. series.

Daniel Brown Trail (Old Squire Brown Trail)

Follow ME 35 to the center of Waterford, then turn northwest onto Plummer Hill Rd. The trail starts 100 yd. beyond and across the road from the Waterford Center Community Building (next to the church). Park there or at the trailhead. A 1979 plaque on the left, reading Daniel Brown Trail, marks the start. Visitors are requested to stay on the trail, because it is on private property.

The trail emerges from the woods with widening views of the hills and lakes of Waterford and Norway. Along with views, the summit has woods and boulders to explore.

Daniel Brown Trail (Old Squire Brown Trail)
Distance from Waterford Center Community Building

   to Tire'm summit: 0.7 mi. (1.1 km.), 40 min.

SABATTUS MOUNTAIN (1253 ft./382 m.)

The chief feature of this summit in Center Lovell is the immense, nearly vertical cliff that forms its southwestern face. From the top of the cliff, impressive views of the countryside spread from Pleasant Mtn. to the Baldfaces. Refer to the USGS Center Lovell quadrangle, 7.5-min. series.

You can reach the trail by following ME 5 north from Lovell to Center Lovell. Take Sabattus Rd. right (east) 0.7 mi. past the Center Lovell General Store and continue to a fork 1.8 mi. from ME 5. Bear right onto Sabattus Mtn. Rd. at the fork and drive 0.6 mi. on this dirt road, to a new, marked parking lot on the right. The trail starts from the parking area and climbs easily, reaching an old firetower site near the open summit ledges. A faint trail to the east leads 0.3 mi. to a large boulder.

Sabattus Mountain
Distance from parking area

   to Sabattus summit: 0.8 mi. (1.3 km.), 30 min.

EVANS NOTCH–CHATHAM REGION

The Cold River runs south from Evans Notch and flows into an extensive valley 3 mi. to the south. The valley floor is no more than 600 ft. above sea level. It is divided between Stow ME, and Chatham NH; the line runs almost directly up the valley. The principal summits in Maine are East Royce (3116 ft.), Ames Mtn. (2686 ft.), Speckled Mtn. (2906 ft.), and, to the north of Evans Notch, Mt. Caribou (2828 ft.).

The AMC Cold River Camp is in North Chatham. Two WMNF campgrounds, Basin and Cold River, are at the northern end of the valley, on the western side of NH/ME 113 about 0.3 mi. west of the Maine/New Hampshire border. The WMNF Hastings Campground entrance is 0.2 mi. south of the junction of NH/ME 113 and Wild River Rd. The Wild River Campground (WMNF) is reached by Wild River Rd. It is about 5.7 mi. southwest of the junction of Wild River Rd. and NH/ME 113. The Kimball Lakes, South Chatham, and Fryeburg offer opportunities for fishing.

To obtain more current information about the condition of trails in the Evans Notch–North Chatham area, contact the WMNF Evans Notch Ranger District, Bridge St., Bethel ME 04217 (207-824-2134).

The 7.5-min. USGS maps are a very valuable addition to the map that comes with this guide. Trails are named on the 7.5-min. quadrangles. See especially those for Wild River in New Hampshire, and for Speckled Mtn., East Stoneham, Bethel, Center Lovell, and Gilead in Maine. In the older 15-min. series, see the Bethel and Fryeburg quadrangles for Maine, and the Gorham and North Conway quadrangles for New Hampshire.

The Chatham Trails Association, Inc. (CTA), has published a 1998 update of its map of the Cold River Valley and Evans Notch. Copies may be obtained from Al Cressy, P.O. Box 74, Bethel ME 04217 (207-824-0508), or in season at the AMC Cold River Campground or Brickett Place. The price is $6.00 per map.

Evans Notch Road (NH/ME 113)

This scenic auto road, NH/ME 113, continues the Valley Rd. of North Chatham northward past Brickett Place, under the impressive cliffs of

East Royce, and through Evans Notch to Hastings. It crosses Evans Brook twice and ends 3.4 mi. farther at US 2, just east of the bridge over the Wild River in Gilead.

Evans Notch Road (NH/ME 113)
Distances from Brickett Place

- *to* Royce Trail (west): 25 yd.
- *to* service road to Speckled Mtn. (east): 0.3 mi.
- *to* Laughing Lion trailhead: 2.1 mi.
- *to* East Royce (west) and Spruce Hill (east) trailheads: 3.1 mi.
- *to* Haystack Notch (east) trailhead: 4.6 mi.
- *to* Mud Brook/Caribou (east) trailhead: 6 mi.
- *to* Wheeler Brook Trail (Little Lary Brook Rd.) (east): 7 mi.
- *to* Hastings (west) trailhead: 7.5 mi.
- *to* Roost (east) trailheads: *est.* 7.1 mi. and 7.8 mi.
- *to* US 2/Gilead: 10.9 mi. (17.4 km.)

THE ROOST (1374 ft./419 m.)

This small hill, near Hastings, has fine views of Wild River Valley, Evans Brook Valley, and many mountains.

Roost Trail (WMNF)

This trail ascends to the Roost from two trailheads about 0.7 mi. apart on the eastern side of ME 113. The northern trailhead is located just north of a bridge over Evans Brook, 0.1 mi. north of the junction of ME 113 and Wild River Rd. at Hastings; the southern trailhead is located just south of another bridge over Evans Brook.

Leaving the northern trailhead, the trail ascends a steep bank for 30 yd., then bears right (east) and ascends gradually along a wooded ridge. It crosses a small brook at 0.3 mi., then rises somewhat more steeply to emerge on a small rock ledge at the summit at 0.5 mi. Here a side trail descends 0.1 mi. west through woods to spacious open ledges, where the views are excellent. The main trail descends generally southeast at a moderate grade and crosses a small brook, then turns right (west) on an old road (no sign) and follows it past a cellar hole and an old clearing back to ME 113.

Roost Trail
Distances from ME 113, northern trailhead

   to Roost summit: 0.5 mi., 30 min.

   to ME 11, southern trailhead: 1.2 mi. (2 km.), 50 min.

Wheeler Brook Trail (WMNF)

The trailheads for this trail are located on the southern side of US 2, 2.3 mi. east of the junction of US 2 and ME 113; and on Little Lary Brook Rd. (FR 8), 1.6 mi. from its junction with ME 113, which is 9.2 mi. north of the road to the Cold River Campground and 3.7 mi. south of the junction of US 2 and ME 113.

From US 2, the Wheeler Brook Trail follows the western side of Wheeler Brook, crossing the brook four times, and rises about 1400 ft., generally following an old logging road, to its highest point on the northwestern slope of Peabody Mtn. at 2.1 mi. (There is no trail to the wooded summit of Peabody Mtn.) The trail then descends generally southwest, swings onto an old logging road, and reaches Little Lary Brook Rd. Turn right (downstream) onto Little Lary Brook Rd. and continue to a locked gate near the bridge over Little Lary Brook, 1.6 mi. from ME 113.

In the reverse direction, proceed along Little Lary Brook Rd. about 100 yd. from the locked gate, then turn right at the junction where FR 8 continues straight ahead. The trail leaves the road on the left in another 0.3 mi. It is very sparsely marked at this end, so exercise care in following it.

Wheeler Brook Trail
Distance from US 2

   to gate on Little Lary Brook Rd.: 3.5 mi. (5.6 km.), 2 hr. 30 min.

MOUNT CARIBOU (2828 ft./862 m.)

This mountain, called Calabo in the 1853 Walling map of Oxford County, is in the town of Mason. The bare, ledgy summit affords excellent views. The Caribou and Mud Brook trails make a pleasant loop. The Caribou summit and much of the surrounding area are part of the Caribou–Speckled Mtn. Wilderness Area.

Caribou Trail (WMNF)

This trail gives access to the attractive ledges of Mt. Caribou. Its west trailhead, which it now shares with the Mud Brook Trail, has a moderate amount of parking and an outhouse. It lies on the eastern side of ME 113 about 6 mi. north of the road to the WMNF Cold River Campground and 4.6 mi. south of US 2. The east trailhead is on Bog Rd. (FR 6), which leaves the southern side of US 2 1.3 mi. west of the West Bethel Post Office (there is currently a sign for Pooh Corner Farm at this junction, but no road sign) and leads 2.8 mi. to the trailhead, where a gate ends public travel on the road. The parking area is small.

From ME 113, the trail runs north, crosses Morrison Brook on a footbridge at 0.3 mi., and follows the brook, crossing it several more times. The third crossing, at 1.9 mi., is located at the head of Kees Falls, a 25-ft. waterfall. The trail levels off at the height-of-land as it crosses the col between Gammon Mtn. and Mt. Caribou at 2.9 mi. There is no camping, to allow for revegetation efforts. Soon the Mud Brook Trail leaves right to return to ME 113 via the summit of Mt. Caribou. The Caribou Trail continues ahead at the junction, descends more rapidly, turns northeast toward the valley of Bog Brook (which lies east of Peabody Mtn.), and follows a succession of logging roads. At 4.8 mi., it bears left in a clearing, then bears left again on the extension of Bog Rd. (FR 6) and continues to the gate.

Caribou Trail
Distances from ME 113

   to Mud Brook Trail: 2.9 mi., 2 hr. 10 min.

to Caribou summit (via Mud Brook Trail): 3.5 mi., 2 hr. 40 min.

to Bog Rd.: 5.4 mi. (8.7 km.), 3 hr. 25 min.

Mud Brook Trail (WMNF)

This trail begins on ME 113 at the same point as the Caribou Trail, about 6 mi. north of the road to the WMNF Cold River Campground, then passes over the summit of Mt. Caribou and ends at the Caribou Trail in the pass between Mt. Caribou and Gammon Mtn. Despite the trail's ominous name, its footing is good.

From ME 113, the trail runs generally south. It then turns east along the north side of Mud Brook, rising gradually; crosses the headwaters of Mud Brook at 2 mi.; and swings left (north) uphill, climbing more steeply. The trail crosses several smaller brooks and, at 3.1 mi., comes out on a small, bare knob with excellent views east. It turns left into the woods and makes a short descent into a small ravine, then emerges above timberline and crosses ledges to the summit of Mt. Caribou at 3.5 mi. It then descends north and meets the Caribou Trail in the pass.

Mud Brook Trail
Distances from ME 113

to Caribou summit: 3.5 mi., 2 hr. 55 min.

to Caribou Trail junction: 4.1 mi. (6.6 km.), 3 hr. 10 min.

Haystack Notch Trail (WMNF)

This trail, with good footing and easy grades but some potentially difficult brook crossings, runs through Haystack Notch. Its western trailhead lies on the east side of ME 113, 4.8 mi. north of the road to the WMNF Cold River Campground. The east trailhead is located on the Miles Notch Trail 0.2 mi. from the trail's northern terminus. From the post office in West Bethel, go south on Flat Road; turn right at 2.6 mi. at a fork, or continue another 0.5 mi. and turn right at a crossroads. These routes merge just after a bridge and cemetery, respectively, and the road continues up the east bank of the West Branch. Just over a mile from the merger, the pavement ends, and the road becomes gradually worse. About 0.8 mi. from the end of pavement, turn right at a Forest Service sign; in another 0.3 mi., the road reaches a clearing (former log yard). The left fork here is the Miles Notch Trail and the right fork is the Haystack Notch Trail, with no sign and with blazes only to the right.

Leaving right, the trail ascends the valley of the West Branch of the Pleasant River, making several crossings of that brook, some of which may be difficult at high water. At 3.3 mi., it crosses through Haystack Notch and descends generally west along the East Branch of Evans Brook, crossing it several times before reaching ME 113. The last crossing, in particular, may be difficult at high water.

In the reverse direction, follow the right fork of the logging road, then follow the trail as it soon leaves right on a woods road and descends to the river. The trail crosses the West Branch and a major tributary four times in the next half-mile, then ascends south and crosses a woods road at 1.2 mi. from the clearing (high-water access). It then ascends along the edge of the valley, with several more minor brook crossings, to Miles Notch.

Haystack Notch Trail
Distances from Miles Notch Trail

   to Haystack Notch: 3.3 mi., 1 hr. 35 min.

   to ME 113: 5.4 mi. (8.7 km.), 3 hr. 5 min.

ALBANY MOUNTAIN (1910 ft./582 m.)
Views from the open summit ledges are excellent in all directions. Refer to the USGS Bethel quadrangle, 15-min. series, and the East Stoneham quadrangle, 7.5-min. series.

Albany Notch Trail (WMNF)
This trail passes through the notch west of Albany Mtn. Parts of its northern section still suffer from invasion by berry bushes as a result

of the loss of mature forest in the windstorm of 1980, and are wet from beaver-dam flooding. The southern section, which is located mostly on old, overgrown logging roads and is disrupted by recent logging, is poorly marked, is wet, and requires much care to follow. Most hikers use the northern section, which makes possible a loop hike over Albany Mtn. in combination with the Albany Mtn. Trail and the branch trail that runs from the height-of-land in Albany Notch to the base of the ledges on the Albany Mtn. Trail.

To reach the north trailhead, follow the road that leads south from US 2 opposite the West Bethel Post Office, which becomes FR 7 when it enters the WMNF at 4.5 mi. At 5.8 mi., turn right onto FR 18, following signs for the Crocker Pond Campground. The trailhead is located on the right in another 0.6 mi., just past the end of an extensive beaver swamp; the sign is hard to see from the road, because it is located at the back of a small clearing and blocked by a large tree. To reach the southern trailhead, leave ME 5 at the western end of Keewaydin Lake, 2.4 mi. west of the East Stoneham Post Office and 0.7 mi. east of the Lovell/Stoneham town line, and follow Bartlettboro Rd. north. Bear right onto Birch Ave. at 0.4 mi. from ME 5. Park carefully to avoid blocking any roads; the road that the trail follows is passable for at least another 0.2 mi., but parking is extremely limited.

Leaving the clearing on FR 18, the trail follows an old logging road that becomes well defined after the first few yards. At 0.6 mi., the Albany Notch Trail bears right at the junction where the Albany Mtn. Trail diverges left (south). At 1.2 mi., it enters the region damaged by blowdown, where berry bushes are a nuisance, though the trail becomes markedly drier underfoot. Returning to mature woods at 1.4 mi., it climbs at a moderate grade to the left of a small brook, and at 1.7 mi., it reaches the junction where a branch trail leads left (east) 0.4 mi. to the Albany Mtn. Trail at the base of the ledges.

The trail now descends moderately, with a few steeper patches just below the pass, and crosses a small brook several times. It then runs mostly on a very old road until it reaches a much newer logging road at 2.4 mi. and turns left onto this road (when *ascending*, turn sharply right). The road, which is fairly easy to follow but rather wet and over-grown, with little evident footway, passes junctions with a snowmobile trail on the left at 2.8 mi. and 3.1 mi.; at the second junction, the road bears right and improves greatly, then crosses Meadow Brook on a snowmobile bridge at 3.6 mi. and continues to the trailhead.

Albany Notch Trail

Distances from FR 18

to   Albany Mtn. Trail: 0.6 mi., 25 min.

to   branch trail junction in Albany Notch: 1.7 mi., 1 hr. 15 min.

to   trailhead on Birch Ave.: 4.2 mi. (6.7 km.), 2 hr. 30 min.

Albany Mountain Trail (WMNF)

This trail ascends the northern slope of Albany Mtn. to an open ledge near its summit that affords good views east and north. It begins on the Albany Notch Trail 0.6 mi. from FR 18.

Leaving the Albany Notch Trail, it soon turns left onto a skidder road that it follows for 20 yd., then leaves to the right. It continues to ascend moderately through woods that have seen some light to mod-erate wind damage. At 0.6 mi., the trail turns right at the foot of a small, mossy rock face, and climbs to a junction at 0.9 mi. where a branch trail leads right (west) 0.4 mi. to the Albany Notch Trail at the height-of-land in Albany Notch. Soon the trail passes a ledge with a good view of the Baldfaces and Mt. Washington and continues to the northeastern outlook, where regular marking ends. The true summit, wooded and not reached by any well-defined trail, is located about 100 yd. south. The summit area has other viewpoints not reached by the trail that repay efforts devoted to cautious exploration by experi-enced hikers. The best viewpoint, somewhat overgrown, lies about 0.1 mi. southwest of the true summit; a sketchy and incomplete line of cairns leads to it.

Albany Mountain Trail

Distance from Albany Notch Trail

   to Albany upper outlook: 1.3 mi. (2.1 km.), 1 hr. 5 min.

Albany Brook Trail (WMNF)

This short, easy trail follows the shore of Crocker Pond and then leads to attractive, secluded Round Pond. It begins at the turnaround at the end of the main road at the Crocker Pond Campground (do not enter the actual camping area). You can reach this by following the road that runs south from US 2 opposite the West Bethel Post Office, which becomes FR 7 when it enters the WMNF at 4.5 mi. At 5.8 mi., turn right onto FR 18, following signs 1.5 mi. to the campground entrance.

    Leaving the turnaround, the trail descends to a small brook and follows the western shore of Crocker Pond for 0.2 mi., then joins and follows Albany Brook with gentle ups and downs. At 0.9 mi., it goes straight through a logging-road intersection with a clearing visible on the right, and soon reaches the northern end of Round Pond.

Albany Brook Trail

Distance from Crocker Pond Campground

   to Round Pond: 1 mi. (1.6 km.), 30 min.

SPECKLED MOUNTAIN (2906 ft./886 m.)

This mountain lies east of Evans Notch, in Batchelder's Grant and Stoneham. It is one of at least three mountains in Maine that have been known by this name. The summit's open ledges have excellent views in all directions. There is a *spring* about 0.1 mi. northeast of the summit, off the Red Rock Trail.

Miles Notch Trail (WMNF)

This trail runs through Miles Notch, giving access to the eastern end of the ledgy ridge that culminates in Speckled Mtn. To reach its southern terminus, near which the Great Brook Trail also begins, leave ME 5 in North Lovell on a road with signs for the Evergreen Valley Ski Area; follow that road northwest for 1.8 mi., then turn right onto Hut Rd. just before the bridge over Great Brook and continue 1.5 mi. to the trailhead.

To reach the northern terminus from the West Bethel Post Office, go south on Flat Rd. and turn right at 2.6 mi. at a fork, or continue another 0.5 mi. and turn right at a crossroads. These routes merge just after a bridge and cemetery, respectively, and the road continues up the eastern bank of the West Branch. Just over a mile from the merger, the pavement ends, and the road becomes gradually worse. About 0.8 mi. from the end of pavement, turn right at a Forest Service sign; in another 0.3 mi., the road reaches a clearing (former log yard). The left fork here is the Miles Notch Trail and the right fork is the Haystack Notch Trail, with no sign and with blazes only to the right.

Take the left fork. The trail ascends moderately, crossing Miles Brook repeatedly. At 2.4 mi., the Red Rock Trail leaves right for the summit of Speckled Mtn. The Miles Notch Trail ascends gradually and reaches Miles Notch at 2.7 mi. Continuing, the trail runs down a small brook gully, crosses Beaver Brook, crosses a branch of the same, and joins an old logging road. The trail goes left for 0.2 mi. to another logging road, joins yet another logging road and follows it generally south (right) for 0.3 mi. to reach the southern terminus.

Miles Notch Trail
Distances from northern terminus

   to Red Rock Trail: 2.4 mi., 1 hr. 15 min.

   to southern terminus: 5.6 mi. (9 km.), 3 hr. 30 min.

Red Rock Trail (WMNF)

This trail ascends Speckled Mtn. from the Miles Notch Trail 0.3 mi. north of Miles Notch, 3.2 mi. from its southern trailhead, and 2.4 mi. from its northern trailhead. It traverses the long eastern ridge of the

Speckled Mtn. Range, affording fine views of the surrounding mountains. The trail is sparsely marked, and should be followed with care.

It leaves the Miles Notch Trail, descends to cross Miles Brook in its ravine, then angles up the northern slope of Miles Knob and gains the ridgecrest northwest of that summit. It descends to a col, then ascends to the summit of Red Rock Mtn. at 1.2 mi. and follows the ridge, with several ups and downs, over Butters Mtn. at 2.5 mi. and then on to the next col to the west. Here, at 3.4 mi., the Great Brook Trail diverges left (east) and descends southeast to its trailhead, very close to the southern trailhead of the Miles Notch Trail. The Red Rock Trail swings south, crosses the summit of Durgin Mtn. at 4.4 mi., then runs generally southwest to a junction with the Cold Brook Trail and the Bickford Brook Trail 30 yd. east of the summit of Speckled Mtn. There is a *spring* near the trail about 0.1 mi. east of the summit.

Red Rock Trail

Distances from Miles Notch Trail

   to Great Brook Trail: 3.4 mi., 2 hr. 15 min.

   to Speckled summit: 5.6 mi. (9 km.), 3 hr. 50 min.

Great Brook Trail (WMNF)

This trail ascends to the Red Rock Trail east of Speckled Mtn. To reach its trailhead, leave ME 5 in North Lovell on a road with signs for the Evergreen Valley Ski Area; follow that road northwest for 1.8 mi., then turn right onto Hut Rd. just before the bridge over Great Brook and continue 1.5 mi. to the trailhead, which is located about 100 yd. past the southern trailhead for the Miles Notch Trail.

The trail continues up the gravel road and bears right onto FR 4 at 0.8 mi., just after crossing Great Brook on a bridge with a gate. At 1.8 mi., it turns left onto a grassy, older road and follows Great Brook. At 3 mi., it crosses a branch of Great Brook, then bears left (arrow), becomes steeper, and continues along Great Brook to the ridgecrest, where it joins the Red Rock Trail in the col between Butters Mtn. and Durgin Mtn.

Great Brook Trail

Distances from trailhead

  to Red Rock Trail: 3.7 mi. (5.9 km.), 2 hr. 35 min.

  to Speckled summit (via Red Rock Trail): 5.8 mi. (9.3 km.), 4 hr. 20 min.

Cold Brook Trail (WMNF)

This trail ascends Speckled Mtn. from a trailhead reached from ME 5 in North Lovell. Follow the road with signs for the Evergreen Valley Ski Area for 1.9 mi., take the first right (with an Evergreen Valley sign) just after the bridge over Great Brook, then continue to a gravel road on the right 2.2 mi. from ME 5. The WMNF sign is on the paved road, but you may be able to drive 0.5 mi. on the rough gravel road to a parking area.

Beyond here, the road becomes rougher, and in 0.7 mi. from the paved road, it bears left past a gate. The next 1 mi. is on a muddy road that circles along the contour to an abandoned farmhouse, the Duncan McIntosh House. Continuing ahead on the road, take the left fork, then the right. The trail descends to Cold Brook and crosses it at 1.9 mi., just above a fork. It then climbs and circles along the farther branch, passes west of Sugarloaf Mtn., and ascends the southern side of Speckled Mtn., passing a junction left at 2.7 mi. with the Link Trail from the Evergreen Valley Ski Area. It emerges on semi-open ledges at 3.2 mi., passes two excellent outlooks south, and bears right to reenter the woods at 4.2 mi. It emerges on semi-open ledges again and soon reaches the junction with the Red Rock Trail (right) and the Bickford Brook Trail (left). It follows the latter trail left 30 yd. to the summit of Speckled Mtn.

Cold Brook Trail

Distance from paved road

   to Speckled summit: 4.7 mi. (7.5 km.), 3 hr. 45 min.

Link Trail (WMNF)

Park in the lot just above the Inn at Evergreen Valley resort in East Stoneham. Follow the paved road uphill 400 ft. Where it turns left, take the dirt road (soon gated) straight ahead and continue climbing steeply. Turn left onto a logging road at 0.4 mi., then right onto the Link Trail at 0.7 mi. (sign reading Speckled Mountain via Cold Brook Trail). The trail is blazed in yellow, heads 70 degrees. Pass a woods-road junction at 1 mi.; and reach the Cold Brook Trail junction at 1.2 mi.

Link Trail

Distances from Inn at Evergreen Valley

   to Cold Brook Trail junction: 1.2 mi., 1 hr.

   to Speckled summit: 3.6 mi. (5.8 km.), 3 hr.

BLUEBERRY MOUNTAIN (1820 ft./555 m.)

This mountain is a long, flat, outlying spur running southwest from Speckled Mtn. The top is mostly one big ledge, with sparse and stunted trees. There are numerous open spaces with excellent views, especially the southwestern ledges on the summit. There is *water* in many places at the top, except in dry seasons.

Stone House Trail (CTA)

This trail ascends to the scenic ledges of Blueberry Mtn. from Shell Pond Rd. To reach the trailhead, leave NH 113 on the eastern side 0.7 mi. north of the AMC Cold River Camp and follow Stone House Rd. 1.1 mi. to a padlocked steel gate, which will make it necessary to park your car .

The trail leaves left (north) 0.5 mi. beyond the gate, east of a shed. It follows a logging road, and approaches Rattlesnake Brook. At 0.2 mi., it merges with a private road (*descending,* bear right at arrow) and immediately reaches the junction with a spur path that leads right 30 yd. to a bridge overlooking Rattlesnake Flume, a small, attractive gorge. The main trail soon swings right (arrow), and at 0.5 mi., another spur leads right 0.1 mi. to Rattlesnake Pool, which lies at the foot of a small cascade. The main trail soon enters the WMNF and, at 1.2 mi., begins to climb rather steeply straight up the slope, running generally northwest to the top of the ridge. There it ends at the Blueberry Ridge Trail, only a few steps from the top of Blueberry Mtn. To reach Speckled Mtn., turn right on the Blueberry Ridge Trail.

Stone House Trail
Distance from Shell Pond Rd.

   to Blueberry summit: 1.5 mi. (2.4 km.), 1 hr. 20 min.

White Cairn Trail (CTA)

This trail provides access to the open ledges on Blueberry Mtn. and, with the Stone House Trail, makes an easy half-day circuit. It begins on Stone House Rd., which leaves the eastern side of NH 113, 0.7 mi. north of the AMC Cold River Camp, and runs 1.1 mi. to a padlocked steel gate that makes it necessary for you to park your car. The trail leaves Shell Pond Rd. at a clearing 0.3 mi. beyond the gate. It follows old logging roads north and west to an upland meadow, passing into the WMNF at 0.3 mi. At 0.8 mi., it begins to climb steeply up the right (east) margin of the cliffs visible from the road, then turns sharply left and begins to climb on ledges. The grade moderates as the trail runs northwest along the crest of the cliffs to the west, with views to the south. At 1.2 mi., it passes a *spring,* then swings right (north) and passes another *spring* before ending at the junction with the Blueberry Ledge Trail, 0.2 mi. west of the upper terminus of the Stone House Trail. A loop trail near its junction with this trail provides a scenic alternative route to the Stone House Trail.

White Cairn Trail

Distance from Shell Pond Rd.

   to Blueberry Ridge Trail: 1.4 mi. (2.3 km.), 1 hr. 20 min.

Blueberry Ridge Trail (CTA)

This trail begins and ends on the Bickford Brook Trail, leaving at a sign 0.6 mi. from its trailhead at Brickett Place on ME 113, and rejoining 0.5 mi. below the summit of Speckled Mtn. (The upper part of the Blueberry Ridge Trail can also be reached from Shell Pond Rd. via the Stone House or White Cairn trails.) It descends toward Bickford Brook, and at 0.1 mi., just before the main trail crosses Bickford Brook, it crosses the Bickford Slides Loop.

   Bickford Slides Loop. This loop path, 0.5 mi. long, leaves the Blueberry Ridge Trail 0.1 mi. from its lower junction with the Bickford Brook Trail. At this junction, a spur path descends along Bickford Brook 50 yd. to the Lower Slides, while the main path crosses Bickford Brook and climbs along it 0.3 mi. to another junction near the base of the Upper Slides. Here, the main path recrosses the brook at the base of the Upper Slides and joins the Bickford Brook Trail 0.9 mi. from NH 113, while a spur path 0.3 mi. long continues up along the brook and the Upper Slides, then crosses the brook above the slides and joins the Bickford Brook Trail 1.1 mi. from ME 113. The loop trail is obscure in places.

   From the junction with Bickford Slides Loop, the Blueberry Ridge Trail crosses the brook (may be difficult in high water) and ascends southeast to an open area just over the crest of Blueberry Ridge, where the White Cairn Trail enters right at 0.7 mi. An overlook loop 0.5 mi. long, with excellent views to the south, leaves the Blueberry Ridge Trail shortly after this junction and rejoins it shortly before the Stone House Trail enters on the right at 0.9 mi., a few steps past the high point of the trail on Blueberry Mtn. From this junction with the Stone House Trail, marked by signs and a large cairn, the Blueberry Ridge Trail bears left and descends to a spring *(unreliable water source)* a short distance from the trail on the left (north). Here it turns sharply right and continues over ledges marked by cairns, through occasional patches of woods, passing over several humps. The trail ends at the Bickford Brook Trail in the shallow pass at the head of Rattlesnake Brook Ravine, about 0.5 mi. below the summit of Speckled Mtn.

Blueberry Ridge Trail

Distances from Bickford Brook Trail, lower junction

- *to* Stone House Trail: 0.9 mi., 55 min.
- *to* Bickford Brook Trail, upper junction: 3.1 mi. (5 km.), 2 hr. 25 min.

Bickford Brook Trail (WMNF)

This trail ascends Speckled Mtn. from Brickett Place on ME 113, 0.2 mi. north of the road to the WMNF Cold River Campground. The trail enters the woods near the garage, then turns right onto an old WMNF service road to Speckled Mtn. at 0.3 mi.; the two footways coincide for the next 2.5 mi. At 0.7 mi., the Blueberry Ridge Trail leaves right (east) for the lower end of the Bickford Slides and Blueberry Mtn.; it rejoins the Bickford Brook Trail 0.5 mi. below the summit of Speckled Mtn., affording the opportunity for a loop hike. At 0.9 mi., the Bickford Slides Loop enters on the right from the lower end of the Upper Slides, and at 1.1 mi., the spur path along the Upper Slides enters on the right. The Bickford Brook Trail soon swings away from the brook and winds up a southwestern spur to the crest of the main west ridge of the Speckled Mtn. Range, where the Spruce Hill Trail enters left at 3.1 mi. The Bickford Brook Trail then passes west and north of the summit of Ames Mtn. into the col between Ames Mtn. and Speckled Mtn., where the Blueberry Ridge Trail rejoins right at 3.8 mi. The Bickford Brook Trail then continues upward to the summit.

Bickford Brook Trail

Distances from ME 113

- *to* Blueberry Ridge Trail, lower junction: 0.7 mi., 35 min.
- *to* Spruce Hill Trail: 3.1 mi., 2 hr. 30 min.
- *to* Blueberry Ridge Trail, upper junction: 3.8 mi., 2 hr. 55 min.
- *to* Speckled summit: 4.3 mi. (6.9 km.), 3 hr. 20 min.

Spruce Hill Trail (WMNF)

This trail begins on the eastern side of ME 113, 3 mi. north of the road to the WMNF Cold River Campground, opposite the start of the East Royce Trail. It ascends to the summit of Spruce Hill at 1.5 mi. It then descends into a sag and climbs to meet the Bickford Brook Trail on the ridgecrest west of Ames Mtn. This forms the shortest route (though not a particularly scenic one) to Speckled Mtn.

Spruce Hill Trail

Distances from ME 113

- *to* Bickford Brook Trail: 1.9 mi., 1 hr. 30 min.
- *to* Speckled summit (via Bickford Brook Trail): 3.1 mi. (5 km.), 2 hr. 20 min.

MOUNT ROYCE (eastern summit 3116 ft. and western summit 3202 ft.)

This mountain north of North Chatham has two distinct summits. While the summit of West Royce is in New Hampshire, this section includes the trail description from the junction of the trails to the two summits. For descriptions of other trails to New Hampshire summits from the Evans Notch–Chatham region, see section 10 of the 1998 edition of the *AMC White Mountain Guide*.

East Royce Trail (AMC)

This trail, blazed in blue, leaves the western side of NH/ME 113 (off-road parking) just north of the height-of-land and 3.1 mi. north of Brickett Place. It immediately crosses Evans Brook and rises steeply, crossing several other brooks in the first half-mile. At a final brook crossing at 1 mi. *(last water),* the Royce Connector Trail to West Royce enters from the left. The East Royce Trail emerges on open ledges at about 1.1 mi., reaches an open subsidiary summit at 1.3 mi., and arrives at the true summit, also bare, 0.1 mi. farther. A spur trail, leaving the summit at approximately 60 degrees down a steep ledge, can be followed over several more ledges to a large, open ledge with beautiful outlooks to the north and west.

East Royce Trail

Distance from NH/ME 113 (Evans Notch Rd.)

   to   East Royce summit: 1.4 mi. (2.3 km.), 1 hr. 50 min.

Royce Trail (AMC)

This trail starts on the western side of NH/ME 113 about 25 yd. above the entrance to Brickett Place (about 0.3 mi. north of the entrance to the WMNF Basin Campground). Follow the narrow logging road for about 0.3 mi. Cross the Cold River and bear right on the trail, which is blazed in blue. At 1.4 mi., the trail crosses and recrosses the river; then, crossing the southern branch of the Mad River, it rises more steeply and soon passes Mad River Falls. A side trail leads left 23 yd. to a viewpoint. About 0.8 mi. above the falls, the logging road becomes a trail—rather rough with large boulders—and rises steeply below the imposing ledges for which this mountain is famous. At 1 mi. beyond the falls, the Laughing Lion Trail enters on the right. At a height-of-land 0.2 mi. farther, after a very steep climb, a connecting trail to the East Royce Trail leads right 50 yd. to open ledges that offer excellent views of Chatham Valley. The connecting trail continues for 200 yd. to join the East Royce Trail.

From there, the Royce Trail levels off, turns left (west), descends slightly, and, in 0.1 mi., crosses a brook. After that, it descends, then climbs to the height-of-land between the peaks, where the Burnt Mill Brook Trail to Wild River Rd. (see the *AMC White Mountain Guide*) bears slightly right, while the Royce Trail turns abruptly left (west) and climbs the steep wall of the col. It then continues by easy grades over ledges and through stunted spruce to the summit, where it meets the Basin Rim Trail (see the *AMC White Mountain Guide*).

Royce Trail
Distances from NH/ME 113 (Evans Notch Rd.)

- *to* Mad River Falls: 1.6 mi., 1 hr.
- *to* Laughing Lion Trail junction: 2.6 mi., 2 hr.
- *to* Royce Connector Trail junction: 2.8 mi., 2 hr. 20 min.
- *to* West Royce summit: 4 mi. (6.4 km.), 3 hr. 30 min.

Laughing Lion Trail (CTA)

This trail leaves the western side of NH/ME 113 just north of a roadside picnic area, about 2.1 mi. north of Brickett Place. It descends in a northerly direction to the Cold River, then climbs steeply, mostly southwest and west, with occasional fine views down the valley. The trail continues north, generally steep, leveling off just before it ends at the Royce Trail, south of the col between East and West Royce.

Laughing Lion Trail (CTA)
Distances from NH/ME 113 (Evans Notch Rd.)

- *to* Royce Trail junction: 1 mi., 1 hr.
- *to* East Royce summit (via Royce Trail): 1.8 mi. (2.9 km.), 2 hr.

Royce Connector Trail (AMC)

This short trail connects the Royce Trail and the East Royce Trail. (Distance from Royce Trail junction to East Royce Trail junction: 0.2 mi.)

Leach Link Trail (CTA)

This trail gives access to Little Deer Hill and Big Deer Hill from Shell Pond Rd., which leaves NH 113 on the eastern side 0.7 mi. north of the AMC Cold River Camp. The trail leaves Shell Pond Rd. just east of the bridge over the Cold River and, at 0.4 mi., crosses Shell Pond Brook (may be difficult at high water). On the far bank, the Shell Pond Brook Trail enters on the left; this is an alternative route from Shell Pond Rd., 0.5 mi. long, that makes the Shell Pond Brook crossing on a snowmobile bridge (useful at high water). At 1.1 mi., a spur path leads right to the Little Deer–Big Deer Trail, which is crossed in another 50 yd.; to the left, the Little Deer–Big Deer Trail ascends Little Deer Hill, and to the right, it leads to the dam at the AMC Cold River Camp. From there, the Leach Link Trail continues along the river, ending at the Ledges Trail.

Leach Link Trail

Distance from Shell Pond Rd.

   to Ledges Trail: 1.5 mi. (2.4 km.), 45 min.

Ledges Trail (CTA)

The Ledges Trail passes interesting ledges and a cave, but is very steep and rough, dangerous in icy conditions, and not recommended for descent. It leaves the southern end of the Leach Link Trail and climbs steeply with numerous outlooks. At 0.2 mi., the connecting path that leads in 0.8 mi. to the Little Deer–Big Deer Trail south of Big Deer diverges right, affording an alternative route to the summit of Little Deer via the spur path (0.2 mi. long) that leaves it 0.2 mi. from the Ledges Trail. At 0.4 mi., the Ledges Trail divides; the right branch, which is slightly longer, rejoins in about 100 yd. Just above the point where these branches rejoin, the spur path from the connecting path mentioned above enters on the right, and soon the trail reaches the summit of Little Deer Hill.

Ledges Trail

Distance from Leach Link Trail

   to Little Deer summit: 0.5 mi. (0.8 km.), 35 min.

Little Deer–Big Deer Trail (CTA)

This trail ascends Little Deer Hill and Big Deer Hill, running from the AMC Cold River Campground to Deer Hill Rd. (FR 9). It leaves the Cold River Camp on a gravel road that runs east, passing the Conant Path on the right, the Tea House Path on the left, and then a spur left to the Leach Link Trail just after crossing the Cold River on the dam. It crosses the Leach Link Trail at 0.3 mi. and climbs moderately past an outlook west, then bears left onto ledges and reaches the summit of Little Deer Hill at 0.9 mi. Here, the Ledges Trail enters on the right. The main trail descends into a sag, then climbs to the summit of Big Deer Hill at 1.6 mi. It then descends the southern ridge with several fine outlooks, turning left at 2.1 mi., where a connecting path to the Ledges Trail and Little Deer Hill leaves on the right. (This connecting path descends to a spur path at 0.6 mi., which leads right 0.2 mi. to the summit of Deer Hill, and then continues from the spur junction to end at the Ledges Trail at 0.8 mi.) Soon the main trail turns left again, then turns right onto an old logging road at 2.3 mi. Here, a spur path follows the logging road left for a few steps, then descends in 0.2 mi. to Deer Hill Spring (Bubbling Spring), an interesting shallow *pool* with air bubbles rising through a small area of light-colored sand. The main trail descends from the junction to Deer Hill Rd.

Little Deer–Big Deer Trail

Distances from Cold River Campground

   to Little Deer summit: 0.9 mi., 45 min.

   to Big Deer summit: 1.6 mi., 1 hr. 20 min.

   to Deer Hill Rd.: 2.9 mi. (4.7 km.), 2 hr.

Conant Trail (CTA)

This loop path to Pine Hill and Lord Hill is frequently referred to (and may be signed as) the Pine-Lord-Harndon Trail, though it does not go particularly close to the summit of Harndon Hill; it should not be confused with the Conant Path, a short trail near the AMC Cold River Campground. It is an interesting and fairly easy walk with a number of good outlooks. It is reached by following Deer Hill Rd. (FR 9) and making a right turn 1.5 mi. from NH 113, then turning left almost immediately and parking near a dike.

The trail runs straight ahead along the dike across Colton Brook—the Colton Dam is located several hundred yards to the right from here—and continues to the loop junction at 0.4 mi., where the path divides. From here, the path is described in a counterclockwise direction. The south branch turns right and follows a logging road (Hemp Hill Rd.) to a level spot at 1 mi. near the old Johnson cellar hole, then turns left onto a logging road, and then left again in a few steps. The trail turns left again at 1.2 mi. and ascends Pine Hill, rather steeply at times, passing a ledge with a fine view to the west at 1.4 mi. It reaches the western end of the summit ridge and continues to the easternmost knob, which has a good view north, at 0.2 mi. The trail zigzags down past logged areas, crosses Bradley Brook at 2.3 mi. and then climbs, crossing the logging road that provides access to the mine on Lord Hill and passing an outlook over Horseshoe Pond. It reaches ledges near the summit of Lord Hill at 3 mi.; here, the Mine Loop leaves on the left.

Mine Loop. This path is 1 mi. long, 0.1 mi. shorter than the section of the Conant Trail that it bypasses. Except for one critical turn mentioned below, it is fairly easy to follow. From the junction with the Conant Trail near the summit of Lord Hill, it climbs briefly to the ledge at the top of the old mica mine and then descends on a woods road. At 0.1 mi., it passes a spur path leading right 30 yd. to the mine. At 0.3 mi., it turns sharply left onto a logging road, then at 0.5 mi., it reaches a fork and turns sharply right back onto the other branch of the road, which shows less evidence of use. This turn is easily missed, because it is difficult to mark adequately and the correct road is less obvious than the main road. (The main road, continuing straight at this fork, crosses the Conant Trail between Pine Hill and Lord Hill and continues south toward Kezar Lake.) At a clearing, the Mine Loop leaves the road on the right and descends 50 yd. to rejoin the Conant Trail 1.1 mi. from its trailhead.

From Lord Hill, the Conant Trail descends to the junction with the Horseshoe Pond Trail on the right at 3.2 mi., where it turns left, then soon turns left again and runs at a fairly level grade along the southern side of Harndon Hill. It passes a cellar hole, and the Mine Loop rejoins on the left at 4.1 mi. At 4.5 mi., the road passes a gate, becomes wider, reaches the loop junction, and continues straight ahead across the dike to the trailhead.

Conant Trail
Distance from trailhead off Deer Hill Rd.
   Complete loop: 5.2 mi. (8.3 km.), 3 hr. 10 min.

Horseshoe Pond Trail (CTA)
This trail, blazed with bright yellow paint, starts from Deer Hill Rd. (FR 9), 4.6 mi. from NH 113, at a parking area at a curve in the road, where the pond is visible; it ends on the Conant Trail. It descends moderately past the Styles grave, enclosed by a stone wall, then enters a recent logging road and turns right onto it. In a few steps, the Horseshoe Pond Loop, 0.4 mi. long, leaves left for the northwestern shore of Horseshoe Pond. The main trail continues on the logging road at 0.3 mi., and the Horseshoe Pond Loop rejoins on the left at an incipient apple orchard in 100 yd. The trail ascends through the clear-cut resulting from timber salvage operations after the 1980 windstorm, following cairns and overgrown skid roads back into the woods to the old trail, which continues to the Conant Trail between Lord Hill and Harndon Hill.

Horseshoe Pond Trail
Distance from Deer Hill Rd.
   to Conant Trail: 1.1 mi. (1.8 km.), 50 min.

Section 8

Grafton Notch and Mahoosuc Range Areas

This section covers the area bounded on the south and west by the Androscoggin River; on the north by Umbagog, Richardson, and Mooselookmeguntic lakes of the Rangeley Lakes chain; and on the east by ME 17. Grafton Notch, in the heart of this area, lies between Old Speck (4180 ft.) on the west and Baldpate Mountain (3812 ft.) on the east. It is traversed by ME 26.

The Mahoosuc Range, which appears on the Carter-Mahoosuc map that comes with this guide, extends southwest from Old Speck across the Maine/New Hampshire line to Mt. Hayes near Gorham NH. As the crow fly, the range is about 17 mi. long, but it is nearly 30 mi. long by trail. Mt. Goose Eye (3870 ft.) and Mahoosuc Notch are among the many interesting features of the Mahoosuc Range. Both lie on the Maine side of the border, but the usual access is via the Mahoosuc Trail, which involves overnight camping, or via trails from Success Pond Rd., which leads east from Berlin NH to ME 26 north of Grafton Notch.

Rumford Whitecap (2197 ft.) is the most popular of the low range of mountains lying between Andover and Rumford.

To provide detailed descriptions of alternative approaches from the west to the trails in the Mahoosuc Range, this guide incorporates relevant trail descriptions from the Mahoosuc Range Area section of the latest edition of the *AMC White Mountain Guide*. In addition to the map in this guide, refer to the USGS Old Speck and Gorham NH/ME quadrangles, 15-min. series; Old Speck Mtn., Puzzle Mtn., Shelburne, and Success Pond quadrangles, 7.5-min. series; or map 7 in the MATC's *Appalachian Trail Guide to Maine.*

GRAFTON NOTCH STATE PARK

Grafton Notch State Park contains 3132 acres extending on both sides of ME 26, west and north, from the Newry/Grafton town line to about 1.5 mi. north of the Appalachian Trail crossing. It includes the summit and northeastern slopes of Old Speck and the lowest western and southwestern slopes of Baldpate, including Table Rock.

The area is now a major hiking center. In addition to the mountain trails, short, graded trails and paths lead from some parking areas to points of interest nearby. *Note:* There is *no camping* in the park.

Scenic Areas and Short Walks

Step Falls

At the lower (southern) end of Grafton Notch, a short trail from the east side of the road leads 0.5 mi. to Step Falls, a series of cascades, with a total drop of 200 ft. The falls are on Wight Brook, which drains the southeastern slope of Baldpate Mtn. The area is a Nature Conservancy reservation. There is parking on the eastern side of ME 26 where the trail (sign) starts.

Screw Auger Falls and the Jail

Farther north, in the Pools, a parking area and picnic tables overlook Screw Auger Falls. The Jail, a large pothole, is just above the picnic area (about 0.4 mi. west of the falls). It is not visible from the road, and nothing marks its location, but you can find it easily by entering the woods to the south (left) of the highway about 100 yd. east of the first highway bridge above Screw Auger Falls. To reach the Jail from below, enter the woods about 150–200 yd. farther east of the bridge and go south to the brook. Follow the brook upstream to a falls. The Jail is on the right (north) bank.

Mother Walker Falls and Moose Cave
Mother Walker Falls are 1.2 mi. north of Screw Auger Falls. There is a parking area on the northern side of ME 26. Moose Cave, a narrow and deep flume, is about 0.2 mi. farther north and 0.6 mi. south of the Old Speck Trail (Appalachian Trail). It is about 0.1 mi. from the parking area via a series of trails, walks, and steps. There is a grand view of Table Rock from the highway at this point.

Grafton Notch Parking Area
Near the height-of-land 2.7 mi. northwest of Screw Auger Falls, there is a Maine Department of Parks and Recreation parking area (sign reading Hiking Trails) on the left (west) side of ME 26. All trails on Old Speck and Baldpate Mtn. leave from this point. The Appalachian Trail crosses ME 26 at this point.

Spruce Meadow Picnic Area
The Spruce Meadow Picnic Area is approximately 0.6 mi. farther on ME 26 and offers outstanding views down the Notch. It also provides excellent facilities for picnicking.

OLD SPECK (4180 ft./1274 m.)
Old Speck, so named to distinguish it from the Speckled mountains in Stoneham and Peru, dominates the western side of Grafton Notch. Long thought to be the second-highest peak in the state, after Hamlin Peak on Katahdin, Old Speck has now yielded that honor to Sugarloaf Mtn. and ranks third. There is an open observation tower on the wooded summit. Refer to the Carter-Mahoosuc map with this guide; the USGS Old Speck quadrangle, 15-min. series; or the Old Speck Mtn. quadrangle, 7.5-min. series.

Old Speck Trail
This trail, part of the Appalachian Trail and blazed in white, ascends Old Speck Mtn. from a well-signed parking area on ME 26 at the

height-of-land in Grafton Notch. From the northern side of the parking lot, follow the left trail (the right trail goes to Baldpate Mtn.). In 0.1 mi., the Eyebrow Trail leaves right to circle over the top of an 800-ft. cliff shaped like an eyebrow. The Old Speck Trail crosses a brook and soon begins to climb, following a series of switchbacks, to approach the falls on Cascade Brook. Above the falls, the trail, now heading more north, crosses the brook for the last time *(last available water)*. At 1.1 mi., it passes the upper terminus of the Eyebrow Trail on the right. The main trail bears left and ascends gradually to the northern ridge, where it bears more left and follows the ridge, which has occasional views southwest. High up, the trail turns southeast toward the summit, and at 3.1 mi., the Link Trail (no sign) diverges left. The Old Speck Trail turns more south and ascends to the Mahoosuc Trail, where it ends. The flat, wooded summit of Old Speck, where an observation tower affords fine views, is 0.3 mi. left (east); the Speck Pond Shelter is located 1.1 mi. to the right.

Old Speck Trail
Distances from ME 26

- *to* Eyebrow Trail, upper junction: 1.1 mi., 1 hr. 5 min.
- *to* Link Trail: 3.1 mi., 2 hr. 40 min.
- *to* Mahoosuc Trail: 3.5 mi., 3 hr. 10 min.
- *to* Old Speck summit (via Mahoosuc Trail): 3.8 mi. (6 km.), 3 hr. 20 min.

Eyebrow Trail

The Eyebrow Trail provides an alternative route to the lower part of the Old Speck Trail, passing along the edge of the cliff called the Eyebrow that overlooks Grafton Notch. The trail leaves the Old Speck Trail on the right 0.1 mi. from the parking area off ME 26. It turns right at the base of a rock face, crosses a rockslide (potentially dangerous if icy), then turns sharply left and ascends steadily, bearing right where a side path leaves straight ahead for an outlook. Soon the trail runs at a moderate grade along the top of the cliff, with good views, then descends to an outlook and runs mostly level until it ends at the Old Speck Trail.

Eyebrow Trail
Distance from Old Speck Trail, lower junction

  to Old Speck Trail, upper junction: 1.2 mi. (1.9 km.), 1 hr. 10 min.

Speck Pond Trail (AMC)

This trail ascends to Speck Pond from Success Pond Rd.; take the right fork of the road 11.4 mi. from Hutchins St. and continue 0.8 mi. to the trailhead. The trail leaves the road, enters the woods, and follows the northern side of a small brook for 1.4 mi. It then swings left away from the brook, climbing steeply at times; passes a relatively level section; then climbs steeply to a junction at 3.1 mi. with the May Cutoff, which diverges right and leads over the true summit of Mahoosuc Arm to the Mahoosuc Trail. The Speck Pond Trail passes an excellent outlook over the pond and up to Old Speck, then descends steeply to the pond and reaches the campsite and the Mahoosuc Trail.

Speck Pond Trail

Distance from branch of Success Pond Rd.

  to Speck Pond Campsite: 3.6 mi. (5.8 km.), 3 hr.

May Cutoff (AMC)

This short trail runs 0.3 mi. (10 min.) from the Speck Pond Trail to the Mahoosuc Trail, across the probable true summit of Mahoosuc Arm, with only minor ups and downs.

MOUNT GOOSE EYE (3870 ft./1177 m.)

Mt. Goose Eye in Riley shares a common trailhead with Mt. Carlo (see below) and makes possible a very interesting loop hike.

Notch Trail (AMC)

This trail ascends to the southwestern end of Mahoosuc Notch, providing the easiest access to this wild and beautiful place. It begins on a spur road that leaves Success Pond Rd. 10.9 mi. from Hutchins St. and runs 0.3 mi. to a small parking area. The trail continues on the spur road across two bridges, then turns left (sign) onto an old logging road at 0.3 mi. It ascends easily along a slow-running brook with many signs of beaver activity, following logging roads much of the way with bypasses at some of the wetter spots. At the height-of-land, it meets the Mahoosuc Trail. Turn left for the notch; very soon after entering the Mahoosuc Trail, the valley, which has been ordinary, changes sharply to a chamber formation, and the high cliffs of the notch, not visible earlier on the Notch Trail, come into sight.

Notch Trail

Distance from spur road off Success Pond Rd.

   to Mahoosuc Trail: 2.2 mi. (3.5 km.), 1 hr. 30 min.

Wright Trail

This new Maine Bureau of Public Lands trail, rated strenuous or difficult, climbs the eastern side of Goose Eye Mtn. from Sunday River Rd. in Ketchum. For a loop, it splits near its upper end into a north-fork ascent through old-growth forest and a south-fork descent affording particularly scenic valley views from the ridge.

From Bethel, take US 2/ME 26 north for 3 mi. Turn left onto Sunday River Rd. and follow it past the Artist Covered Bridge for about 7 mi. The road turns left at a junction with Twin Bridges (steel). Cross the bridges and immediately turn right. Follow this dirt road for another 1.5 mi., until it crosses Goose Eye Brook on the only bridge. The trailhead, with a parking lot 50 yd. beyond, is on the left 200 yd. up the road.

The Wright Trail, with blue blazes, leaves the southern side of this parking lot and heads toward Goose Eye Brook. It follows along the northern side of the brook for 0.5 mi. past several large pools and a 30-ft. gorge before turning left onto an old logging road. It follows this road for 0.3 mi., again turns left, and descends 0.1 mi. to the confluence of Goose Eye Brook and an unnamed feeder stream. Stay on the northern side of this stream for 150 yd., turn sharply left, and cross it. For the next 1.3 mi., the trail more or less follows the northern bank of Goose Eye Brook. Then it splits into two sections of a loop.

The northern fork continues along Goose Eye Brook for 0.2 mi., crossing it twice before veering right and climbing moderately from the valley floor. The trail then passes beneath several large rock slabs, and comes out on one (0.3 mi.). From here, the whole of a cirque formation can be seen. The trail descends off the lower slabs, crosses the valley, and begins a steep climb to the ridge (0.5 mi.). It lightens to a moderate climb and turns sharply right to cross the *last year-round stream* at about 3100 ft. Continuing at a moderate to steep climb for 0.3 mi., it meets the Appalachian Trail. Turn left and climb the steep slabs of the East Peak 0.1 mi. to the summit. Continue south on the Appalachian Trail for another 0.1 mi. to the junction with the southern fork of the Wright Trail.

Descending off Mahoosuc Ridge down a subsidiary ridgeline for 1.7 mi., the Wright Trail crosses over two peaks and one exposed slab before descending steeply into a saddle, 0.2 mi. It weaves its way through to the northern side of the saddle and descends moderately for 0.6 mi. to Goose Eye Brook. Cross the brook obliquely to the right and down to the junction of the forks.

Wright Trail

Distances from parking area

to Goose Eye (East Peak) summit: *est.* 4 mi., 3 hr. 30 min.

Complete loop: 8 mi. (12.8 km.), 7 hr. (add 0.5 mi. each way for West Peak)

Goose Eye Trail (AMC)

This trail ascends Goose Eye Mtn. from Success Pond Rd., starting with the Carlo Col Trail 8.1 mi. from Hutchins St., and reaches the Mahoosuc Trail 0.1 mi. beyond the summit. This is a generally easy trail to a very scenic summit, but there is one fairly difficult scramble up a ledge just below the summit. From the road, the two trails follow a broad logging road, and in 100 yd., the Goose Eye Trail diverges sharply left down an embankment. It then turns sharply right onto another logging road, while the Carlo Col Trail continues straight ahead on the first road. The Goose Eye Trail follows the logging road, crosses two brooks, and enters a more recent gravel road that comes in from the right (*descending,* bear right). In 100 yd., it diverges right (watch carefully for sign) from the gravel road, passes through a clear-cut area, crosses a wet section, and, at 1.4 mi., reaches the yellow-blazed Maine/New Hampshire state line. The trail angles up the southern side of a ridge at a moderate grade through hardwoods, climbs more steeply uphill, then becomes gradual at the crest of the ridge; at 2.6 mi., there is a glimpse of the peak of Goose Eye ahead. The trail ascends moderately along the northern side of the ridge, then steeply, scrambling up a difficult ledge that may be dangerous if wet or icy, then comes out on the open ledges below the summit. From the summit, which has magnificent views, the trail continues 0.1 mi. to the Mahoosuc Trail, which turns right (southbound) and runs straight ahead (northbound).

Goose Eye Trail

Distances from Success Pond Rd.

- *to* Goose Eye summit: 3.1 mi., 2 hr. 40 min.
- *to* Mahoosuc Trail: 3.2 mi. (5.2 km.), 2 hr. 45 min.

MOUNT CARLO (3562 ft./1086 m.)

Mt. Carlo, in Riley, can be climbed from a common trailhead with the Goose Eye Trail on Success Pond Rd., 8.5 mi. from Berlin NH and 11.5 mi. from ME 26.

Carlo Col Trail (AMC)

This trail ascends to the Mahoosuc Trail at the small box ravine called Carlo Col; it leaves Success Pond Rd. in common with the Goose Eye Trail 8.1 mi. from Hutchins St. From the road, the two trails follow a broad logging road. In 100 yd., the Goose Eye Trail diverges sharply left down an embankment, while the Carlo Col Trail continues straight ahead on the road, which it follows east for 0.8 mi. with little gain in elevation. Turning left off the road at a log yard, the trail immediately crosses the main brook (may be difficult at high water), continues near it for about 0.3 mi., then turns away from the brook and bends east up the rather steep southern bank of the south branch. Avoiding several false crossings of the brook, it climbs to the Carlo Col Shelter at 2.4 mi. (*last water*, perhaps, for several miles). The trail continues up the dry ravine and ends at the Mahoosuc Trail at Carlo Col. There is a fine outlook ledge a short distance to the right (west) on the Mahoosuc Trail.

Carlo Col Trail
Distance from Success Pond Rd.

   to Mahoosuc Trail: 2.6 mi. (4.1 km.), 2 hr. 5 min.

MOUNT SUCCESS (3565 ft./1087 m.)

Mt. Success, in Success NH (reached also from Shelburne on the south via the Austin Brook and Mahoosuc trails), is accessible from Success Pond Rd., 5.5 mi. from Berlin NH and 14.5 mi. from ME 26.

Success Trail (AMC)

This trail ascends to the Mahoosuc Trail 0.6 mi. north of Mt. Success from Success Pond Rd. 5.4 mi. from Hutchins St. Note that the trail sign is easy to miss. The trail follows a logging road, bears right at a fork at 0.1 mi., and passes straight through a clearing, entering the woods at a sign in 0.4 mi. Soon the trail starts to climb steadily on the road, and at 1.4 mi., it reaches the upper edge of an area of small second-growth trees, swings right, and ascends more steeply. At 1.6 mi., a loop path 0.3 mi. long diverges right to a spectacular ledge outlook with fine views of the Presidentials and the mountains of the North Country. In a little over 100 yd., the upper end of the loop path rejoins, and the main trail ascends to a ridgecrest, from which it descends very gradually to a brook *(unreliable water source)* at an old logging campsite. The trail now makes an easy climb up a shallow ravine, part of the way in the bed of a small, unreliable brook (follow paint blazes carefully), and soon reaches the Mahoosuc Trail at the main ridgecrest.

Success Trail

Distances from Success Pond Rd.

   to Mahoosuc Trail: 2.4 mi., 2 hr.

   to Success summit (via Mahoosuc Trail): 3 mi. (4.8 mi.), 2 hr. 30 min.

Austin Brook Trail (AMC)

This trail ascends to the Mahoosuc Trail at Gentian Pond from North Rd., 0.6 mi. west of Meadow Rd. (which crosses the Androscoggin at Shelburne Village). There is limited parking on the southern side of the road. The trail passes through a turnstile on private land and follows the western side of Austin Brook, crossing the Yellow Trail at 0.4 mi. The trail follows logging roads along the brook, then crosses it and reaches gravel Mill Brook Rd., which is normally gated at North Rd., at 1.1 mi. (Austin Stream). Turn left onto the logging road and continue past a brook crossing to the junction (left) with the Dryad Fall Trail at 1.9 mi. At 2.1 mi., the trail turns left onto an old logging road. At 3.1 mi., the trail crosses the brook that drains Gentian Pond and climbs steeply to the Mahoosuc Trail at the Gentian Pond Shelter.

Austin Brook Trail

Distance from North Rd.

   to Gentian Pond: 3.5 mi. (5.7 km.), 2 hr. 30 min.

Lary Flume

This is a wild chasm in the southern slope of the Mahoosuc Range that resembles the Ice Gulch and Devils Hopyard, with many boulder caves and one fissure cave.

There is no trail, but experienced climbers have followed the brook, which can be reached by going east where the Austin Brook Trail begins its last 0.5 mi. of ascent to Gentian Pond.

Dryad Fall Trail (AMC)

This trail runs from the Austin Brook Trail to the Peabody Brook Trail near Dream Lake, passing Dryad Fall, one of the highest cascades in the mountains. Dryad is particularly interesting for a few days after a rainstorm, since its several cascades fall at least 300 ft. over steep ledges. The trail is blazed in yellow.

The trail leaves the Austin Brook Trail on the left 1.9 mi. from North Rd., just past the third brook crossing. (*Note:* Plans call for a relocation of this trail in the near future; it will probably leave the Austin Brook Trail about 0.5 mi. farther north in order to bypass an eroded section of the current trail.) It gradually ascends old logging roads, then drops down (right) to Dryad Brook, which it follows nearly to the base of the falls at 0.5 mi. *Caution:* Rocks in the vicinity of the falls are very slippery and hazardous. From here, the trail climbs steeply northeast of the falls. At 0.6 mi., it turns right away from the falls, then turns left onto an old road and comes back to the top of the falls. Here, it turns left on another road and crosses Dryad Brook at 0.9 mi., then climbs at mostly moderate grades to the Peabody Brook Trail near Dream Lake 0.1 mi. east of the Mahoosuc Trail. (*Descending*, watch carefully for the junction where the trail turns down steeply to the right off the logging road above the falls.)

Dryad Fall Trail

Distances from Austin Brook Trail

   to Dryad Fall: 0.5 mi., 35 min.

   to Peabody Brook Trail: 1.8 mi. (2.9 km.), 1 hr. 45 min.

Peabody Brook Trail (AMC)

This trail ascends to the Mahoosuc Trail at Dream Lake from North Rd., 1.3 mi. east of US 2. Overnight parking is not permitted at the base of this trail.

The trail follows a logging road between two houses and turns right onto an old logging road at 0.5 mi. It continues north along the brook and bears right at a fork at 0.8 mi., soon becomes a trail, and begins to ascend moderately. At 1.2 mi., a path leaves left and leads, in 0.3 mi., to Giant Falls. The main trail rises more steeply, and at 1.5 mi., you will see a glimpse of Mt. Washington and Mt. Adams through open trees. The trail climbs a short ladder just beyond. At 2.1 mi., it crosses the eastern branch of the brook, then recrosses it at 2.4 mi. From here, the trail climbs easily to Dream Lake and the junction on the right with the Dryad Fall Trail at 3 mi., then continues to the Mahoosuc Trail.

Peabody Brook Trail
Distance from North Rd.

   to Mahoosuc Trail: 3.1 mi. (5 km.), 2 hr. 20 min.

Centennial Trail (AMC)

This trail, part of the Appalachian Trail, begins on Hogan Rd.; this dirt road turns west from North Rd. north of where it crosses the Androscoggin River, just before it swings abruptly to the east. There is a small parking area 0.2 mi. from North Rd., and parking is also permitted at the junction of North Rd. and Hogan Rd.; in either case, do not block the road. The Centennial Trail was constructed by the AMC in 1976, its centennial year.

From the parking area on Hogan Rd., the trail runs generally northwest. After 50 yd. on an old road, it bears left up a steep bank into the woods, levels off, and reaches the first of many stone steps in 0.1 mi. The trail ascends rather steeply, then more gradually, with a limited view of the Androscoggin River. It turns left onto a woods road and crosses a brook at 0.7 mi. *(last available water)*. The trail then crosses a logging road and climbs past several restricted viewpoints, then descends to a sag in a birch grove at 1.6 mi. Climbing again, it soon turns sharply left and continues upward past ledges that provide increasingly open views. At 2.8 mi., the trail reaches an easterly summit of Mt. Hayes, where there is an excellent view of the Carter–Moriah Range and northern Presidentials from open ledges. The trail descends slightly, then ascends across a series of open ledges to end at the Mahoosuc Trail at 3.1 mi. The summit of Mt. Hayes, with fine views, is 0.2 mi. left; the Appalachian Trail turns right (north) on the Mahoosuc Trail.

Centennial Trail

Distance from Hogan Rd.

   to Mahoosuc Trail: 3.1 mi. (5 km.), 2 hr. 30 min.

MAHOOSUC RANGE AREA

This section includes the region along the Maine/New Hampshire border from Lake Umbagog southward to the big loop of the Androscoggin River from Gorham to Bethel. The area is drained principally by this river and its branches.

   The Mahoosuc Trail extends the entire length of the Mahoosuc Range, from Gorham to Old Speck, and there are many side trails. All of the trails in this section are east of NH 16, north of US 2, and west of ME 26.

   Grafton Notch State Park includes the highway corridor of ME 26 and the summit of Old Speck. The remainder of the ridgecrest, followed by the Appalachian Trail from the Maine/New Hampshire boundary to Dunn Notch, passes through Maine Public Reserve Land.

   In 1976, the state of Maine negotiated an exchange of land with the Brown Paper Company, now the James River Corporation, which had owned most of the Mahoosuc Range summits. The state gave up rights in public lots and lands in various townships along the Mahoosuc Range extending west and south from the boundary of Grafton Notch State Park.

State laws restrict wood and charcoal fires to designated sites (shelters and Trident Col).

ACCESS ROADS

Success Pond Road

This road runs from the eastern side of the Androscoggin River in Berlin NH to Success Pond in about 14 mi., and continues to ME 26 north of Grafton Notch. Over the years, this has been perhaps the most difficult road in the White Mountains for someone unfamiliar with the region to find; important landmarks have disappeared or changed, and the first section of the road itself was moved with astounding but unpredictable regularity. However, it now appears that the situation has become sufficiently stable to give cause for hope, though even at the best of times, following Success Pond Rd. requires a good deal of care and often some trial and error. To find it, leave NH 16 just south of the city of Berlin, 4.5 mi. north of the eastern junction of US 2 and NH 16 in Gorham, and cross the Androscoggin on the Cleveland Bridge. At the eastern end of the bridge, the road (Unity St.) swings left and passes straight through a set of traffic lights in 0.7 mi. from NH 16. At 0.8 mi., the road bears right across railroad tracks and becomes Hutchins St. It turns sharply left at 1.6 mi. at Frank's Village Store and continues past the Crown Vantage mill yard. At 1.9 mi. from NH 16, where there has usually been a large sign reading OHRV Parking 1 Mile, Success Pond Rd. begins on the right (east). It no longer winds among the huge wood piles of the mill yard, but you should still watch out for large trucks, especially those entering from the right. The first part of the road has frequently been difficult to distinguish from branch roads, but once you are past this area, it is well defined—though it is often easy to take a dead-end branch road by mistake. The road is not generally open to public vehicular use in winter, and it can be very rough and muddy, particularly in spring and early summer before yearly maintenance is carried out. Trailheads are marked only with small AMC standard trail signs, often at old diverging logging roads with no well-defined parking area, so you must look for them carefully. The lower parts of the trails originating on this road have been disrupted frequently in the past by construction of new logging roads; great care is necessary to follow the blazes that mark the proper roads, ascending or descending.

Success Pond Rd. leaves ME 26 southwesterly about 2.8 mi. north of the Old Speck trailhead in Grafton Notch.

Success Pond Road
Approximate distances from ME 26

- *to* Speck Pond Trail, marked by a blue blaze and sign on low post, leaves left at about 7 mi.

- *to* Notch Trail spur road (sign), about 8.5 mi.

- *to* Carlo Col/Goose Eye trailhead, about 11.5 mi. (signs)

- *to* Success Trail (unmarked), about 14 mi.

- *to* Hutchins St., Berlin NH, about 20 mi.

North Road

This road provides access to the trails on the southern side of the Mahoosuc Range. It leaves US 2 about 2.8 mi. east of its easterly junction with NH 16 in Gorham, and crosses the Androscoggin River on the Lead Mine Bridge; the Appalachian Trail follows this part of the road. North Rd. then swings east and runs along the northern side of the river to rejoin US 2 just north of Bethel ME. Bridges connect North Rd. with US 2 at the villages of Shelburne NH and Gilead ME.

MAHOOSUC TRAIL (AMC)

The trail, here described from southwest to northeast, extends along the entire length of the Mahoosuc Range, from Gorham NH to the summit of Old Speck. Beyond its junction with the Centennial Trail, the Mahoosuc Trail is a link in the Appalachian Trail. To protect fragile soils and vegetation, camping is limited to the tentsites at Trident Col and to the four shelters: Gentian Pond, Carlo Col, Full Goose, and Speck Pond (all of which also have tentsites). These sites may have a caretaker, in which case a fee is charged. Some of these shelters are slated for removal, but the tentsites will remain. *Water is scarce,* particularly in dry weather, and its purity is always in question. Do not be deceived by the relatively low elevations; this trail is among the most rugged of its kind in the White Mountains, a very strenuous route—particularly for those with heavy packs—with numerous minor humps and cols, and many ledges, some of them quite steep, that are likely to be slippery when wet. Many parts of the trail may require significantly more time than that listed here, particularly for backpackers, and Mahoosuc Notch may require several extra hours, depending in part on how much time you spend enjoying the spectacular scenery. Mahoosuc Notch is regarded by many who have hiked the entire length of the Appalachian Trail as its most difficult mile. *Caution:* Mahoosuc Notch can be hazardous in wet or icy conditions, and can remain impassable due to unmelted snowdrifts through the end of May—perhaps even longer.

Part I. Gorham to Centennial Trail

To reach the trail, cross the Androscoggin River by the footbridge under the Boston & Maine Railroad bridge, 1.3 mi. north of the Gorham Post Office on NH 16. On the eastern bank, follow the road to the right (southeast) along the river for 0.4 mi., then cross the canal through the open upper level of the powerhouse (left of entrance). At the eastern end of the dam, continue straight ahead for about 100 yd. to the woods, where you will find the trail sign. The trail is sparsely blazed in blue. Turn left and follow an old road north along the side of the canal for 0.1 mi., then turn right uphill onto an old logging road. At 0.8 mi. from NH 16, the trail crosses a power-line clearing, then bears right and reaches but does not cross a brook, following it closely for 100 yd. Avoid side paths from recent logging operations. The trail ascends at only a slight grade to a side path at 1.1 mi. that leads right 0.2 mi. to Mascot Pond, just below the cliffs seen prominently from Gorham. The Mahoosuc Trail crosses a woods road, then ascends the valley of a brook, which it crosses several times. At 2.5 mi., it passes a short spur (sign) that leads left to Popsy Spring, then climbs steeply and emerges on the southwestern side of the flat, ledgy summit of Mt. Hayes. An unmarked footway leads a few yards right to the best viewpoint south over the valley. A cairn marks the true summit of Mt. Hayes at 3.1 mi. The trail descends on open ledges with good views north to the junction (right) with the Centennial Trail at 3.2 mi.

Part II. Centennial Trail to Gentian Pond

From here north, the Mahoosuc Trail is part of the Appalachian Trail, marked with white blazes. It descends north to the col between Mt. Hayes and Cascade Mtn. at 4.1 mi.; here, there is sometimes *water*. The trail then ascends Cascade Mtn. by a southwestern ridge, over ledges and large fallen rocks, emerging on the bare summit ledge at 5.1 mi. It turns back sharply into the woods, descending gradually with occasional slight ascents to the eastern end of the mountain, then enters a fine forest and descends rapidly beside cliffs and ledges to Trident Col at 6.3 mi., where a side path leads left 0.2 mi. to the Trident Col Tentsite. *Water* is available about 50 yd. below (west of) the site. The bare ledges of the rocky cone to the east of Trident Col repay the effort required to scramble to its top; a route ascends between two large cairns near the tentsite side path.

The trail descends rather steeply to the southeast and runs along the side of the ridge at the base of the Trident, which is made up of the previously mentioned cone, the ledgy peak just west of Page Pond, and a somewhat less prominent peak between them. The trail crosses several small brooks, at least one of which usually has *water.* It follows a logging road for 0.1 mi., then turns left off the road at a sign and ascends to Page Pond at 7.3 mi. The trail passes the southern end of the pond, crosses a beaver dam, and climbs gradually, then more steeply, to a short spur path at 7.9 mi. that leads left to a fine outlook from ledges near the summit of Wocket Ledge, a shoulder of Bald Cap. The main trail crosses the height-of-land and descends east, crosses the upper (west) branch of Peabody Brook, then climbs around the nose of a small ridge and descends gradually to the head of Dream Lake. The trail bears left here, then right around the northern end of the lake, and crosses the inlet brook at 9 mi. Just beyond, the Peabody Brook Trail leaves on the right.

From this junction, the Mahoosuc Trail follows a lumber road left for 100 yd. It soon recrosses the inlet brook, passes over a slight divide into the watershed of Austin Brook, ascends through some swampy places, and descends to Moss Pond at 10.5 mi. It continues past the northern shore of the pond and follows an old logging road down the outlet brook, then crosses the brook, turns abruptly right downhill from the logging road, and descends to Gentian Pond. It skirts the southwestern shore of the pond, then drops to cross the outlet brook. A few yards beyond, at 11.2 mi., is the Gentian Pond Campsite (shelter and tentsites); here, the Austin Brook Trail diverges right for North Rd. in Shelburne.

Part III. Gentian Pond to Carlo Col

From the Gentian Pond Shelter, the trail climbs to the top of the steep-sided hump whose ledges overlook the pond from the east, then descends moderately to a sag. It next starts up the western end of Mt. Success, climbing steeply at first to the lumpy ridge, and passes a small stream at 12.6 mi. in the col that lies under the main mass of Mt. Success. The trail now climbs rather steeply and roughly for about 0.5 mi. to the relatively flat upper part of the mountain, then ascends over open ledges with an outlook to the southwest, passes through a belt of high scrub, crosses an alpine meadow, and finally comes out on the summit of Mt. Success at 14 mi.

The trail turns sharply left here and descends through scrub, then forest, to the sag between Mt. Success and a northern subpeak, where the Success Trail enters left at 14.6 mi. The main trail climbs slightly, then descends moderately to the main col between Mt. Success and Mt. Carlo at 15.3 mi. The trail then rises over a low hump and descends to a lesser col; here it turns right, then left, passes the Maine/New Hampshire border signs, and ascends moderately again. At 16.4 mi., it drops sharply past a fine outlook ledge into the little box ravine called Carlo Col. The Carlo Col Trail from Success Pond Rd. enters left here; the Carlo Col Campsite is located 0.3 mi. down the Carlo Col Trail, at the head of a small brook.

Part IV. Carlo Col to Mahoosuc Notch

From Carlo Col, the trail climbs steadily to the bare southwestern summit of Mt. Carlo at 16.8 mi., where there is an excellent view. It then passes a lower knob to the northeast, descends through a mountain meadow—from which there is a fine view of Goose Eye ahead—and reaches the col at 17.4 mi. The trail turns more north and climbs steeply to a ledgy knoll below Goose Eye, then passes through a sag and climbs steeply again to the narrow ridge of the main peak of Goose Eye Mtn. at 18.2 mi. Use care on the ledges. Here, at the ridgetop, the Goose Eye Trail branches sharply left, reaching the open summit and its spectacular views in 0.1 mi. and continuing to Success Pond Rd. From the ridgetop junction, the Mahoosuc Trail turns sharply right (east) and follows the ridgecrest through mixed ledge and scrub to a col at 18.5 mi., where it meets the southern branch of the Wright Trail to Bull Branch Rd. in Ketchum ME. The Mahoosuc Trail then climbs steeply through woods and open areas to the bare summit of the East Peak of Goose Eye Mtn. Here it turns sharply left (north) down the open ledges of the ridge and enters the scrub at the eastern side of the open part, meeting the northern branch of the Wright Trail at 18.8 mi. Beyond the col, the trail runs in the open nearly to the foot of the North Peak, except for two interesting box ravines, where there is often *water.* At the summit of the North Peak, at 19.8 mi., the trail turns sharply right (east) along the ridgecrest, then swings northeast down the steep slope, winding through several patches of scrub. At the foot of the steep slope, it enters the woods and angles down the western face of the ridge to the col at 20.8 mi. The Full Goose Campsite is located on a ledgy shelf near here; there is a *spring* 80 yd. to the right (east of the campsite). The trail then turns sharply left and ascends, coming into the open about 0.3 mi. below the summit of the South Peak of Fulling Mill Mtn., which is reached at 21.3 mi. Here the trail turns sharply left and runs through a meadow. It descends northwest through woods, first gradually, then steeply, to the head of Mahoosuc Notch at 22.3 mi. Here the Notch Trail to Success Pond Rd. diverges sharply left (southwest).

Part V. Mahoosuc Notch to Old Speck

From the head of Mahoosuc Notch, the trail turns sharply right (northeast) and descends the length of the narrow notch along a rough footway, passing through a number of boulder caverns, some with narrow openings where your progress will be slow and where ice remains into the summer. The trail is blazed on the rocks with white paint. *Caution:* Use great care when traveling through the notch, because of its numerous slippery rocks and dangerous holes; the notch may be impassable through early June because of snow, even with snowshoes. Heavy backpacks will impede progress considerably.

At the lower end of the notch, at 23.4 mi., the trail bears left and ascends moderately but roughly under the eastern end of Mahoosuc Mtn. along the valley that leads to Notch 2, then crosses to the northern side of the brook at 23.9 mi. The trail then winds upward among rocks and ledges on the very steep wooded slope of Mahoosuc Arm with a steep, rough footway. A little more than halfway up, it passes the head of a little flume, in which there is sometimes *water.* At 25 mi., a few yards past the top of the flat ledges near the summit of Mahoosuc Arm, the May Cutoff diverges left and leads 0.3 mi. over the true summit to the Speck Pond Trail. The Mahoosuc Trail swings right and wanders across the semi-open summit plateau for about 0.5 mi., then drops steeply to Speck Pond (3430 ft.), one of the highest ponds in Maine, bordered with thick woods. The trail crosses the outlet brook and continues around the eastern side of the pond to the Speck Pond Campsite at 25.9 mi. (in summer, there is a caretaker and a fee for overnight camping). Here, the Speck Pond Trail to Success Pond Rd. leaves on the left.

The trail then climbs to the southeastern end of the next hump on the ridge, passes over it, and runs across the eastern face of a second small hump. In the gully beyond, a few yards east of the trail, is an *unreliable spring.* The trail climbs on the western shoulder of Old Speck, reaching an open area where the footway is well defined on the crest. Near the top of the shoulder, the trail bears right, reenters the woods, and follows the wooded crest with blue blazes marking the boundary of Grafton Notch State Park. The Old Speck Trail, which continues the Appalachian Trail northward, diverges left to Grafton Notch at 27 mi., and the Mahoosuc Trail runs straight ahead to the summit of Old Speck and its observation tower, where the poorly marked East Spur Trail enters.

Mahoosuc Trail

Distances from NH 16 in Gorham

to Hayes summit: 3.1 mi., 2 hr. 25 min.

to Centennial Trail: 3.3 mi., 2 hr. 30 min.

to Cascade summit: 5.1 mi., 3 hr. 45 min.

to Trident Col: 6.3 mi., 4 hr. 25 min.

to Page Pond: 7.3 mi., 5 hr. 5 min.

to Wocket Ledge: 7.9 mi., 5 hr. 40 min.

to Dream Lake, inlet brook crossing: 9 mi., 6 hr. 20 min.

to Gentian Pond Campsite: 11.2 mi., 7 hr. 30 min.

to Success summit: 14 mi., 9 hr. 55 min.

  to Success Trail: 14.6 mi., 10 hr. 10 min.

  to Carlo Col Trail: 16.4 mi., 11 hr. 20 min.

  to Carlo: 16.8 mi., 11 hr. 45 min.

  to Goose Eye Trail: 18.2 mi., 12 hr. 45 min.

  to Wright Trail, southern junction: 18.5 mi., 12 hr. 55 min.

  to Goose Eye Mtn., East Peak: 18.6 mi., 13 hr. 5 min.

  to Wright Trail, northern junction: 18.8 mi., 15 hr. 50 min.

  to Full Goose Campsite: 20.8 mi., 14 hr. 20 min.

  to Notch Trail: 22.3 mi., 15 hr. 15 min.

  to foot of Mahoosuc Notch: 23.4 mi., 15 hr. 45 min.

  to Mahoosuc Arm summit: 25 mi., 17 hr. 25 min.

  to Speck Pond Campsite: 25.9 mi., 17 hr. 50 min.

  to Old Speck Trail junction: 27 mi., 18 hr. 45 min.

  to Old Speck summit: 27.3 mi. (43.9 km.), 19 hr.

Table Rock Trail

The Table Rock Trail, which climbs 900 ft., offers a short, fairly steep, but spectacular climb to the prominent rock ledge on Baldpate Mtn., which is on the eastern side of Grafton Notch. From this ledge, the trail continues onward to rejoin the Appalachian Trail. There is an extensive slab-cave system, possibly the largest in the state, on this trail.

The trail leaves the Appalachian Trail to the right (south) 0.1 mi. from the trailhead on ME 26 (described below). For 0.3 mi. from this junction, the trail rises gently along the side of a hill above a marsh until it reaches a drop-off. From there, it climbs steadily through mature hardwoods and reaches a rocky, caribou moss–covered area called the boulder patch at 0.6 mi. After several switchbacks along rocky ledges, the trail enters a deep ravine between two rock faces. At the top of the ravine, bear right. The trail climbs less steeply to a prominent outlook at 0.8 mi. At 0.9 mi., it reaches the base of the ledges that form Table Rock, where the slab caves begin. *Caution:* Be careful if you explore the caves. Some are quite deep, and a fall could mean serious injury.

On the trail, continue south around the bottom of Table Rock. (On the ledges above, note the weather-formed rock that looks like a shark's fin.) At 1 mi., after swinging behind Table Rock, you will meet a blue-blazed trail. Table Rock is 20 yd. to the left.

To the right, the blue-blazed upper Table Rock Trail continues, with only a slight change in elevation, about 0.5 mi. to the Appalachian Trail. Turn right (east) to reach Baldpate; go left (west) to return to the trailhead on ME 26.

Table Rock Trail
Distances from state parking area on ME 26

  to start (via Baldpate Mountain Trail): 0.1 mi.

  to Table Rock and junction with upper trail: 1 mi.

  to state parking area, ME 26 (via Baldpate Mountain Trail): 2.4 mi. (3.9 km.), 1 hr. 45 min.

BALDPATE MOUNTAIN (East Peak 3812 ft./1162 m. and West Peak 3680 ft./1122 m.)

Baldpate Mtn., once known as Saddleback and Bear River Whitecap, rises to the east of Grafton Notch. There are two main summits: the fine open East Peak, and the West Peak. The Appalachian Trail traverses both. Refer to the USGS Old Speck Mountain quadrangle, 15-min. series; the Old Speck quadrangle, 7.5-min. series; AMC map 6, North Country–Mahoosuc Range; or map 7 in the MATC's *Appalachian Trail Guide to Maine.*

Baldpate Mountain via Appalachian Trail

The Appalachian Trail, which traverses the range, is maintained by the MATC and blazed in white. The following describes approaches from both the west and east.

From Grafton Notch

The trail leaves the northern side of the state-park parking lot on ME 26 (take the trail to the right). It soon crosses ME 26. Then it runs briefly through woods and beside a marsh until, at 0.1 mi., it crosses a brook on a log footbridge. Almost immediately after this crossing, the trail passes the start of the Table Rock Trail, which leaves right. The trail rises gradually on an old woods road. At 0.9 mi., it passes another blue-blazed trail on the right leading to Table Rock. The main trail climbs steadily and then more steeply to the western knob of Baldpate, with good views to the northwest. The trail then slabs the northern side of the knob to a ridge extending toward the West Peak, soon descending to a brook where, at about 2 mi., a side trail leads south to the new Baldpate Shelter. Then it climbs steeply over rough terrain to the West Peak, which is covered with tiny scrub but offers vistas in almost all directions. The trail, turning in a more northerly direction, drops only about 240 ft. before climbing to the East Peak nearly a mile beyond. From there, it continues to Andover–East B Hill Rd.

From Andover–East B Hill Road

The trail leaves the left (south) side of East B Hill Rd. about 8 mi. west of Andover Village. It descends from the road, crosses a small brook, then turns south along the edge of a progressively deeper gorge cut by this brook, which it follows for 0.5 mi. before turning west into the mouth of Dunn Notch. At 0.8 mi., the trail crosses the West Branch of the Ellis River (a large stream at this point) at the top of a double waterfall plunging 60 ft. into Dunn Notch. You can reach the bottom of the falls via an old logging road across the stream. (Upstream, you will find a small, rocky gorge and the beautiful upper falls.) The Appalachian Trail crosses the old road and climbs steeply up the eastern rim of the notch. It then climbs moderately to the south.

At 1.3 mi., the trail turns left and climbs gradually through open hardwoods along the edge of the northern arm of Surplus Mtn. At 3 mi., it slabs right (southwest) around the nose of Surplus, climbs gently along a broad ridge, and passes near the summit. In another 1.6 mi., it descends steeply over rough ground to the Frye Notch Lean-to, near the head of Frye Brook. At 1.7 mi. from the lean-to, the trail reaches and climbs the crest of a ridge to the open summit of Baldpate's East Peak. The trail then drops down, climbs the West Peak, and descends into Grafton Notch via the trail from the west (described above).

Baldpate Mountain via Appalachian Trail

Distances from state parking area on ME 26

> *to* lower side trail to Table Rock: 0.1 mi., 5 min.
>
> *to* upper side trail to Table Rock: 0.9 mi., 45 min.
>
> *to* Baldpate, West Peak: 2.9 mi., 2 hr. 30 min.
>
> *to* Baldpate, East Peak: 3.8 mi., 3 hr. 10 min.
>
> *to* Andover–East B Hill Road: 10.1 mi. (16.3 km.), 6 hr. 40 min.

Distances from Andover–East B Hill Rd.

> *to* waterfall: 0.8 mi., 55 min.
>
> *to* Frye Notch Lean-to: 4.6 mi., 3 hr.
>
> *to* Baldpate, East Peak: 6.3 mi., 4 hr. 30 min.
>
> *to* Baldpate, West Peak: 7.2 mi., 5 hr. 15 min.
>
> *to* state parking area on ME 26: 10.1 mi. (16.3 km.), 7 hr.

MOUNT WILL (1736 ft.)

The mountain is located in Bethel on the border of Newry. The blue-green-blazed trails are maintained by the Bethel Conservation Commission. Except for the North Ledge Trail section, the trail is on private land. Refer to the USGS Bethel quadrangle, 7.5 min.-series. The marked trailhead is on the western side of ME 2, 1.9 mi. north of the state rest area, just opposite the Bethel Transfer Station.

Not far from the trailhead, the trail divides. The right fork goes up a nature trail to the North Ledges, continuing in a loop around to the South Cliffs after passing just under the summit.

From the cliffs, the trail drops steeply and then more easily back to the junction and out to ME 2.

Mount Will

Distances from trailhead

to North Ledges: 0.75 mi., 45 min.

to South Cliffs: 1 mi., 45 min.

Complete loop: 3.25 mi., 2 hr. 15 min.

RUMFORD WHITECAP (2197 ft./670 m.)

This mountain is a long, bare-topped ridge in the northwestern part of Rumford. It yields excellent views with relatively little effort. Refer to the USGS East Andover quadrangle, 7.5-min. series.

The trail climbs up from the west. From US 2, 0.5 mi. west of Rumford Point, go north on ME 5 toward Andover. About 3 mi. from US 2, turn right (east) onto the side road that crosses the Ellis River. In 0.3 mi., turn left (north), and then in 1.6 mi., turn right (east) onto Coburn Brook Rd. toward Roxbury Notch. At 0.7 mi., the trail leaves the right side of the road on a logging road (not passable for cars) and climbs steeply. Cross a logging yard then continue up. Bear left with the road. Just after two badly drained dips, turn right up the trail. Climb steeply through the woods to open ledges, following flags and cairns. At a large boulder, the trail turns right through the woods to more open ledges.

The final 1 mi. is a delightful walk along the open ridge to the summit. From the summit, the antenna on Black Mountain and the satellite station at Andover are visible. The trail through the woods and along the ridge is marked by ribbons and cairns with few paint blazes. *Descending,* take great care to find and follow the correct trail west into the woods; there are many cairns and paths leading in different directions. Ribbons mark the critical points.

Rumford Whitecap

Distances from Coburn Brook Rd.

to left turn off logging road: 0.5 mi.

to ledges: 1 mi.

to Rumford Whitecap summit: 2 mi. (3.2 km.), 1 hr. 40 min.

OLD BLUE MOUNTAIN (3600 ft./1097 m.)

The Appalachian Trail (AT) crosses Old Blue Mtn., which is south of Elephant Mtn. and east of the road from Andover to the South Arm of Lower Richardson Lake. The summit of Old Blue is covered with dense evergreen trees 2–3 ft. high, allowing excellent views in all directions. Refer to the USGS Old Speck Mtn. and Rangeley quadrangles, 15-min. series; the East Andover quadrangle, 7.5-min. series, or map 7 in the MATC's *Appalachian Trail Guide to Maine.*

To reach the AT, follow the road to the South Arm for 8.5 mi. north of Andover to Black Brook Notch. *Note:* There is a *spring* a half-mile north on South Arm Rd. at the foot of the hill before the AT crossing. From South Arm Rd., the AT climbs very steeply up the eastern wall of Black Brook Notch. At 0.6 mi., the trail reaches the top of the notch, then it gradually climbs to the base of Old Blue, which it reaches at 2.3 mi. Here, the trail begins its final 0.5-mi. ascent to the summit.

From the summit, the AT descends north 800 ft. into the high valley between Old Blue Mtn. and Elephant Mtn. In this valley, the AT runs through a virgin red spruce forest for more than a mile.

For detailed information about the AT north of Old Blue, see the latest edition of the MATC's *Appalachian Trail Guide to Maine.*

Old Blue Mountain

Distances from South Arm Rd.

to top of Black Brook Notch: 0.6 mi.

to base of Old Blue: 2.3 mi.

to Old Blue summit: 2.8 mi. (4.5 km.), 2 hr. 40 min.

BEMIS MOUNTAIN (3592 ft./1095 m.)

Bemis Mtn. is an open ridge with outstanding views. It rises south of Mooselookmeguntic Lake. The ridge, which runs northeast–southwest, has four peaks descending in elevation to the northeast. The highest peak is wooded. The three lower peaks all have excellent views. The Appalachian Trail crosses Bemis Ridge, and there is a new lean-to near Third Peak. Refer to the USGS Oquossoc and Rangeley quadrangles, 15-min. series; the Houghton and Metallak Mtn. quadrangles, 7.5-min. series; or map 7 in the MATC's *Appalachian Trail Guide to Maine.*

Via Appalachian Trail

Access is from ME 17 at a turnout 11 mi. south of Oquossoc and 26 mi. north of Rumford. Park at a clearing 0.6 mi. south at the Bemis Stream trailhead.

The trail descends 0.8 mi. to the ford where Bemis Stream splits. There are two long crossings, difficult at high water. At 1 mi., cross the gravel logging road, which was the bed of the old Rumford and Rangeley Lakes Railroad in the 1930s. There is a small *spring* at 1.1 mi. After climbing through woods, emerge onto open ledges at 1.5 mi. and cross a series of rocky knobs, the first at 1.7 mi. The ridge trail crosses three peaks: First Peak (2604 ft.) at 2.2 mi.; Second Peak (2923 ft.) at 3.1 mi.; the lean-to at 4.6 mi.; and Third Peak (3138 ft.) at 5 mi. At 5.1 mi., the trail begins the ascent to the two wooded knobs of Fourth Peak (3592 ft.), which are reached at 6.2 and 6.3 miles.

For an interesting loop hike, climb Bemis by way of the Appalachian Trail and return via the Bemis Stream Trail, a total of almost 14 mi.

Via Bemis Stream Trail

This trail starts from a cleared parking area off ME 17, 0.6 mi. south of the Appalachian Trail crossing mentioned above. Hikers on either trail should park here.

The trail fords a brook at 0.2 mi., winds down to the gravel rail-road-bed road at 1.2 mi., and climbs to reach Bemis Stream. It follows the western bank up to ford the stream at about 2 mi., recrossing to the western side at 2.8 mi. Climbing, it crosses again at 4.6 mi. and 5 mi. Then the trail swings up and west to join the Appalachian Trail at 6.5 mi. (This point is 7.3 mi. along the Appalachian Trail from ME 17.)

For a detailed description of the Appalachian Trail beyond Fourth Peak, see the latest edition of the MATC's *Appalachian Trail Guide to Maine.*

Bemis Mountain

Distances from ME 17 via Appalachian Trail

to Fourth Peak: 6.3 mi., 4 hr. 30 min.

to Bemis Mountain Lean-to: 4.6 mi.

Complete loop (via Appalachian Trail, Bemis Stream Trail, and ME 17): 14 mi. (22.4 km.), 8 hr. 30 min.

Section 9

Weld Region

Weld Village lies on the eastern shore of Lake Webb (678 ft.) and is almost encircled by mountains. Tumbledown Mtn. (3068 ft.), with its tremendous cliffs, three peaks, and high pond, is the most interesting mountain in the area and one of the state's outstanding summits. Little Jackson Mtn. (3434 ft.), Jackson Mtn. (3535 ft.), and Blueberry Mtn. (2942 ft.) are also in the Tumbledown Range, which forms the northern and northwestern walls of the valley. Mt. Blue (3187 ft.) lies to the east. The ledgy summits of Bald Mtn. (2386 ft.) and Saddleback Wind Mtn. (2572 ft.) close the valley on the southeast. Brush Mtn. (2430 ft.) and West Mtn. (2782 ft.) are to the west.

Mt. Blue State Park (1273 acres) has two sections. The area along the western shore of Lake Webb offers picnicking, swimming, and camping facilities. The section east of the lake and Weld includes the Center Hill parking overlook and picnic area, and Mt. Blue itself. Information on accommodations and trail conditions can be obtained at the supervisor's headquarters 1.5 mi. from Weld on the road toward Center Hill and Mt. Blue.

TUMBLEDOWN MOUNTAIN (3068 ft./935 m.)

Although not the highest peak of the Tumbledown Range, Tumbledown Mtn., at the southwestern end, is in many ways the most interesting. The enormous cliff on the southern side of this mountain attracts many rock climbers. Of the three summits, the 3068-ft. West Peak is slightly higher than the others. Another feature of the mountain is Tumbledown Pond (called Beaver or Crater by some), located on the eastern slope of the mountain and surrounded on three sides by higher elevations. The views from the summit ridges are good, except where higher mountains in the range block them to the north and northeast. There are four trails to the pond. In addition to the map in this guide, you can refer to the USGS Dixfield and Rangeley quadrangles, 15-min. series, and the Roxbury quadrangle, 7.5-min. series.

Loop Trail

The Loop Trail leaves Byron Notch Rd. 5.8 mi. west of Weld Corner, heading north on the eastern side of a brook. There is a sign at the start of the trail, as well as a clearing diagonally opposite the trail's entrance into the woods. The trail (blue-blazed) rises gradually, crossing a brook twice, and at 1 mi. passes the huge Tumbledown Boulder. From there, it rises steeply, coming out on the open Great Ledges, from which there are splendid views of the 700-ft. cliffs of Tumbledown Mtn. On the ledges, at a large cairn, the Loop Trail to the saddle turns right.

The trail crosses a brook and then climbs steeply in a gully. Near the top of the gully, a side trail leads right to a fissure cave (Fat Man's Misery). Above this is an opening in the boulders with iron rungs. (This section makes the trail unsuitable for dogs.) At 0.6 mi. from the Great Ledges cairn, reach the saddle with a *spring* (unreliable in dry weather). From here, the trails lead east and west.

There are no trails on the North Peak of Tumbledown, but you can reach it by bushwhacking through the valley between the East and North peaks or by going east around Tumbledown Pond and up the upper reaches of Parker's Ridge. See section on Bushwhacking in the Maine Mountains in the Introduction.

Loop Trail

Distances from Byron Notch Rd.

  to Tumbledown Boulder: 1 mi.

  to Great Ledges (cairn): 1.3 mi.

  to saddle (Tumbledown Ridge Trail): 1.9 mi. (3.1 km.), 1 hr. 45 min.

Brook Trail

This is a direct route to Tumbledown Pond from Byron Notch Rd. It leaves the road 1.8 mi. west of the start of the Parker's Ridge Trail and 4.4 mi. west of Weld Corner. The trail diverges north just before the spot where the road crosses a large double-steel culvert over Tumbledown Brook. The trail is marked Brook Trail on a rock at the start and is blue-blazed throughout its length. For the first mile, it is a logging road passable for jeeps. At 1 mi., the trail diverges to the right into a low spot; then it climbs steeply, generally following the brook to the pond.

Brook Trail

Distances from Byron Notch Rd.

    to right turn off logging road: 1 mi.

    to Tumbledown Pond: 1.5 mi. (2.4 km.), 1 hr. 30 min.

Parker's Ridge Trail

This is the oldest of the trails up Tumbledown. Take the road to the right (northwest) from Byron Notch Rd., about 2.7 mi. west of Weld Corner and about 0.3 mi. west of a cemetery. Follow the road northwest about 0.9 mi. to a clearing and shelter. Park here. From this area, the Little Jackson Trail leaves on a logging road, northwest.

The Parker's Ridge Trail, blazed blue, enters the woods left (west), crosses a brook, and turns northwest, joining a logging road. For 1 mi., the trail rises gently through second growth, then steeply for a short distance over three ledges. After that, the trail rises steadily. Then it crosses the open ledges of Parker's Ridge with views of Tumbledown's three peaks ahead, and descends west to Tumbledown Pond.

Parker's Ridge Trail

Distances from parking area

    to Parker's Ridge: 1.9 mi., 2 hr.

    to pond (outlet): 2.2 mi. (3.5 km.), 2 hr. 10 min.

Tumbledown Ridge Trail

From the pond outlet junction with the Brook Trail and Parker's Ridge Trail, the Tumbledown Ridge Trail ascends west over mostly open ledge to East Peak and to the junction with the Loop Trail. A short spur extends to the summit of the West Peak, offering views into the Swift River Valley and to Old Blue and Elephant mountains to the west.

Tumbledown Ridge Trail
Distances from pond outlet

   to East Peak: 0.4 mi.

   to Loop Trail junction: 0.6 mi.

   to West Peak: 0.7 mi. (1.1 km.), 45 min.

Pond Link Trail

From the Parker's Ridge Trail 0.1 mi. east of the pond, the Pond Link Trail, blazed blue, heads north, skirting the eastern end of the pond for about 100 yd. It then turns east to ascend to the height-of-land between Parker's Ridge and Little Jackson Mtn. at 0.3 mi. from the pond. The trail continues generally east to a junction with the Little Jackson Trail. This makes an interesting loop.

Pond Link Trail
Distances from the pond

   to start of Pond Link Trail: 0.1 mi.

   to height-of-land: 0.3 mi.

   to Little Jackson Trail: *est.* 1 mi. (1.6 km.), 40 min.

LITTLE JACKSON MOUNTAIN (3434 ft./1047 m.)

For the road approach, see the Parker's Ridge Trail section. If you want to supplement the map in this guide, refer to the USGS Rangeley quadrangle, 15-min. series, and the Roxbury quadrangle, 7.5-min. series.

The trail leaves the shelter area northwest on a logging road.

There are no trail signs along the way, but the trail is well blazed and fairly well worn. There are many intersecting logging roads. Stay close to the edge of the valley that leads toward the Jacksons. About 0.5 mi. from the shelter, the route heads north toward the col between Little Jackson on the west and Jackson on the east. At about 1.5 mi., the trail turns right (northeast), and the blue-blazed Pond Link Trail leads straight ahead (northwest). At about 2.3 mi., the trail crosses a brook and continues onto open ledges 0.3 mi. beyond. At the ledges, the trail turns left and, ascending across open ledges with fine outlooks, climbs to the summit of Little Jackson.

Descending from the open areas on Little Jackson, the trail bears well to the right and is somewhat hard to see, so it is easy to get confused in the puckerbrush.

The distance from the col to the summit is about 1 mi. There is a clearing with a UHF jumper tower on top.

Little Jackson Mountain
Distances from parking area

> *to* Pond Link Trail junction: *est.* 1.5 mi.

> *to* col: 2.5 mi., 2 hr.

> *to* Jackson summit (via bushwhack from col): *est.* 3.5 mi.

> *to* Little Jackson summit (via trail): 3.3 mi. (5.3 km.), 2 hr. 30 min.

JACKSON MOUNTAIN (3535 ft./1077 m.)

Jackson is a large, rambling mountain partially covered with spruce, with a 100-ft.-diameter clear-cut, a building, and a radio structure on top. A trail has been cut to the summit of Jackson from the col between it and Little Jackson Mtn. Local enthusiasts plan more trails surrounding the Weld area.

Jackson Mountain
Distance from col

> *to* Jackson summit: *est.* 1 mile.

BLUEBERRY MOUNTAIN (2942 ft./897 m.)

See the USGS Phillips quadrangle, 15-min. series, or the Madrid quadrangle, 7.5-min. series, if you want to supplement the map in this guide.

The trail leaves ME 142 1.5 mi. from Weld Corner toward Phillips. Blueberry Mtn. Bible Camp maintains a road that runs 1.8 mi. to a clearing above the buildings. A gate near the base may be locked, blocking cars, but to date, personnel at the camp have been cooperative about letting people use their road. They ask that you park near the main building, not up in the clearing. From the middle of the northern side of the clearing, follow a logging road to a trail with blue blazes, which soon splits right. Trail maintenance has been sporadic. The trail rises steeply, first through conifers and then over ledges, to the summit. There are interesting geological formations at the top, which is bare and offers excellent views in all directions. There is *no water* on the trail.

Blueberry Mountain Trail

Distances from ME 142

to clearing (via Bible camp road): 1.8 mi.

to Blueberry summit: 3.5 mi. (5.6 km.), 2 hr. 30 min.

MOUNT BLUE (3187 ft./971 m.)

From Mt. Washington, this peak is one of the most perfect cones on the skyline. The former firetower on the summit has no cab. In addition to the map in this guide, you can refer to the USGS Dixfield quadrangle, 15-min. series, and the Mt. Blue quadrangle, 7.5-min. series.

In Weld Village, take the road that leads uphill east from the four corners and bear left at the fork at 0.5 mi. Take the right fork at a little over 3 mi. and continue to the parking place at about 6 mi. (signs). The trail crosses a field northeast of the woods, where it is joined by an old telephone line. The path is broad and well worn and passes the old firewarden's cabin, where there is a fine *spring*. Above the cabin site, the gradient is the same for a half-mile; it then begins to lessen as the ridge is approached, although the footway becomes narrower and rougher. The board shelter has collapsed and the stairs have been removed from the tower frame, but there are paths to four rock outcrops, which offer views in various directions.

Mount Blue
Distances from parking place

> *to* firewarden's cabin: 0.6 mi.

> *to* Mt. Blue summit: 1.7 mi. (2.7 km.), 1 hr. 40 min.

BALD MOUNTAIN (2386 ft./727 m.)

The trail up Bald Mtn. leaves the southern side of ME 156 about 8.5 mi. west of Wilton and about 5 mi. east of Weld, just southeast of two bridges and a logging road. In addition to the map in this guide, you can refer to the USGS Dixfield quadrangle, 15-min. series, and the Mt. Blue quadrangle, 7.5-min. series.

Cross the brook immediately *(last sure water)* and enter the woods. The trail climbs steadily through the woods, marked by occasional red paint blazes. On the open ledges, it is marked by paint and cairns to the summit, where there are fine views in every direction. A faint trail may be followed 2 mi. farther to the summit of Saddleback Wind Mtn., which is slightly higher but attracts fewer visitors.

Bald Mountain
Distances from ME 156

> *to* ledges: 0.9 mi., 45 min.

> *to* Bald Mtn. summit: 1.5 mi. (2.4 km.), 1 hr. 15 min.

SUGARLOAF MOUNTAIN (1521 ft./464 m.)

Sugarloaf Mtn. in Dixfield is conspicuous because of its two prominent summits. It offers fine vistas from its open northern summit. Refer to the USGS Dixfield quadrangle, 7.5- and 15-min. series.

For the shortest route to the summit go north from the corner of Main St. (US 2) and Weld St. in Dixfield. Take ME 142 for 1.7 mi. The blue-blazed trail starts in back of a brown house across ME 142 from CMP utility pole J 17. Climbing steadily, the trail reaches the Bull Rock Trail on the right at 0.4 mi. *Note:* In this area, a 1992 logging operation destroyed part of the Sugarloaf and Link trails. Bearing left and climbing more steeply for 0.2 mi., reach the col between the northern and southern peaks. By a large boulder, a trail to the right has been cut to the southern peak. Continue left out of the col and climb to the northern summit. Explore north of this summit to find more open-ledge viewpoints.

Sugarloaf Mountain
Distances from ME 142

>   *to*   Link Trail junction: 0.4 mi.

>   *to*   col: 0.6 mi.

>   *to*   northern summit: 0.9 mi. (1.4 km.), 45 min.

BULL ROCK (920 ft./280 m.)

Perched on the side of Sugarloaf Mtn. in Dixfield, Bull Rock offers a delightful preview of the views from Sugarloaf. Hang-glider pilots now fly from Bull Rock and land in the field by the road.

Start from Dixfield as for the trail to Sugarloaf, and proceed 1.5 mi. north on ME 142 to a driveway on the right just before CMP utility pole J 10 and a blue house with a swimming pool. Only 20 yd. from ME 142, turn right onto the blue-blazed trail for 50 yd. Turn left, cross a small brook, pass a white house on the right, and climb a steep hogback to the open ledge.

Bull Rock
Distance from ME 142

>   *to*   Bull Rock ledges: 0.4 mi. (0.6 km.), 20 min.

Section 10

Rangeley and Stratton Area

This section includes the mountains north of Rangeley Lakes; the area westward to Lake Aziscohos and the New Hampshire border; the isolated mountains north toward the Canadian border, reached by a network of private logging roads and ME 27; and the important and outstanding cluster of 4000-ft. mountains, including Saddleback, Abraham, Sugarloaf, Crocker, Spaulding, Reddington, and Bigelow, reached through the towns of Rangeley, Stratton, Kingfield, and Phillips. This last group includes ten of the state's 4000-ft. peaks. Sugarloaf Mtn., at 4237 ft., is Maine's second-highest mountain (aside from the subsidiary summits of Katahdin), although Mt. Abraham (4049 ft.), Saddleback Mtn. (4116 ft.), and especially Bigelow Mtn. (4150 ft.) are more interesting for hiking.

There are two large ski areas in this region, on Sugarloaf Mtn. and Saddleback Mtn.

Accommodations are ample along ME 16/27 between Rangeley, Stratton, and Kingfield. Rangeley Lake State Park on the southern shore opened in 1967, with full camping, boating, and swimming facilities. You can drive to the park via ME 17 or ME 4. There are additional public facilities at Mt. Blue State Park in Weld, just south of this section.

The town of Eustis maintains the Cathedral Pines Campground and trailer park, with laundry facilities and a recreation building, on ME 27, 3 mi. north of the ME 16 and ME 27 junction at Stratton and 2.3 mi. south of Eustis.

The MFS maintains the following camping areas (fires permitted): on the northern side of ME 16 about 5 mi. east of Rangeley and near Dallas; on the western shore of Flagstaff Lake at the end of Old Flagstaff Rd., 2 mi. east of a junction with ME 27 (near Flagstaff Memorial Church) and 0.8 mi. north of the Cathedral Pines Campground; on the western side of ME 27 about 3 mi. south of the Chain of Ponds; at Upper Farm on the eastern shore of the Chain of Ponds just off ME 27; and on the eastern shore of the Chain of Ponds at its northern end, off ME 27.

MOUNT AZISCOHOS (3215 ft./980 m.)

South of Lake Aziscohos, this mountain offers excellent views of the Rangeley Lakes region. Fifteen lakes are visible from the summit. The trails lead to the eastern, and slightly lower, of the two peaks, where an abandoned MFS firetower is down. Refer to the USGS Oquossoc and Errol quadrangles, 15-min. series, and the Richardson Pond and Wilsons Mills quadrangles, 7.5-min. series.

There are two routes up the mountain. Both have discreet blue blazes. Opinions differ as to what they should be named; therefore, the descriptions here are titled simply From the Northwest and From the North.

From the Northwest

Sometimes called the Tower Man's Trail or South Trail, this route begins on the southern side of ME 16, at a small parking area 100 yd. east of the bridge over the Magalloway River at the Aziscohos Dam. The trail, gated by a cable, follows a relatively large logging road; at about 0.7 mi., it turns left (east) onto a narrower, older logging road. At 0.8 mi., it crosses the remains of a bridge at and continues gradually uphill. Then, after crossing extensive open space, it bears left into the woods. Cross the small stream at 1.1 mi. and take the left (south) fork. At 1.7 mi., the road reaches the clearing at the site of the former MFS firewarden's cabin, where there is an enclosed *spring*. Hike on the left side of the clearing and enter the open softwood forest. The trail continues on steeper but relatively easy grades, and at 2.4 mi., the trail from the north comes in on the left. Turn right and continue to the summit at 2.5 mi.

Mount Aziscohos from the Northwest
Distances from ME 16

> *to* cabin site: 1.7 mi.
>
> *to* junction with trail from the north: 2.4 mi.
>
> *to* Aziscohos summit: 2.5 mi. (4 km.), 2 hr. 30 min.

From the North

The route from the north begins on ME 16, 1 mi. east of the bridge over the Magalloway River at the Aziscohos Dam. Approximately 50 paces east of a graveled logging road, the trailhead is marked with a sign and registration box about 10 yd. south of the roadway. It leads gradually uphill on an old tote road through open hardwood and mixed forest, then turns sharply left at 0.5 mi. At 1 mi., the trail enters conifers, and it crosses a brook at 1.1 mi. After that, it continues more steeply, becoming rougher over boulders and exposed roots. It reaches the Tower Man's Trail coming in from the northwest at 2 mi. To the left, it is 0.1 mi. over ledges to the summit.

Mount Aziscohos from the North
Distances from ME 16

> *to* brook crossing: 1.1 mi.
>
> *to* Tower Man's Trail junction, from the northwest: 2 mi.
>
> *to* Aziscohos summit: 2.1 mi. (3.4 km.), 2 hr. 10 min.

BALD MOUNTAIN (2443 ft./745 m.)

This small mountain is in a prime location between Mooselookmeguntic and Rangeley lakes. A ski area on the northern slope has been out of business for many years, and the ski trails are overgrown. Refer to the USGS Oquossoc quadrangle, 15-min. series and 7.5-min. series.

To reach the hiking trail, go west from Oquossoc on ME 4 about 1 mi. to the terminus of that highway at Haines Landing. Turn left (south) onto Bald Mtn. Rd. before the landing and follow it for about 0.8 mi. to the parking area and trail on the left. A short distance from the start of the trail, take the right fork and climb east and southeast to the summit. The blue-blazed trail is well used and easy to see in the hardwood forest at the base of the mountain. Some minor boulder scrambling is required at the higher elevations, where you must take a little care to stay on the main trail. The bedrock summit has a variety of terrain and excellent views from different outlooks through the spruce.

Bald Mountain

Distance from road

   to Bald Mtn. summit: 1 mi. (1.6 km.), 1 hr.

WEST KENNEBAGO MOUNTAIN (3705 ft./1129 m.)

This isolated mountain is north of the Rangeley Lakes and west of Kennebago Lake. There is a firetower on the southern peak, which also offers fine views of the area and is the highest of the several summits of the north–south ridge that forms the mountain. Refer to the USGS Cupsuptic quadrangle, 15-min. series, and the Kennebago quadrangle, 7.5-min. series.

Access to the firewarden's trail is via the Brown Paper Company (now the James River Corporation) system of private roads. Turn north from ME 16 onto a company road 4.9 mi. west of the ME 4 and ME 16 junction in Oquossoc and 0.3 mi. west of the MFS buildings at Cupsuptic. Drive 3.2 mi. from ME 16 to a junction with a well-maintained, wide gravel road. Turn right (east); in 5.3 mi., the road reaches the firetower trail, which is marked by an MFS sign.

The trail starts as a road but soon becomes a path and climbs rather steeply. At 0.9 mi., it levels out among conifers and bears left. Then it begins to climb again, crosses a small stream, and turns sharply right. At 1.4 mi., the trail reaches the warden's camp (3186 ft.), a picturesque log cabin built in 1911. There is a *spring* behind the camp 100 yd. to the left. The trail leaves the camp from the upper right (northwest) corner of the clearing. At 1.7 mi., it reaches the ridge, where the trail turns left (south) to follow the ridge to the firetower.

West Kennebago Mountain
Distances from road

> *to* warden's camp: 1.4 mi.

> *to* West Kennebago, southern summit: 2.1 mi. (3.4 km.), 2 hr.

EAST KENNEBAGO MOUNTAIN (3791 ft./1155 m.)

East of Kennebago Lake, this is a long, wooded ridge running east–west in T 2 R 4 and T 2 R 5. (*T* and *R* stand for "township" and "range"; Maine uses this system to designate its unincorporated towns.)

This is in part a bushwhack trip. Refer to the USGS Kennebago Lake quadrangle, 15-min. series, and the Kennebago Lake and Quill Hill quadrangles, 7.5-min. series. East Kennebago also appears on the Rangeley-Stratton map in this guide.

On ME 16, 9 mi. from ME 16/27 in Stratton, or 9.6 mi. from ME 4/16 in Rangeley, turn northwest onto a logging road, cross a bridge over the river, and turn right. Set altimeter at 1320 ft. Follow the road and take the right fork at 0.9 mi. (1380 ft.). Cross the stream and take an immediate left (formerly gated). At 2.2 mi. (1440 ft.), keep left at the intersection. Continue straight where the road turns left toward a sandpit (2.5 mi., 1620 ft.). Take a left at a triangle intersection (2.9 mi., 1900 ft.). Pass through a log yard at 3.5 mi. (2100 ft.). Ignore two left-branching roads at 3.8 mi. (2200 ft.) and 4.2 mi. (2500 ft.). Beyond this, the road is deteriorated and brushy; it has dips for water control. Cross a stream at 2640 ft. and enter another log-yard clearing at 2700 ft. The road then climbs abruptly for a short distance. Go left at a fork and continue on an overgrown path. At a left-curling turn, come to a stream crossing, which may be dry (2980 ft.). There are two popular bushwhack routes. One starts just left of the stream, the other about 30 yd. beyond it. On a 340-degree heading, the brushy terrain gives way to open forest. Continue the bushwhack into the middle of the col between peaks (3600 ft.). Turn left to 230 degrees and climb through some scrub, then open woods, about 0.5 mi. to the flat summit and register.

Suggestion: Return by reversing your route; the southeastern slopes of this peak are steep and ringed with thick spruce.

East Kennebago Mountain

Distance from gate

   to East Kennebago summit: *est.* 5 mi. (8.1 km.), 3 hr. 45 min.

SNOW MOUNTAIN (3960 ft./1207 m.)

Snow Mtn. is southwest of the Chain of Ponds. There is an abandoned MFS firetower on the summit. The mountain offers extensive views in all directions, including an extended sweep into Canada over Lake Megantic. From the summit, you can see many miles of Benedict Arnold's route to Quebec in 1775, which followed the headwaters of the Dead River past the Chain of Ponds and into Quebec Province. Refer to the USGS Chain Lakes quadrangle, 15-min. series, and the Chain of Ponds and Jim Pond quadrangles, 7.5-min. series.

The approach is via a dirt road leading left (west) from ME 27, 0.3 mi. north of the Alder Stream/Jim Pond town line and 7.5 mi. north of Eustis. The road is gated and sometimes locked near ME 27. At 0.3 mi., pass a road on the left to Round Pond. Cross and recross a stream. At 2.1 mi., turn left at a yarding area and cross a stream. At 3.6 mi., turn sharply left and cross a brook. At 4 mi., the road to the left leads to Snow Mtn. Pond. The former firewarden's cabin there is now private property. Turn right to the firewarden's trail (sign) and climb steeply north, passing a *spring*. At 5.2 mi., the trail from Big

Island Pond comes in on the left. Turn right and climb northeast to the summit.

Descending, don't miss the point where the firewarden's trail turns left and the trail from Big Island Pond goes right.

Snow Mountain
Distances from ME 27

   to   Snow Mtn. Pond: 5 mi., 2 hr. 30 min.

   to   Snow summit: 5.4 mi. (8.7 km.), 3 hr. 10 min.

KIBBY MOUNTAIN (3654 ft./1114 m.)

This remote mountain is in the heart of the wilderness area north of Flagstaff Lake, east of the Chain of Ponds, and south of the Canadian Atlantic Railroad, which runs through Lac-Megantic in Quebec and Jackman. The Kibby Mtn. Trail was restored in 1989, and is periodically maintained. Refer to the USGS Kibby Mtn. quadrangle, 7.5-min. series, and the DeLorme *Maine Atlas and Gazetteer* maps 28, 29, 38, and 39.

   From the junction with ME 16 in Stratton, drive northwest on ME 27 for 17 mi. (3.1 mi. northwest from the Snow Mtn. Rd. entrance). Turn right onto the wide dirt Beaudry Rd., which runs parallel to Gold Brook. Drive 9.2 mi. to an abandoned road on the right. Look for a small cairn or possible marking by the rock ledge to the left of the entrance. Park here. This former jeep trail ascends about 2 mi. at an easy grade via two long switchbacks on grassy terrain—delightful hiking and superb winter skiing. The upper 0.5-mi. section to the summit is a steeper footpath. There is an old MFS firetower stand with outstanding, extensive views of the surrounding wilderness.

Kibby Mountain
Distance from parking area

   to   Kibby summit: *est.* 2.5 mi. (4 km.), 1 hr. 30 min.

EUSTIS RIDGE (1623 ft./495 m.)

Eustis Ridge is a fine outlook over Flagstaff Lake, the Bigelow Range, and other peaks to the south. It is right on the road, and there is a state picnic area. Refer to the USGS Stratton and Kennebago Lake quadrangles, 15-min. series, and Tim Mtn. quadrangle, 7.5-min. series, if you want to supplement the map in this guide.

From Stratton, drive north on ME 27 to Cathedral Pines. About 3.5 mi. from Stratton, turn left onto a paved road (signs) and drive west 2 mi. to the picnic area.

SADDLEBACK MOUNTAIN AND THE HORN
(summit 4116 ft./1255 m. and The Horn 4023 ft./1226 m.)

Saddleback Mtn., southeast of Rangeley, is one of Maine's outstanding mountains. It is a long range extending east–west. Pronounced saddles separate its several peaks. Two of the peaks are over 4000 ft.—the Saddleback summit and The Horn. The bare summits of both offer far-flung views in all directions. Saddleback, with its widespread areas above treeline, is also unusually exposed. *Caution:* High winds and restricted visibility can be dangerous. You can refer to the USGS Phillips and Rangeley quadrangles, 15-min. series, and the Redington and Saddleback Mtn. quadrangles, 7.5-min. series, as well as to the map in this guide or map 6 in the MATC's *Appalachian Trail Guide to Maine.*

There are several points of interest on the southwestern side of the mountain. Piazza Rock is an enormous overhanging flat boulder with a growth of mature trees; nearby, the Caves offer ample opportunities for exploration. Both are on the Appalachian Trail, 1.4 mi. north of ME 4. Eddy Pond, one of several small ponds on Saddleback, is particularly attractive.

The Saddleback Mountain Ski Area is on the northwestern slope of the mountain.

Appalachian Trail (AT)

To approach Saddleback from the west, follow ME 4 for 32 mi. north from the ME 4 and US 2 junction in Farmington or for 9.9 mi. south from the ME 4 and ME 16 junction in Rangeley. The AT crosses ME 4 in a steep, winding section of the road. Use the parking lot on the western side of the highway.

From ME 4, the AT descends and crosses the Sandy River at 0.1 mi. The trail climbs out of the valley, crossing a gravel logging road at 1.1 mi. At 1.4 mi., the trail passes the Piazza Rock Lean-to (built in 1935 by the Civilian Conservation Corps; reconditioned by the MATC; accommodates six; MFS campsite). A side trail leads left 167 yd. to the top of Piazza Rock. Not far beyond, on the AT, a side path leads left 100 yd. to the Caves, a series of boulder caves with narrow passages. The AT then climbs steeply, passes along Ethel Pond's western shore, and turns sharply left, away from the end of the pond. The trail then continues to rise, passes Mud Pond, and descends slightly to Eddy Pond (*last sure water*). Watch for a point near the eastern shore of Eddy Pond about 3.2 mi. from ME 4 where the trail, after turning left onto a road for a few feet, turns sharply right from the road onto a trail. It rises steeply through conifers, emerging in 0.8 mi. on a scrub-covered slope.

This open crest is particularly interesting, but the cairns are small, the path is not well worn, and the trail is fully exposed. It should not be traveled in bad weather. After nearly 0.8 mi. over rocky slopes and heath, the trail descends slightly into a sag, where a blue-blazed side path (may be hard to see) leads right (south) about 0.1 mi. through scrub to a *spring* (not dependable). The main trail climbs 0.1 mi. farther to the summit.

The AT continues over open slopes, descends steeply into the col between Saddleback and The Horn, and reaches the summit of The Horn 1.6 mi. from the main summit.

For the continuation of the AT beyond The Horn, see the 1997 edition of the MATC's *Appalachian Trail Guide to Maine.*

Appalachian Trail, Saddleback Mountain

Distances from ME 4

- *to* junction with logging road: 1.1 mi.
- *to* Piazza Rock Lean-to: 1.4 mi.
- *to* Piazza Rock (via side trail): 1.5 mi.
- *to* Saddleback summit: 5.1 mi., 3 hr. 45 min.
- *to* The Horn summit: 6.7 mi. (10.8 km.), 4 hr. 15 min.

MOUNT ABRAHAM (4049 ft./1234 m.)

Mt. Abraham (or Abram) lies northwest of Kingfield and south of Sugarloaf Mtn. and Spaulding Mtn. It is an impressive ridge about 4.5 mi. long that runs on a northwest–southeast axis and consists of about eight peaks ranging from 3400 to more than 4000 ft. The highest peak, with an abandoned MFS firetower, lies north of the middle of the ridge. The extensive areas above timberline on Abraham give it an unusually alpine appearance for its height. Although the trailless ridge south of the tower has been traversed, that route is not advisable, since the distances are deceptive and the scrub is very dense between peaks. *Caution:* The mountain's openness makes sudden electrical storms unusually dangerous. Watch your weather!

Two trails ascend to the abandoned firetower. The Fire Warden's Trail approaches the mountain from Kingfield. The Mt. Abraham Side Trail, cut in 1987, approaches from the Appalachian Trail north of Mt. Abraham and west of Spaulding Mtn. Refer to the USGS Kingfield and Phillips quadrangles, 15-min. series, and Mt. Abraham quadrangle, 7.5-min. series, or map 6 in the MATC's *Appalachian Trail Guide to Maine,* if you want to supplement the map in this guide.

Fire Warden's Trail

To reach the trail, follow ME 27 north from Kingfield. Turn left (west) onto the paved road (West Kingfield St.) at the Jordan's Lumber Company store, 0.2 mi. north of the bridge over the Carrabassett River. At 3 mi. from ME 27, the road becomes gravel. Go straight through a crossroads at 3.5 mi. to 3.7 mi., where the road forks. From this point, the road is partially private. At 6 mi., a road turns left to a new bridge over Rapid Stream. Cross the stream and follow the road for about 0.5 mi. to the trailhead at a crossroads. The trail begins straight into the woods.

The trail follows the southern bank of Norton Brook, crosses the brook, and continues along the northern bank, gradually climbing. In another 0.3 mi., it turns northwest and then crosses another logging road. To reach this point by car, turn right at the trailhead and bear left. The next 2 mi. of the trail, to the abandoned warden's cabin, skirt the northeastern flank of the mountain, crossing four major brooks. Grades are easy. There is a good *spring* to the right of the cabin.

From the old cabin (2127 ft.), the trail turns left straight up the slope and climbs steeply through the woods for a mile, then comes out on an old slide with good views. At about 0.1 mi. above the cabin, a side trail leads left to a brook *(last sure water)*. The remainder of the trail is completely exposed, except for a few short stretches of scrub. In this section, an abandoned telephone line and the few cairns should be followed carefully in bad weather. The trail rises steadily across a boulder field to the firetower.

Fire Warden's Trail
Distances from Rapid Stream

   to crossroads near Norton Brook: 0.5 mi.

   to firewarden's cabin: 3 mi.

   to Abraham summit: 4.5 mi. (7.2 km.), 3 hr. 45 min.

Mount Abraham Side Trail

For the approach to this trail, see the description of the Appalachian Trail route to Spaulding Mtn. in this guide.

From the junction of the Appalachian Trail and the blue-blazed side trail to the Spaulding Mtn. summit, continue south on the Appalachian Trail, descending the cone of Spaulding Mtn. to the site of the Spaulding Mtn. Lean-to, with two tentsites, a *spring*, and a privy. A temporary side trail marked by orange tape leads 0.6 mi. north to the old Spaulding Mtn. Lean-to, which is still functional.

Continue south on the Appalachian Trail to the junction of the Mt. Abraham Side Trail. The Appalachian Trail continues southwest, climbing Lone Mtn. Refer to map 6 in the 1992 edition of the MATC's *Appalachian Trail Guide to Maine*. The Mt. Abraham Side Trail leads 1.7 mi. southeast following a very old tote road, climbing gradually then steeply up the southern ridge of Mt. Abraham, which is characterized by very dense forest. The trail emerges from the trees and ascends a rock field to the tower.

Mount Abraham Side Trail
Distances from Caribou Valley Rd.

- *to* junction of Appalachian Trail and Spaulding summit trail: 3.9 mi.

- *to* site of new Spaulding Mtn. Lean-to: *est.* 4.5 mi.

- *to* junction of Appalachian Trail and Mt. Abraham Side Trail: *est.* 4.9 mi.

- *to* Abraham summit: 6.6 mi. (10.6 km.), 5 hr. 25 min.

CROCKER MOUNTAIN (northern peak 4168 ft./ 1270 m. and southern peak 4000 ft./1219 m.)

The northern extension of the Crocker–Redington Pond Range, these mountains are 3.5 mi. west of Sugarloaf Mtn. and separated from it by Caribou Valley (South Branch of the Carrabassett). The summit of Crocker, despite its height, has few views and is heavily wooded to the top. South Crocker Mtn., 1 mi. to the south, has a definite summit with fine views and rises 380 ft. above the col between it and Crocker Mtn. Hikers can approach the mountain via the Appalachian Trail from ME

27 or Caribou Valley Rd., which in early 1998 was poorly maintained and later had work done to make it passable. Drive it with caution.

Approach via ME 27

For the approach from the north and ME 27, follow the highway 2.6 mi. northwest from the Sugarloaf access road. Park off the highway at this point (sign reading Appalachian Trail Crossing). Leaving the southern side of the highway, the Appalachian Trail climbs steadily through woods for nearly 1.5 mi. before reaching the northernmost knoll of Crocker. A spruce section begins at about 1 mi. and continues to about 2 mi., where the trail slabs the western side of the ridge through birches. It continues up the western side of the ridge, reenters conifers at about 3.5 mi., and passes a small stream (usually reliable— *last water*). After that, the trail rises more steeply to the crest and reaches the summit of Crocker at 5.2 mi. The descent into the col begins immediately. The trail leads to the low point of the col and soon begins to climb toward the rocky summit of South Crocker. To reach the summit, take the 50 yd., blue-blazed path (sign) to the right (west), where the Appalachian Trail makes a sharp left turn for the descent to Caribou Valley.

Crocker and South Crocker via Appalachian Trail
Distances from ME 27

- *to* Crocker, northern ridge: 1.5 mi.
- *to* stream in conifers: *est.* 3.5 mi.
- *to* Crocker summit: 5.2 mi., 4 hr.
- *to* South Crocker summit (via blue-blazed summit trail): 6.2 mi., 4 hr. 30 min.
- *to* Caribou Valley Rd.: 8.3 mi. (13.4 km.), 5 hr. 30 min.

Approach via Caribou Valley Road

This road leads south from ME 27, 1 mi. northwest of the entrance to Sugarloaf. The Appalachian Trail crosses the road 4.5 mi. south of ME 27; 50 yd. beyond this crossing, an old metal gate is usually open.

The Appalachian Trail leaves the road to the right (west) and climbs steadily but not too steeply through birch woods. Nearly a mile from the road, a blue-blazed trail leads right 0.2 mi. to the Crocker Cirque Campsite (built by the MATC in 1975; it has a two-tent platform, fireplace, and latrine). On the side trail to this campsite is the *last sure water.* Beyond the turnoff to the campsite, the Appalachian Trail begins the steep climb to the shoulder of South Crocker. The trail leads up the shoulder through woods for the next mile to the crest of South Crocker. Then it turns sharply right, and at the same point, the 50-yd. side trail (sign) to the actual summit of South Crocker leaves to the left. The Appalachian Trail then descends into the col, from which it climbs steadily to the summit of North Crocker.

South Crocker and North Crocker via Caribou Valley Road
Distances from Caribou Valley Rd.

   to side trail to campsite: 0.9 mi., 35 min.

   to South Crocker summit: 2.1 mi., 2 hr.

   to Crocker summit: 3.1 mi., 2 hr. 45 min.

   to ME 27: 8 mi. (12.9 km.), 5 hr.

SUGARLOAF MOUNTAIN (4237 ft./1291 m.) **and** SPAULDING MOUNTAIN (3988 ft./1216 m.)

Sugarloaf Mountain

Sugarloaf Mtn. is the second-highest mountain in Maine. Many other peaks are more popular with hikers, however; Sugarloaf is known and frequented chiefly for skiing. The ski area is on the northern slope, and since it is in one of the heaviest snowbelts in the northeastern

United States, spring skiing is frequently good after other areas farther to the south have closed for the season. For the hiker, the view from the symmetrical, bare cone is well worth the climb of almost 2500 ft. The number of peaks visible is perhaps unequaled in the state, except from Katahdin. Spaulding Mtn. is about 2.5 mi. to the south of Sugarloaf and is connected with it by a high ridge.

A rough road (not good enough for cars but easy to follow on foot in bad weather) has been built to the summit. It starts behind the maintenance-vehicle storage building at the base, near the ski-area parking lot, and climbs at first west, then south, and finally east to the summit. This road, or the network of ski trails on the mountain, provides an approach from the north. The road is about 4 mi. long; the ski trails are shorter but steeper.

For ski-trail route, drive in toward the ski area off ME 27. Take a right at the fork. Stay left at sign reading Country Club Condos. Go to the very top of the big loop, and take the dead-end road right at the highest point. Park at 75 yd. A summer mountain-bike trail leads to the woods and ski slope. Stay right and pass Bullwinkles, then follow power lines to a building (weather shelter) and the summit.

You can also approach Sugarloaf from the south. The Appalachian Trail leaves Caribou Valley Rd. 4.5 mi. south of ME 27. After leaving the road to the east, the trail soon crosses the South Branch of the Carrabassett (dangerous in high water), follows up the stream for a time, and then begins to climb, at first gently and then more steeply. After that, it crosses ledges and skirts the top of a cirque on the western side of Sugarloaf. The *last water* is a stream 1.8 mi. from the road. At 1.9 mi., the Appalachian Trail turns right toward Spaulding Mtn., while the blue-blazed Sugarloaf Side Trail leaves to the left and reaches the summit in 0.6 mi.

Sugarloaf Side Trail

Distances from Caribou Valley Rd.

   to Sugarloaf Side Trail junction (via Appalachian Trail): 1.9 mi., 1 hr. 45 min.

to Sugarloaf summit: 2.5 mi. (4 km.), 2 hr. 15 min.

Spaulding Mountain

From its junction with the Sugarloaf Side Trail, the Appalachian Trail (south) traverses the crest of the ridge between Sugarloaf and Spaulding, with views and steep cliffs on the left. At 1.5 mi., the trail begins the ascent of Spaulding, first steeply, then gradually. Near the top, a blue-blazed trail leads left 167 yd. to the summit.

For a description of the Appalachian Trail south of Spaulding, see the Mt. Abraham Side Trail description in this guide or the 1997 edition of the MATC's *Appalachian Trail Guide to Maine.*

Spaulding Mountain

Distance from Caribou Valley Rd.

to Spaulding summit (via Appalachian Trail): 4 mi. (6.4 km.), 3 hr. 25 min.

BIGELOW RANGE

LITTLE BIGELOW (3040 ft./927 m.)
AVERY PEAK (4088 ft./1246 m.)
WEST PEAK (4150 ft./1265 m.)
SOUTH HORN (3831 ft./1168 m.)
NORTH HORN (3810 ft./1161 m.)
CRANBERRY PEAK (3213 ft./979 m.)

The Bigelow Range runs east–west for some 12 mi. It is second only to the Katahdin region in interest and opportunities for superb ridge walking. The central features are the twin "cones," Avery Peak and West Peak, which project above the ridge. The equally symmetrical twin "horns," farther west and only slightly lower, are North Horn and South Horn. Still farther west is Cranberry Peak, with its bare ledges.

To the east of Avery Peak, but separated from it by a deep notch, lies Little Bigelow Mtn.

The Bigelow Mtn. Preserve, established by the people of Maine in a June 1976 referendum, includes the Bigelow Range and the land surrounding it. The 33,000-acre preserve is administered by the Maine Bureau of Parks and Lands.

Backpackers can find campsites at Cranberry Stream, and Moose Falls (both stoves only; no fires) and Safford Notch, with Horns Pond Lean-to and Avery Memorial Lean-to (both stoves only; no fires), and Little Bigelow Lean-to. Prior to the New England hurricane of 1938, the western portion of the range was an almost unbroken, uncut softwood forest. That and subsequent storms greatly damaged the forest, and only small uncut sections remain. Water is scarce in some areas of this range.

From Avery Peak, there is a magnificent outlook over the rugged wilderness of peaks, ponds, streams, and extensive Flagstaff Lake— perhaps the best view in the state, except for the one from Katahdin.

Flagstaff Lake, a man-made reservoir (Maine's fourth-largest body of water), lies just north of the Bigelow Range. Like the range, the lake stretches east–west.

West of the Horns lies Horns Pond, a beautiful mountain tarn. Cranberry Pond, Arnolds Well, and other landmarks are farther west.

In addition to the map in this guide, you can refer to the USGS Stratton and Little Bigelow quadrangles, 15-min. series; the Little Bigelow Mtn. and Horns quadrangles, 7.5-min. series; or map 5 in the MATC's *Appalachian Trail Guide to Maine.*

The Fire Warden's Trail is the shortest approach to the main peaks of the Bigelow Range, but the Horns Pond Trail is less steep and more interesting. It leads to the Horns Pond, where it joins the Appalachian Trail (AT) to follow the ridge between the Horns, over South Horn and West Peak, and on to Avery Peak. As a third approach to the west of the first two trails, the AT runs from ME 27 to the ridge west of Horns Pond. These trails approach from the south (ME 16/27). A fourth and longer approach, the Bigelow Range Trail from Stratton east to the AT, east of Cranberry Pond, involves more ridge travel up and down the many peaks of the range. It extends the range's full length, from the western end to Avery Peak. A road runs along the southern shore of Flagstaff Lake from Long Falls Dam Rd. toward Stratton. It offers a fifth approach to the highest peaks via the Safford Brook Trail.

Fire Warden's Trail

A rough dirt road, Stratton Brook Rd. (usually passable) runs east from ME 27 about 3.2 mi. northwest of the Sugarloaf ski area access road and 4.5 mi. southeast of Stratton. Drive in, cross the AT at 1 mi., and continue straight ahead, turning left at 1.6 mi. into a limited parking area. The road beyond is very rough. The bridge over Stratton Brook is washed out. Cross Stratton Brook and continue on the road. At 0.2 mi., reach a fork and go left. (The right fork descends to a partially destroyed bridge.) From this point, the trail leads north for 0.2 mi., then runs east on the level for about 0.5 mi. After that, it climbs steeply over ledges to a shelf. The grade is easy for the next 1.5 mi., during which the trail crosses several brooks. At 1.6 mi. from the parking area, the Horns Pond Trail leaves left (northwest). At 3.1 mi. from Stratton Brook, the trail runs under the West Peak of Bigelow, and its grade becomes increasingly steep. The trail gains nearly 1700 ft. in the next 1.5 mi. as it climbs north-northeast to Bigelow Col, where it meets the AT at 4.6 mi. The caretaker uses the old firewarden's cabin, which is kept locked.

From the col, go right (east) via the AT 0.4 mi. to reach Avery Peak and its abandoned firetower. To reach West Peak from the col, go left (west) on the AT about 0.4 mi.

Descending, the trail diverges from the AT in Bigelow Col and goes down to the southwest.

Fire Warden's Trail
Distances from parking area

   to Horns Pond Trail junction: 1.6 mi., 1 hr. 10 min.

   to Bigelow Col and AT junction: 4.6 mi., 4 hr. 50 min.

   to Avery Peak summit: 5 mi., 4 hr.

to West Peak summit: 4.9 mi., 4 hr.

Horns Pond Trail

This trail starts at the same point as the Fire Warden's Trail (see above). The Horns Pond Trail diverges left (northwest) from the Fire Warden's Trail 1.6 mi. from Stratton Brook. The Horns Pond Trail heads northwest, climbing gradually. At 3 mi., the trail skirts the southern edge of a former bog area with an excellent view of the South Horn. The trail continues to rise gradually, then gets steeper. At 4.1 mi., the Horns Pond Trail intersects the white-blazed AT. Bear right on the AT for 0.2 mi. to the two Horns Pond lean-tos (caretaker; accommodate six each; MFS campsite). A 50-yd., blue-blazed trail behind the eastern lean-to leads to Horns Pond.

Horns Pond Trail

Distances from Stratton Brook

   to start (via Fire Warden's Trail): 1.6 mi., 1 hr. 10 min.

   to AT: 4.1 mi.

   to Horns Pond lean-tos: 4.3 mi. (6.9 km.), 3 hr.

Appalachian Trail from the South

This trail (partly maintained by the Maine Chapter of the AMC) leaves ME 27 2.6 mi. northwest of the Sugarloaf Mtn. access road. In the first mile, the trail descends slowly and crosses Stratton Brook Rd. at 0.9 mi. (This road and the so-called Jones Pond Rd., soon after it, form alternative starting points for the hike.) After Jones Pond Rd., the trail descends immediately to cross Stratton Brook on a footbridge. In the next mile, the trail passes through spruce woods and then joins an old tote road. Turn left on the tote road, which soon crosses a stream. At 1.9 mi., turn right off the road and cross a tote road 2.5 mi. from ME 27. The trail passes an abandoned beaver pond and then climbs gradually but steadily as it approaches the basin of Cranberry Pond, where it passes a spring (*last sure water* before Horns Pond).

At 3.4 mi., the AT turns sharply right (north). The Bigelow Range Trail (sign) continues straight ahead (west). The AT climbs steeply through a boulder field. At 4 mi., it reaches the crest of the ridge. There, it turns right (east) and follows the ridge, crossing a minor summit. At 5 mi., where the trail takes a sharp left, there is a lookout 17 yd. to the right over Horns Pond to the Horns. The trail descends steeply. At 5.1 mi., the Horns Pond Trail comes in on the right. The AT continues along the southern shore of Horns Pond, passing the two Horns Pond lean-tos at 5.3 mi.

From Horns Pond, the AT continues east, climbing South Horn. At 5.8 mi., the blue-blazed North Horn Trail leads 0.2 mi. left to the North Horn. A little farther on, the AT crosses the South Horn. Then it continues along the crest of the Bigelow Range, reaching West Peak at 8 mi. The trail then descends to the Avery Memorial Lean-to at 8.4 mi.; the Fire Warden's Trail comes in on the right directly in front of the lean-to. The AT continues east, climbing to the summit of Avery Peak at 8.8 mi.

From Avery Peak, the AT descends east to its junction with the Safford Brook Trail. For a description of the AT east of the Safford Brook Trail, see the 1997 edition (map 5) of the MATC's *Appalachian Trail Guide to Maine.*

Appalachian Trail from the South

Distances from ME 27

to Stratton Brook Rd.: 0.9 mi.

to Stratton Brook: 1 mi.

to Bigelow Range Trail junction: 3.4 mi.

to Horns Pond Trail junction: 5.1 mi.

to Horns Pond lean-tos: 5.3 mi. (8.5 km.), 3 hr. 40 min.

to South Horn summit: 5.9 mi.

to West Peak summit: 8 mi.

to Avery Lean-to and Fire Warden's Trail junction: 8.4 mi., 5 hr. 55 min.

to Avery Peak: 8.8 mi. (14.2 km.), 6 hr. 15 min.

Bigelow Range Trail

This blue-blazed trail starts at the western end of the range, on ME 27/16, 0.5 mi. southeast of Stratton and about 100 yd. northwest of the Eustis/Coplin town line. From the highway, follow a dirt road east. At 0.5 mi. from ME 27/16, the road ends at a clearing. The trail passes through woods for 0.3 mi. Then it climbs gradually about 0.2 mi. on a wide logging road. The trail reaches the first barren ledges at 1.9 mi. and bears right. Arnolds Well (a deep cleft in the rocks; *no drinking water*) is 7 yd. to the right. The trail turns up the ledges. There is a good view from the top of the first ledges. The trail leads through scrub and logged areas along the northern edge of the ridge with fine views. After reaching open ledges, it makes a short, steep ascent to Cranberry Peak at 3.2 mi.

After a short, steep descent, the trail descends more gradually. Then it follows the northern shore of Cranberry Pond, to end at a junction with the AT at 4.9 mi.

Bigelow Range Trail
Distances from ME 27

to clearing: 0.5 mi.

to first ledges: 1.9 mi.

to Cranberry Peak: 3.2 mi., 2 hr. 40 min.

to AT junction: 4.9 mi. (7.9 km.), 3 hr. 50 min.

Bigelow Range from the North (Safford Brook Trail and Appalachian Trail)

This trail begins at Round Barn Field on the shore of Flagstaff Lake, crosses East Flagstaff Rd., and climbs to the AT at Safford Notch.

The trail can be approached by water or by road. Round Barn Field is located on the easternside of a cove on the southern shore of

Flagstaff Lake; this cove can be identified from the lake by a large sawdust pile on the lakeshore. To reach the trail by road, turn north off ME 16 onto the blacktop Long Falls Dam Rd. in North New Portland. At 16.7 mi., turn left (northwest) onto Bog Brook Rd. (gravel). At about 0.8 mi., East Flagstaff Rd. leads left (north and west); it crosses Safford Brook at 4 mi. and the trail at 4.5 mi.

From Round Barn Field, the trail passes through the woods and crosses East Flagstaff Rd. at 0.3 mi. The trail follows a graded tote road, then climbs steeply, crosses Safford Brook, and enters Safford Notch. At 2.6 mi., you will reach a junction with the AT.

Fifty yd. east (left) on the AT is a blue-blazed trail that leads south (right) 0.2 mi. to the Safford Notch Campsite, with two tent platforms and a privy. (The AT east reaches the highest peak of Little Bigelow at 3.7 mi.) The AT west rises steeply toward Avery Peak for a mile, with several excellent vistas. At 3.4 mi., it reaches the crest of the ridge. There, a side trail leads left 167 yd. to the top of Old Man's Head (a cliff on the side of the mountain). The trail continues to climb steeply, reaching the timberline and, shortly thereafter, the abandoned tower on Avery Peak.

Safford Brook Trail and Appalachian Trail
Distances from Round Barn Field

- *to* East Flagstaff Rd.: 0.3 mi.
- *to* AT junction (via Safford Brook Trail): 2.6 mi.
- *to* Little Bigelow summit (via AT east): 6.3 mi., 4 hr.
- *to* Avery Peak (via AT west): 4.5 mi. (7.2 km.), 3 hr. 45 min.

LITTLE BIGELOW MOUNTAIN (3040 ft./927 m.)

Little Bigelow lies to the east of the main Bigelow Range, separated from it by a deep notch, known as Safford Notch. It is a long, narrow ridge, with steep cliffs along its southern side. The northern slope descends steadily for some 2 mi. to Flagstaff Lake. The natural structure of the mountain makes extremely rough terrain. The trail is part of the Appalachian Trail and therefore marked with white paint blazes. Refer to the USGS Little Bigelow Mtn. quadrangle, 15-min. series and 7.5-min. series, or map 5 in the MATC's *Appalachian Trail Guide to Maine,* if you want to supplement the map in this guide.

The approaches are via the AT. See the Safford Brook description above for Avery Peak for the approach from the west. To approach from the east, follow Long Falls Dam Rd. north from North New Portland. At 16.7 mi., the former route of ME 16, Bog Brook Rd. (flooded out by Flagstaff Lake), diverges left. Follow this well-graded road for 0.8 mi. Turn left onto East Flagstaff Rd., which crosses the Appalachian Trail in 0.1 mi. The Appalachian Trail leads through hardwoods and follows a brook. At 1.2 mi., a blue-blazed side trail leads right 0.1 mi. across the brook to the Little Bigelow Lean-to. The trail continues through the woods, leaving the brook, and climbs on a series of open ledges that comprise the northeastern buttress of the mountain. At 3 mi., it reaches a viewpoint at the southeastern end of the summit ridge. The true summit is about 0.5 mi. farther northwest along the trail.

Little Bigelow Mountain

Distances from East Flagstaff Rd. (via Appalachian Trail)

   to Little Bigelow Lean-to: 1.3 mi.

   to Little Bigelow summit: 3.5 mi., 2 hr. 45 min.

   to Avery Peak: 7.5 mi. (12.1 km.), 6 hr.

Section 11

Kennebec Valley

This section includes several mountains on the lower and middle sections of the Kennebec River, and other mountains accessible from US 201 and roads running off this highway. There are MFS firetowers on several of these summits. US 201 generally follows the Kennebec River as far as The Forks. It then runs through mountainous country past Parlin Pond to Jackman and on to the Quebec border. ME 15 diverges east from US 201 at Jackman and follows down the Moose River Valley to reach Moosehead Lake at Rockwood.

The highest mountain in this section is Coburn Mtn. (3718 ft.). Boundary Bald Mtn. is 3640 ft., but the majority of the rest are much lower. Most of the mountains described in this section are in Somerset County; two are in Kennebec County.

MOUNT PISGAH (809 ft./246 m.)

On the summit of Mt. Pisgah in Winthrop are a MFS firetower and a relay tower, both with microwave dishes, and a log-cabin equipment building. Refer to the USGS Wayne quadrangle, 7.5-min. series.

From the intersection of US 202 and ME 41 in Winthrop, go 3 mi. west on US 202. Turn right (northwest) at Knights of Columbus (formerly St. Stanislas Catholic Church) on the road to North Monmouth. Continue past the Tex Tech Industries factory on the left. At 0.7 mi., the road reaches the crossroads in North Monmouth. (A dam and a bridge over a stream are on the left.) Turn right onto New Rd. and go 0.2 mi. to the point where it becomes Pisgah Rd. Continue for 2 mi. to the warden's cabin on the right. The trail (sign reading Trail to Fire

Tower) follows the line of the driveway, crosses the yard to the rear of the cabin, and immediately crosses a brook (dry in dry weather). After a 0.3-mi. climb following telephone wires, the trail bears left, levels out at a stone wall, and joins a snowmobile road coming in from the right (sign). From this junction, the trail gently rises over a distance of about 0.7 mi., at times following the telephone wires or a jeep road, which also runs from the warden's cabin to the tower. The trail's last 33 yd. traverse open ledges to the summit, where views open up to the west. From the firetower platforms, views in all directions take in the entire sweep of western Maine's mountains, from Pleasant Mtn. to Sugarloaf, as well as the Presidentials in New Hampshire. Views of surrounding lakes add sparkle to the scene.

Mount Pisgah

Distance from warden's cabin

   to Pisgah summit: 1 mi. (1.6 km.), 45 min.

MONUMENT HILL (660 ft./201 m.)

Monument Hill in Leeds is just west of Androscoggin Lake and offers good views to the south and southwest from its summit, though in other directions views are largely obscured by trees. On the summit is a granite monument to Leeds soldiers and sailors of the Civil War. Refer to the USGS Turner Center quadrangle, 7.5-min. series.

To reach the trail from US 202 between Lewiston and Augusta, take ME 106 north for 8.2 mi. to Leeds. Take Church Hill Rd. left for 1 mi. to North Rd. on the right. The trailhead is at 0.9 mi. (sign), and the well-worn trail is marked by faded and sporadic blue blazes. It leads east and southeast through varied forest and berry patches to the rocky summit.

Monument Hill

Distance from North Rd.

   to Monument summit: 1 mi. (1.6 km.), 30 min.

COOK HILL (472 ft./143 m.)

Cook Hill, in Vassalboro, is topped by a 60-ft. MFS firetower with a 360-degree view, and microwave facilities. Refer to the USGS Vassalboro quadrangle, 15-min. and 7.5-min. series.

From US 201/ME 100 in Vassalboro, take the road northeast at Coburn–Oak Grove School and drive 2 mi. to an unsurfaced service road on the left (northwest) with a double overhead wire. From ME 32 in North Vassalboro, take the same road southwest at the brick factory building and drive 1.2 mi. to the same side road on the right (northwest). For a pleasant walk, or in wet weather, leave the car on the main road. Walk 1 mi., avoiding left turns, to the summit, where, (besides the towers), you will find a picnic grove with a table and fireplace.

Cook Hill

Distance from main road

   to Cook summit: 1 mi. (1.6 km.), 30 min.

CHASE HILL (774 ft./235 m.)

This summit in Canaan offers a 360-degree view from the firetower on its summit. Refer to the USGS Skowhegan quadrangle, 15-min. series, or the Canaan quadrangle, 7.5-min. series.

From the junction of US 2 and ME 23 east of Canaan Village, drive 4 mi. northeast on ME 23 to a town road (gravel) on the left (west). From the junction of ME 151 and ME 23 in Hartland, drive 6 mi. southwest on ME 23 to the same road on the right. After turning onto the town road, drive 0.3 mi. to a fork. Follow the right fork (a small cemetery is just past the junction) for 0.9 mi. to a house on the right, with a jeep road on the left. Park by the jeep road and walk past the warden's cabin and an excellent picnic area with a fireplace and a table (*spring* nearby). It is 0.2 mi. to the tower rising above the trees on the wooded summit.

Chase Hill

Distance from parking lot

   to Chase summit: 0.2 mi. (0.3 km.), 10 min.

KELLY MOUNTAIN (1675 ft./511 m.)

This mountain is in Brighton Plantation, east of Bingham. There is an abandoned MFS firetower on its summit. The present approach is from the northeast. Refer to the USGS Kingsbury quadrangle, 7.5-min. series.

Since use of the firetower ceased, the trail has become overgrown; check with the MFS firewarden supervisor in Caratunk before you drive to the mountain. To reach the trail, take a woods road leading west from ME 151, 2.7 mi. north of Brighton and 1.6 mi. south of the ME 151 and ME16 junction (Mayfield Corner). Park off the highway at the locked gate at the start of the road. Follow the road around the northern end of Smith Pond to the start of the trail. The warden's cabin is 0.1 mi. farther and straight ahead *(water)*.

The trail goes right, following the telephone line. It climbs gradually through open woods for about 1 mi. and then more steeply for 0.5 mi. to the summit.

Kelly Mountain

Distances from ME 151

   to start of trail (via woods road): 2 mi., 1 hr.

   to Kelly summit: *est.* 3.6 mi. (5.8 km.), 2 hr.

MOXIE BALD MOUNTAIN (2630 ft./802 m.)

This mountain, located in Bald Mtn. Township northeast of Bingham, is a long ridge running north–south for about 4 mi. Although the summit is not very high, it has many features of above-timberline summits because of its extended ledges and open crest. The trailless North Peak, easy to reach from the Appalachian Trail, is worth exploring.

Refer to the USGS The Forks and Bingham quadrangles, 15-min. series; the Bald Mtn. Pond and Moxie Pond quadrangles, 7.5-min. series; or map 4 in the MATC's *Appalachian Trail Guide to Maine*.

The views from the summit are excellent. Katahdin is to the northeast, beyond many other peaks in Piscataquis County; Bigelow, Sugarloaf, and Abraham are to the west; and Coburn and Boundary Bald are to the north.

The approach is via the Appalachian Trail, which leaves from a point on a paper-company road just south of Joe's Hole, the southernmost point on Moxie Pond. To reach the trailhead from the south, turn off US 201 in Bingham onto ME 16 and follow it for 0.8 mi. Turn north onto a gravel paper-company road. Two roads join the highway at this point; take the right, which follows Austin Stream for much of its length. At the stop sign, 1.7 mi. from the highway, proceed straight; at 9.9 mi., join the power line for a short distance; and at 10.3 mi., where the road forks, take the left fork. At 14.8 mi., you will see the Appalachian Trail sign on the right. There is little room to park here, although there are some places farther up the road. Be careful not to block camp driveways. (The Appalachian Trail approach to Pleasant Pond Mtn. from the east begins a little more than 100 yd. north, just beyond a power-line crossing and across from a small boat landing.)

To reach the trailhead from the north, leave US 201 at The Forks and take the road toward Indian Pond. At Lake Moxie Station, 5.3 mi. from the highway, turn south onto the road that follows the old railroad bed along Moxie Pond. This road is rough and very narrow in places, and there are many camps located on this shore of the lake, so drive carefully. At 8.1 mi. from Lake Moxie Station, the sign for the Appalachian Trail and Moxie Bald is located on the left.

The Appalachian Trail up Moxie Bald leaves the eastern side of the road and crosses Baker Brook (in times of high water, you might choose to use a tricky two-cable footbridge located just downstream near Joe's Hole). At 0.5 mi., a power line is crossed. The trail ascends gradually, then more steeply over open ledges before breaking out above the treeline. At 4.2 mi., reach a junction with a 0.5-mi., blue-blazed side trail used to bypass the summit in bad weather. It rejoins the Appalachian Trail north of the summit along the crest of the mountain. At 4.8 mi., reach the open summit of Moxie Bald. The former tower has been removed.

Moxie Bald Mountain
Distance from paper-company road via Appalachian Trail

   to Moxie Bald summit: 4.8 mi. (7.7 km.), 3 hr. 15 min.

PLEASANT POND MOUNTAIN (2480 ft./756 m.)

On the Appalachian Trail between Moxie Pond and the Kennebec River at Caratunk, Pleasant Pond Mtn. has open ledges that offer fine views in all directions. Hikers can approach the mountain from either the east or the west, although the western approach is generally favored. Refer to the USGS The Forks quadrangle, 15- or 7.5-min. series.

From the east, the approach by road is the same as for Moxie Bald Mtn. The Appalachian Trail, relocated in 1987 to avoid a 2-mi. road walk along Moxie Pond Rd., leads west up the mountain from a spot on the paper-company road near Joe's Hole, the southernmost tip of Moxie Pond. The trail crosses a power line after 0.1 mi. and ascends to a long ridge, which it follows to the summit 4.9 mi. from the gravel road. A small *spring* is 0.1 mi. east.

The road approach from the west starts by turning off US 201 by the MFS station in Caratunk. At a spot 0.5 mi. from the highway, reach a junction and turn left (northeast), following the signs to Pleasant Pond. At 3.1 mi., take the left fork; at 3.4 mi., the pavement ends. Continue another 0.8 mi. on the noticeably rougher gravel road, past a gated road right to a left curve in the road where, a narrower gravel road leaves right. Take this road to the right and park soon at a grassy opening. At 5.6 mi. from US 201, the Pleasant Pond Mtn. Lean-to is on the left. The Appalachian Trail leaves the gravel road to the east about 100 yd. beyond it. The trail leads steeply uphill. At about 1 mi., pass the remains of an old warden's cabin, and shortly thereafter break out onto open ledges, where all that remains of the old firetower are a couple of concrete and rock footings and some broken glass.

Pleasant Pond Mountain from the East
Distances from paper-company road via Appalachian Trail

to power line: 0.1 mi.

to Pleasant Pond summit: 4.9 mi. (7.4 km.), 3 hr. 10 min.

Pleasant Pond Mountain from the West
Distances from Pleasant Pond Mountain Lean-to

to old cabin remains: 0.9 mi.

to Pleasant Pond summit: 1.2 mi. (1.9 km.), 1 hr. 15 min.

COBURN MOUNTAIN (3718 ft./1130 m.)

This mountain, west of US 201 between The Forks and Jackman, is the highest in the region. The cab has been removed from its abandoned MFS firetower. Coburn formerly supported the Enchanted Mtn. ski area, but this has been shut down for several years, and the ski trails are rapidly growing in; all buildings have been removed.

Turn west off US 201 onto the ski-area access road (no sign) about 11 mi. north of The Forks and about 15 mi. south of the US 201 and ME 15 junction in Jackman. The access road is badly eroded and, as of 1998, only 0.2 mi. is passable by larger autos, although high-clearance front-wheel-drive cars and four-wheel-drive vehicles can make it another 2 mi. to the location of the former ski-area buildings.

At the base of the mountain is a three-way fork in the road. Take the hard right fork about 100 yd. Park and exit from the northwestern corner of a clearing, following a course about 280 degrees mag. up former ski slopes and talus. About 0.7 mi. from the location of the former ski-area buildings, reach the top of the old ski slope, where a new solar-powered radio repeating station is located. Immediately above the station is a narrow but easily followed footpath, marked with alternating orange and blue surveyor's tape, that leads very steeply uphill about 0.4 mi. It exits the woods onto the summit at a second, new repeating station and just south of the firetower. Past the firetower and the summit buildings is the old firewarden's trail, which leads off the northeastern ridge and circles back down past the few remains of the old warden's cabin onto an old logging track that intersects the jeep road about halfway down the mountain. This trail is much more easily found at the top than at the bottom. For those with compass skills and some bushwhacking experience, it can make a nice loop trip when combined with the former trail.

Coburn Mountain

Distances from US 201

> *to* base of mountain (via access road): *est.* 2.2 mi.
>
> *to* top of ski area: *est.* 2.9 mi.
>
> *to* Coburn summit via new trails: *est.* 2.4 mi. (3.9 km.), 2 hr.

SALLY MOUNTAIN (2221 ft./675 m.)

Sally Mt. is southwest of Jackman, between Wood Pond and Attean Pond. It has a long summit ridge running northeast–southwest, with the highest point at the southwestern end. The northeastern and southeastern slopes rise fairly steeply above two ponds, and the climb to the summit ridge is very steep from these directions. The MFS firetower has been demolished, and although the trail is no longer regularly maintained, it gets sufficient use to keep the route clear. Refer to the USGS Attean quadrangle, 15-min. series, and the Attean Pond quadrangle, 7.5-min. series.

Leave US 201 on a road (dirt after 0.2 mi.) to the west just south of Jackman Station and nearly opposite ME 15 east. Follow the road for about 1.5 mi. until it approaches the stream connecting Wood and Attean ponds where the Canadian Pacific Railroad tracks cross the gated road. Park before the tracks and follow the railroad line to the west for about 1.8 mi. The trail crosses the railroad tracks about 67 yd.

beyond a west-facing trail signal post with the marking 770. As of July 1987, the start of the trail is marked by a piece of pipe wrapped in surveyor's tape on the southern side of the tracks; there is no sign. The trail, marked by red surveyor's tape on trees, runs fairly level for a time before climbing steeply through a pleasant forest of· mixed hardwoods to the summit ridge. Among the rocks and scrub growth of the summit ridge, the trail becomes fainter, but it generally runs along the east-facing edge of the ridge on a gradual ascent toward the summit, where four pieces of steel bolted to the rocks mark the former site of the firetower. The views from the top are excellent, taking in several large ponds and mountains, from Katahdin to Bigelow to the border peaks.

A more pleasant alternative to hiking along the railroad tracks is making the approach to the trail by canoe. Follow the dirt road mentioned previously to its end at the public landing on Attean Pond. By boat, follow the northern shore of Attean Pond west. The trail begins at the second established campsite in a small cove directly opposite Birch Island. The trail can be easily followed for about 0.1 mi. to a spot where it crosses the Canadian Pacific tracks.

Sally Mountain

Distances from road

>   *to*   start of trail (via railroad line): 1.8 mi.

>   *to*   Sally summit: 3 mi. (4.8 km.), 2 hr.

BOUNDARY BALD MOUNTAIN (3640 ft./1107 m.)

This rocky summit is north-northeast of Jackman and about 8 mi. southwest of the Canadian border. Its long, open summit ridge offers 360-degree views of the mountain and lake country of northern Somerset County. Over the past decade, the former firewarden's trail has succumbed to logging operations, blowdowns, and lack of maintenance, and it no longer exists. However, the mountain and the collapsed firetower at its top can be reached by a 1.2-mi. bushwhack from the former warden's cabin, now rented to a snowmobile club. Refer to the USGS Penobscot Lake and Long Pond quadrangles, 15-min. series, and the Boundary Bald Mtn. quadrangle, 7.5-min. series.

From the bridge on US 201 in Jackman, drive north 7.7 mi. to The Falls picnic area on the right. Take the second right after the picnic area (the first right leads back, parallel to the highway). This narrow, unmaintained gravel road leads 5.8 mi. to the former warden's cabin. It is generally suitable for pickup trucks and four-wheel-drive vehicles; some front-wheel-drive vehicles with high clearance might be able to make it most of the way. Drivers may want to carry a shovel to deal with deep washouts and drainage dips.

Pass over a height-of-land then, at 2.5 mi., cross the Heald Stream gorge and immediately take a right at the fork. (Don't be drawn left by Heald Stream Rd.) The road passes north of Mud Pond and crosses another small stream. At 1.8 mi. after the gorge, take a left at the junction. Another 1.3 mi. of steady uphill driving brings you to the former warden's cabin on the left. The trail formerly began behind the cabin. Now a trail starts left about 9 minutes beyond the cabin, at a sign reading Bald Mt. Tower. The trail, which heads up a slaty streambed, is marked with blue blazes.

Boundary Bald Mountain

Distance from former warden's cabin

to Boundary Bald summit: 1.2 mi. (1.9 km.)

Glossary

blaze   trail marking on a tree or rock, painted and/or cut

blazed   marked with paint (blazes) on trees or rocks

bluff   high bank or hill with a cliff face overlooking a valley

boggy   muddy, swampy

boulder   large, detached, somewhat rounded rock

box canyon   rock formation with vertical walls and flat bottom

bushwhack   to hike through woods or brush without a trail

buttress   rock mass projecting outward from a mountain or hill

cairn   pile of rocks to mark trail

cataract   waterfall

cirque   upper end of valley with half-bowl shape (scoured by glacier)

cliff   high, steep rock face

col   low point on a ridge between two mountains; saddle

crag   rugged, often overhanging rock eminence

flume   ravine or gorge with a stream running through it

grade   steepness of trail or road; ratio of vertical to horizontal distance

graded trail well-constructed trail with smoothed footway

gulf cirque

gully small, steep-sided valley

headwall steep slope at the head of a valley, especially a cirque

height-of-land highest point reached by a trail or road

knob rounded minor summit

lean-to shelter open on one side

ledge large body of rock; or, but not usually in this book, a horizontal
shelf across a cliff

ledgy having exposed ledges, usually giving views

outcrops large rocks projecting out of the soil

plateau high, flat area

potable drinkable

ravine steep-sided valley

ridge highest spine joining two or more mountains, or leading up to a
mountain

runoff brook brook usually dry (intermittent), except shortly after rain
or snowmelt

saddle lowest, flattish part of ridge connecting two mountains; col

scrub low trees near treeline

shelter building, usually of wood, with roof and three or four sides, for
camping

shoulder point where rising ridge levels off or descends slightly before rising higher to a summit

slab (n.) smooth, somewhat steeply sloping ledge

slab (v.) to travel in a direction parallel to the contour of a slope

slide steep slope where a landslide has carried away soil and vegetation

spur minor summit projecting from a larger one

spur trail side path to a point off a main trail

strata layers of rock

summit highest point on a mountain; or, a point higher than any other point in its neighborhood

switchback zigzag traverse of a steep slope

tarn small pond, often at high elevation or with no outlet

timberline elevation that marks the upper limit of commercial timber

treeline elevation above which trees do not grow

Appendix

Accident Report

Your Name_____**Date** _____**Time**_____

DESCRIPTION OF LOST OR INJURED PERSON:

Name _____**Age/Sex**_____

Address_____**Hair:** _____

_____**Fac. Hair:** _____

Phone: _____

REPORTING PERSON:

Name _____**Phone:** _____

Address _____

WHAT HAPPENED:

_____

_____

_____

_____

_____

POINT LAST SEEN:

Car Description _____**Date** _____

Car Location _____

Itinerary _____

233

WEARING (color/style/size):

Jacket _____ Shirt _____

Shorts/Pants _____ Hat/Gloves _____

Glasses _____ Pack _____

Footgear _____ Crampons _____

CARRYING (color/style/size/quantity):

Map _____ Sleeping Bag _____

Tent/Bivy _____ Rain/Windgear _____

Flashlight/Batts _____ Extra Clothing _____

Food/Water _____ Ski Poles/Ice Axe _____

Experience _____

Physical/Mental Conditions _____

ESSENTIAL PATIENT EXAMINATION

PROBLEM AREAS/INJURIES

❑ Head   ❑ Neck   ❑ Shoulders   ❑ Chest
❑ Abdomen   ❑ Back   ❑ Pelvis

❑ Left Upper Leg   ❑ Left Lower Leg   ❑ Left Foot
❑ Right Upper Leg   ❑ Right Lower Leg   ❑ Right Foot

❑ Left Arm   ❑ Left Hand   ❑ Right Arm   ❑ Right Hand

Chief Complaint and Plan

_____

_____

_____

Problem 2 and Plan

_____

_____

_____

Problem 3 and Plan

_____

_____

_____

BACKGROUND INFORMATION

Allergies _____

Medication _____

Previous Injury/Illness _____

Last 24hr food/water intake _____

Medical Conditions/Other _____

_____

FOR BACK, CHEST, OR ABDOMINAL PAIN, DETERMINE:

History _____

Duration _____

Intensity _____**Changing +/-** _____

VITAL SIGNS

ESSENTIAL				HELPFUL		
TIME	LEVEL OF CONSCIOUSNESS	BREATHING RATE	PULSE	BLOOD PRESSURE	SKIN	PUPILS

NOTES

DATE/TIME	WEATHER/LOCATION AND FINDINGS	ACTION TAKEN

Index

Notes: **Boldface** denotes trail name
ALL CAPS denotes section name

About the
Appalachian Mountain Club

Begin a New Adventure!

Join the Appalachian Mountain Club, the oldest and largest outdoor recreation club in the United States. Since 1876, the Appalachian Mountain Club has helped people experience the majesty and solitude of the Northeast outdoors. Our mission is to promote the protection, enjoyment, and wise use of the mountains, rivers, and trails of the Northeast.

Members enjoy discounts on all AMC programs, facilities, and books.

Outdoor Adventure Programs

We offer more than 100 workshops on hiking, canoeing, cross-country skiing, biking, and rock climbing as well as guided trips for hikers, canoeists, and skiers.

Facilities: Mountain Huts and Visitor Centers

The AMC maintains backcountry huts in the White Mountains of New Hampshire and visitor centers throughout the Northeast, from Maine to New Jersey.

Books and Maps

Guides and maps to the mountains, streams, and forests of the Northeast—from Maine to North Carolina—and outdoor skill books from backcountry experts on topics from winter camping to fly fishing. Call 1-800-AMC-HILL to request a complete catalog.

The Appalachian Mountain Club
5 Joy Street
Boston, MA 02108
617-523-0636

Find us on the web at **www.outdoors.or**org to order books, make reservations, learn about our workshops, or join the club.

Other AMC Titles of Interest

Trail Guides

Guide to Mount Desert Island and Acadia National Park
Hiking Guide to Mount Washington and the Presidential Range
Massachusetts and Rhode Island Trail Guide
North Carolina Hiking Trails
West Virginia Hiking Trails
White Mountain Guide

Paddling Guides

Classic Northeastern Whitewater Guide
Quiet Water Canoe Guide: Maine
Quiet Water Canoe Guide: Massachusetts/Connecticut/Rhode Island
Quiet Water Canoe Guide: New Hampshire/Vermont
Quiet Water Canoe Guide: New York
Sea Kayaking along the New England Coast
Sea Kayaking along the Mid-Atlantic Coast
Whitewater Handbook

Outdoor Skill Guides

Guide to Trail Building and Maintenance
Organizing Outdoor Volunteers
River Rescue
Watercolor Painting on the Trail

NOTES

NOTES